Hegel & the Infinite

INSURRECTIONS: CRITICAL STUDIES IN RELIGION, POLITICS, AND CULTURE

INSURRECTIONS: CRITICAL STUDIES IN RELIGION, POLITICS, AND CULTURE
Slavoj Žižek, Clayton Crockett, Creston Davis, Jeffrey W. Robbins, editors

The intersection of religion, politics, and culture is one of the most discussed areas in theory today. It also has the deepest and most wide-ranging impact on the world. Insurrections: Critical Studies in Religion, Politics, and Culture will bring the tools of philosophy and critical theory to the political implications of the religious turn. The series will address a range of religious traditions and political viewpoints in the United States, Europe, and other parts of the world. Without advocating any specific religious or theological stance, the series aims nonetheless to be faithful to the radical emancipatory potential of religion.

After the Death of God, John D. Caputo and Gianni Vattimo, edited by Jeffrey W. Robbins

The Politics of Postsecular Religion: Mourning Secular Futures, Ananda Abeysekara

Nietzsche and Levinas: "After the Death of a Certain God," edited by Jill Stauffer and Bettina Bergo

Strange Wonder: The Closure of Metaphysics and the Opening of Awe, Mary-Jane Rubenstein

Religion and the Specter of the West: Sikhism, India, Postcoloniality, and the Politics of Translation, Arvind Mandair

Plasticity at the Dusk of Writing: Dialectic, Destruction, Deconstruction, Catherine Malabou

Anatheism: Returning to God After God, Richard Kearney

Rage and Time, Peter Sloterdijk

Radical Political Theology: Religion and Politics After Liberalism, Clayton Crockett

Radical Democracy and Political Theology, Jeffrey W. Robbins

EDITED BY
SLAVOJ ŽIŽEK | CLAYTON CROCKETT | CRESTON DAVIS

Hegel & the Infinite

RELIGION, POLITICS, AND DIALECTIC

COLUMBIA
UNIVERSITY
PRESS
New York

Columbia University Press
Publishers Since 1893
New York   Chichester, West Sussex

Copyright © 2011 Columbia University Press
All rights reserved

Library of Congress Cataloging-in-Publication Data
Hegel and the infinite : religion, politics, and dialectic / edited by Slavoj Zizek, Clayton Crockett, and Creston Davis.
    p. cm. — (Insurrections)
  Includes index.
  ISBN 978-0-231-14334-9 (cloth)
  ISBN 978-0-231-14335-6 (pbk.)
  ISBN 978-0-231-51287-9 (e-book)
  1. Hegel, Georg Wilhelm Friedrich, 1770–1831.   I. Žižek, Slavoj.
II. Crockett, Clayton, 1969–   III. Davis, Creston.   IV. Title.

  B2948.H31787   2011
  193—dc22
                                                    2010045029

To KXMM (the King College Mountain Men)
and James C. Livingston, and to the future readers of Hegel

CONTENTS

Preface: Hegel's Century   ix
                                                 SLAVOJ ŽIŽEK

Acknowledgments   xiii

Introduction: Risking Hegel: A New Reading
for the Twenty-first Century   1
                         CLAYTON CROCKETT AND CRESTON DAVIS

1   Is Confession the Accomplishment of Recognition? Rousseau and
     the Unthought of Religion in the *Phenomenology of Spirit*   19
                                             CATHERINE MALABOU

2   Rereading Hegel: The Philosopher of Right   31
                                          ANTONIO NEGRI

3   The Perversity of the Absolute, the Perverse Core of Hegel,
     and the Possibility of Radical Theology   47
                                         JOHN D. CAPUTO

4   Hegel in America   67
                                         BRUNO BOSTEELS

5   Infinite Restlessness   91
                                         MARK C. TAYLOR

6   Between Finitude and Infinity: On Hegel's Sublationary Infinitism   115
                                                      WILLIAM DESMOND

7   The Way of Despair   141
                                                          KATRIN PAHL

8   The Weakness of Nature: Hegel, Freud, Lacan,
    and Negativity Materialized   159
                                                       ADRIAN JOHNSTON

9   Disrupting Reason: Art and Madness in Hegel and Van Gogh   181
                                                       EDITH WYSCHOGROD

10 Finite Representation, Spontaneous Thought, and the Politics of
    an Open-Ended Consummation   199
                                                        THOMAS A. LEWIS

11 Hegel and Shitting: The Idea's Constipation   221
                                                          SLAVOJ ŽIŽEK

    List of Contributors   233
    Index of Names   235

PREFACE

Hegel's Century

SLAVOJ ŽIŽEK

The ultimate anti-Hegelian argument is the very fact of the post-Hegelian break: what even the most fanatical partisan of Hegel cannot deny is that something changed after Hegel, that a new era of thought began that can no longer be accounted for in the Hegelian terms of absolute conceptual mediation. This rupture occurs in different guises, from Schelling's assertion of the abyss of prelogical Will (vulgarized later by Schopenhauer) and Kierkegaard's insistence on the uniqueness of faith and subjectivity, through Marx's assertion of actual socioeconomic life process and the full autonomization of mathematicized natural sciences, up to Freud's motif of the "death-drive" as a repetition that persists beyond all dialectical mediation. Something happened here; there is a clear break between before and after. And while one can argue that Hegel already announces this break, that he is the last of idealist metaphysicians and the first of postmetaphysical historicists, one cannot really be a Hegelian after this break. Hegelianism has lost its innocence forever. To act like a full Hegelian today is the same as to write tonal music after the Schönberg revolution.

The predominate Hegelian strategy that is emerging as a reaction to this scarecrow image of Hegel as the Absolute Idealist is the "deflated" image of Hegel freed of ontological-metaphysical commitments, reduced to a general theory of discourse, of possibilities of argumentation. This approach is best exemplified by so-called Pittsburgh Hegelians (Brandom, McDowell): no wonder Habermas praises Brandom, since Habermas also avoids directly approaching the "big" ontological question (are humans *really* a subspecies of animals? is Darwinism true?), the question of God or Nature, of idealism or materialism. It would be easy to prove that Habermas's neo-Kantian avoiding of ontological commitment is in itself necessarily ambiguous: while the neo-Kantians treat naturalism as the obscene secret not to be publicly admitted ("of course man developed from nature, of course Darwin was right"), this obscure secret is a lie; it covers up the idealist *form* of thought, the a priori transcendentalism of communication that cannot be deduced from natural being. The truth is here in the form: as with Marx's old example of royalists in the republican form, Habermasians secretly think they are really materialists, while the truth is in the idealist form of their thinking.

Such a deflated image of Hegel is not enough. One should approach the post-Hegelian break in more direct terms. True, there is a break, but in this break Hegel is the "vanishing mediator" between its "before" and its "after," between traditional metaphysics and postmetaphysical nineteenth- and twentieth-century thought. That is to say, something happens in Hegel, a breakthrough into a unique dimension of thought, which is obliterated, rendered invisible in its true dimension, by the postmetaphysical thought. This obliteration leaves an empty space, which has to be filled in so that the continuity of the development of philosophy can be reestablished. Filled in with what? The index of this obliteration is the ridiculous image of Hegel as the absurd "absolute idealist" who "pretended to know everything," to possess Absolute Knowledge, to read the mind of God, to deduce all of reality out of the self-movement of (his) Mind—the image which is an exemplary case of what Freud called *Deck-Erinnerung* (screen memory), a fantasy formation destined to cover up a traumatic truth. In this sense, the post-Hegelian turn to "concrete reality, irreducible to notional mediation" should rather be read as the desperate posthumous revenge of metaphysics, as an attempt to reinstall metaphysics, although in the inverted form of the primacy of concrete reality.

In what, then, resides Hegel's uniqueness? Hegel's thought stands for the moment of passage between philosophy and master's discourse, the philosophy of the One that totalizes the multiplicity and antiphilosophy, which asserts the Real that escapes the grasp of the One. On the one hand, he clearly breaks with the metaphysical logic of counting-for-One; on the other hand, he does not allow for any excess external to the field of notional representations. For Hegel, totalization-in-One always fails, the One is always already in excess with regard to itself, it is itself the subversion of what it purports to achieve; and it is this tension internal to the One, this Twoness, which makes the One One and simultaneously dislocates it, it is this tension which is the movement of the "dialectical process." In other words, Hegel effectively denies that there is no Real external to the network of notional representations (which is why he is regularly misread as an "absolute idealist" in the sense of the self-enclosed circle of the totality of the Notion). However, the Real does not disappear here in the global self-relating play of symbolic representations; it returns with a vengeance as the immanent gap, the obstacle, on account of which representations cannot ever totalize themselves, on account of which they are "non-All."

Is there nonetheless not a grain of truth in the most elementary reproach to Hegel? Does Hegel effectively not presuppose that, contingent and open as the history may be, a consistent story can be told afterward? Or, to put it in Lacan's terms: is the entire edifice of the Hegelian historiography not based on the premise that, no matter how confused the events, a *subject supposed to know* will emerge at the end, magically converting nonsense into sense, chaos into new order? Recall just his philosophy of history with its narrative of world history as the story of the progress of freedom. And is it not true that, if there is a lesson of the twentieth century, it is that all the extreme phenomena that took place over that time cannot ever be unified into a single encompassing philosophical narrative? One simply cannot write a phenomenology of the Twentieth-Century Spirit, uniting technological progress, the rise of democracy, the failed Communist attempt with its Stalinist catastrophe, the horrors of Fascism, and the gradual end of colonialism.

But why not? Is it *really* so? What if, precisely, one can and should write a Hegelian history of the twentieth century, this "age of extremes" (as Eric Hobsbawm calls it), as a global narrative delimited by two epochal constellations: the (relatively) long, peaceful period of capitalist expansion from 1848 to 1914 as its substantial starting point whose subterranean antagonisms then exploded with the First World War and the ongoing global-capitalist "New World Order" emerging after 1990 as its conclusion, the return to a new all-encompassing system signaling to some a Hegelian "end of history," but whose antagonisms already announce new explosions? Are the great reversals and unexpected explosions of the topsy-turvy twentieth century, its numerous "coincidences of the opposites"—for example, the reversal of the October Revolution into the Stalinist nightmare—not the very privileged stuff that seems to call for a Hegelian reading? What would Hegel have made of today's struggle of liberalism against fundamentalist faith? One thing is sure: he would not simply take sides with liberalism, but would have insisted on the "mediation" of the opposites.

(And, let us not forget that, for Hegel himself, his philosophical reconstruction of history in no way pretends to "cover everything" but consciously leaves blanks: the medieval time, for example, is for Hegel one big regression—no wonder that, in his lectures on the history of philosophy, he dismisses the entire medieval thought in a couple of pages, flatly denying any historical greatness to figures like Thomas Aquinas. He does not even mention the destructions of great civilizations like the Mongols' wiping out so much of the Muslim world (the destruction of Baghdad, etc.) in the thirteenth century. There is no "meaning" in this destruction; the negativity unleashed here did not create the space for a new shape of historical life.)

This is why the time of Hegel still lies ahead—Hegel's century will be the twenty-first.

ACKNOWLEDGMENTS

Creston and Clayton would like to acknowledge those who generously supported the efforts without which this work would have never materialized. Most of all, we would like to thank the contributors for their time, work, and inspiration. In addition and in particular, Slavoj Žižek, Mario D'Amato, Jeff Robbins, and Catherine Malabou have encouraged us to pursue the original vision of Hegel seen in this collected volume, and Wendy Lochner and Christine Mortlock have constantly supported us at Columbia University Press. We would like to acknowledge our families, Vicki Bryan Crockett and the Reverend Molly Bosscher Davis, as well as our children, Maria and Bryan Crockett and Asher and Isak Davis, whose patience and love allowed us to labor with our love for risking Hegel in our time. To our respective departments: At the University of Central Arkansas, Clayton wants to acknowledge his colleagues in the Department of Philosophy and Religion, including Charles Harvey, Jesse Butler, Phillip Spivey, Jake Held, Gary Thiher, Jeff Williams, Jim Shelton, Benjamin Rider, Jim Deitrick, Ron Novy, and Tanya Jeffcoat. And at Rollins College, Creston's colleagues Tom Cook, Margaret McLaren, L. Ryan Musgrave, Eric Smaw, Scott Rubarth, Hoyt Edge, Yudit Greenberg, and Mario D'Amato; we thank you for your intellectual and material support. An especial thanks is extended to the dean of the faculty at Rollins College, Dr. Laurie Joyner, for supporting the research that made this book possible. Thanks to Melanie Davis for her amazing work in helping prepare this manuscript for publication. Also thanks to Kelly Kozich and Kira Pack for their inspiration and encouragements. Finally, the Department of Information Technology at Rollins College needs to be acknowledged for their care in providing this project with unwavering support, especially Joseph F. Hughes and Caleb Jones.

Hegel & the Infinite

INTRODUCTION

Risking Hegel: A New Reading for the Twenty-first Century

CLAYTON CROCKETT AND CRESTON DAVIS

It is possible that in reality the future of the world, and thus the meaning of the present and that of the past, depend, in the last analysis, on the way in which the Hegelian writings are interpreted today.
—ALEXANDRE KOJÈVE

Hegel is at the origin of everything great in philosophy for the last century.
—MAURICE MERLEAU-PONTY

This volume presents some of the most prominent readers of Hegel in contemporary philosophy and theology. We assert here that Hegel has become the litmus test of thought and possibility. How one interprets Hegel determines how one fundamentally understands the very force of thought, being, and truth. To be sure there are many different readings of Hegel, but among all the different readings, we suggest that one must finally come down on one of two sides: the Right, conservative side, or the Leftist, revolutionary side.

The conservative side reads Hegel's ontology as finally remaining captive to both the Kantian split between form and content and the notion of rational autonomy. On this view Hegel's doctrine of Being might first appear to be an infinite dialectical becoming that moves ever closer to Absolute Spirit but in *truth* looses it nerve and folds back into the security-domain of a self-enclosed methodology sundered from reality. A representative take on this conservative stance is Charles Taylor's 1975 version of Hegel. Here Taylor argues that Hegel's synthesis cannot

> command adherents today not only because it is built in part on the expressivist reaction to the modern identity which contemporary civilization has tended to entrench more and more, but because it is built on an earlier and outmoded form of this reaction. It belongs to the opposition while claiming to give us a vision of reason triumphant; and it belongs moreover to a stage of this opposition which no longer appears viable.[1]

Here Taylor comes down by saying that basically Hegel's "synthesis" is ultimately controlled by wedding a kind of nostalgic, romantic view of the world as essentially unified *with* a "rational autonomy." But this is a problem because it relegates and confines Hegel's ontology to a Kantian stance premised on the rational-core truth of the universe debarred from disruptive spirit. This conservative reading that reduces Hegel to Kant is true if you understand the former to be saying little more than he did in his very early essay on the "Life of Jesus."[2] In this essay, as T. M. Knox states, "Jesus appears as a teacher of Kant's purely moral religion."[3] Hegel's infatuation with Kantian "Reason" is evident when in this essay he says, "Pure Reason completely free of any limit or restriction whatsoever is the deity itself." Indeed Hegel's Jesus tells humanity to switch "the eternal law of morality and Him whose holy will cannot be affected by anything but by the law."[4] Jesus says: "You were commanded to love your friends and your nation, but you were permitted to hate your enemies—I say however unto you: Respect mankind even in your enemy, if you cannot love him."[5] And again: "Act on that maxim which you can at the same time will to be a universal law among men. This is the fundamental law of morality—the content of all legislation and of the sacred books of all nations."[6] Taylor's Hegel is thus confined to a liberal bourgeois subjectivity grounded in the Kantian idealized split between Reason and the external world. Autonomous reason ascends to the a priori of being which freezes the radicality of an ontology of irruptive becoming that overturns all static categories.

This conservative position further assumes that the heart of Hegel's own structure enacts "the nothing" of Kant's "thing-in-itself" precisely because the structure of Kant's metaphysics collapses: and so spirit is left to tarry with form sundered from content. The Kantian metaphysical collapse takes place because Kant's nerve gives out at the precise moment of truth. For instead of opting for risk, Kant circles the wagons and settles into what basically amounts to a defensive posture that has indelibly left its mark on philosophical structures ever since; indeed one could go even further here and show that it was this Kantian conservative move (which assumes a single version of transcendence, that is, Christian transcendence) which brings the radical nature of thinking under the control of systems which must assume no transcendence, such as the Nation-State, in order to exist.

Of course it remains a viable debate, but is this not the exact stance that Hegel in his mature thinking attempted to traverse? For if form (appearance) is detached from all things beyond itself, then is not the dialectic hijacked by the very *idea* of form as such? That is to say, form left to itself fails to relate to anything outside itself. And this brings us to a decisive difference between Hegel and Kant: namely, whereas Kant circles the wagons in a moment of panic, Hegel pushes form beyond its static definition and with it subverts orthodox Christian transcendence.[7] This stance is what Hegel called *Being-for-itself*, which opposes the situation whereby Method always returns to itself as Method (self-referential and identical return) and so never goes beyond itself to touch the world (which resembles not just the One of Parmenides[8] but also one of the problems that plagues phenomenology).

The notion of Method is here merely an uninterested *interpretation* of the world, a position that Karl Marx roundly criticizes in his *Thesis on Feuerbach* XI: "Philosophers have only interpreted the world, in various ways; the point is to change it." So, this stance assumes that Hegel's philosophy, as brilliant as it is, remains sundered from changing the world.

Then there is the other side, namely the "Leftist" reading of Hegel. Here one can read Hegel as positing an infinite truth that fundamentally revolts against the current and operating ideology incarnated as a social and political ontological-revolutionary act. On this view the very dynamic logic of being is always and already overturning any instantiation of itself in terms that are static and frozen. Moreover, this reading rests on the idea that the internal-core logic of the *concept* (*Begriff*) of Spirit always and perpetually traverses beyond (*Vor-stellung*) the instantiation (or fulfillment) of itself and into the future (as lack). In this regard, not only is Hegel's ontology not a self-referential interpreted "Method" sundered from the world, it actually is the underlying logic of the world's unfolding as such. But it is at this precise juncture that we end up confronting the deadlock hidden in both sides of this Hegelian divide: If the true meaning of Hegel's ontology is a Method sundered from the world (as Marx charged), and if the opposite is true, namely that his ontology is inseparable from the world as such, then what we have here is nothing short of a tale of two totalizing logics. That is, the conservative, apolitical reading of method qua method converges with the Leftist reading of dynamic ontology insofar as Leftist revolutionaries become convulsed with questions of formal method and substitute the theorizing of the revolution for the revolution itself, and conservatives adopt a Hegelian dynamic social ontology to justify the ravages of capitalist repression. This split between Right and Left Hegel forms a perfect circle, just as Hegel's philosophy itself is wrongly seen as totally circular and therefore totalizing in its logic. Nothing is to be done.

On this view, both Method *and* idealized ontology as world are guilty of totalizing and violence because each stance ultimately collapses all forms of otherness into a monolithic horizon of sameness and Identity. For the former the very existence of Method fails to offer up a space within which otherness exists in terms of itself as other and so finally folds into the logic of the same. There are three seminal twentieth-century philosophers who represent this stance: Emmanuel Levinas, as seen in his extraordinary book, *Totality and Infinity*; Jacques Derrida primarily in *Glas*; and Jean-Francois Lyotard in his brilliant analysis of *The Postmodern Condition*. The fundamental question that Levinas raises in *Totality and Infinity* is deceptively simple: is there an outside to the closure of thinking wrought by the history of Western philosophy from the Greeks to the twentieth century? Entertaining such a question as this, as simple as it may seem, really determines how thinkers within the history of Western philosophy fit into Levinas's genealogy of metaphysics. Levinas's assumption is that all metaphysics and ontology are by their very nature infused with violence. From this view of ontology it is all too easy for Levinas to place Hegel into his limited framework of Western philosophers.

For Levinas thinks of Hegel as a thinker who epitomizes the problem that plagues philosophy: he is a totalizing thinker who creates a world in which all things, all forms of otherness are absorbed within the horizon of a single History without an iota of deviation. So, as it turns out, the entire book *Totality and Infinity* is nothing short of a covert challenge to Hegel's (and Heidegger's) ontology.[9] Levinas explicitly says that Hegel thinks that History is the transcendent determiner of all Identity: "Objectivity is absorbed in absolute knowledge, and the being of the thinker, the humanity of man, is therewith conformed to the perpetuity of the solid *in itself*, within a totality where the humanity of man and the exteriority of the object are at the same time conserved and absorbed."[10] The picture of Hegel that Levinas paints here is one of solidity, one that cleaves to the sign of the In-Itself. But this reading is highly problematic, as some of the contributors to this volume demonstrate. Furthermore, Levinas's reading can be seen as violent because he fails to see how his own concept of totality is too quickly attached to Hegel's thought. He is thus able to reduce Hegel to the figure of Sameness.

The other towering figure who pigeonholed Hegel (at least from the late 1960s to the late 1980s) into a totalizing shell is Jacques Derrida. Derrida's principle text in which he engages Hegel is *Glas* (which is the word for the tones of a death knell).[11] Heinz Kimmerle tells us about the opening passages in *Glas*, which begins with the question "what remain(s) today, for us, here, now, of a Hegel?" from which alights another question, "what remain(s) for us to think after absolute knowledge?"[12] For, like Levinas, the Derrida of the late 1960s to the late 1980s thinks little more of Hegel than a complete totalizer devoid of the possibility of exteriority and difference. This can be seen most plainly in *Positions*, where Derrida attempts to distinguish *différance* from Hegelian difference. Derrida asserts that Hegel, "in the greater *Logic* determines difference as contradiction only in order to resolve it, to interiorize it, to lift it up (according to the syllogistic process of speculative dialectics) into the self-presence of an onto-theological or onto-theological synthesis."[13] The third and final thinker of this view that reduces Hegel to a totalizer without remainder is Jean-Francois Lyotard. Lyotard writes that the conditions of modernity requires that

> Philosophy must restore unity to learning, which has been scattered into separate sciences into laboratories and in pre-university education; it can only achieve this in a language game that links the sciences together as moments in the becoming of spirit, in other words, which link them in a rational narration, or rather metanarration. Hegel's *Encyclopedia* (1817–27) attempts to realize this project of totalization.[14]

Thus all three main figures of twentieth-century postmodern philosophical orientation interpret Hegel as the apex of modernity in which difference and exteriority are impossible from within Hegel's structure.

For those who critique the radical side of Hegel, if the world really does unfold inextricably with and as Spirit, then this logic (at first glance) seems to be inherently wedded to a teleological trajectory of all History into which all things (all otherness and difference from otherness) must ultimately fold. And this is precisely where Gilles Deleuze's critique fails to see the radically contingent, fissured ontology located within the heart of Hegel. Deleuze understands Hegel's notion of difference as emerging from the latter's notion of contradiction. Moreover, he explicitly says this when he compares Hegel to Aristotle: "Hegel determines difference by the opposition of extremes or of contraries that is articulated by the difference between Identity (self) and difference (other)."[15] Thus for Deleuze difference for Hegel is premised on a thing's negation from "all that it is not." So for a thing to be, it must first be subtracted from everything else that it is not. That is to say that a thing only is (as possessing the ontological status of existing), as Deleuze understands Hegel, when it is in absolute nonrelation with everything else, and so ultimately everything (all History and so forth) must fold into a total system whose *telos* comes to itself necessarily through a pretend difference, that is, a difference that contains within it a secret singularity which is already part of the *telos* of History as absolute knowledge coming to terms with itself. So for Deleuze (following Levinas, Derrida, and Lyotard), difference for Hegel is really not difference but sameness. Additionally, it is clear that Deleuze understands Hegel as being too conservative, stopping short of pushing the idea of difference beyond the limits encompassed in the idea of contradiction seen in the *Science of Logic*. Deleuze follows Bergson here in the belief that all things don't begin with Identity via negation (as with Hegel) but with the axiom that a "thing differs with itself, first immediately" (and not secondarily). But Slavoj Žižek challenges Deleuze's misreading of Hegel based on Bergson: "If ever there was a straw-man, it is Deleuze's Hegel: is not Hegel's basic insight precisely that every external opposition is grounded in the thing's immanent self-opposition, i.e., that ever external difference implies self-difference? A finite being differs from other (finite) things because it is already not identical with itself."[16] Deleuze is much closer to Hegel than he wants to think.

Thus we can see that these two different twentieth-century takes on Hegel, working together, basically spell out the completion and exhaustion of his thought and by extension the death of metaphysics and finally, according to Badiou, the end of philosophy for our time.[17] On the other hand, suppose that this double threat (which culminates in the work of Levinas, Derrida, Lyotard, and Deleuze) entirely misses the point precisely because each critical side does not believe in the very idea of risk itself? To put it differently, suppose that the force of the critique leveled at Hegel (that he is a totalizer and wedded to a historical teleology that neutralizes all difference) is actually presupposed within these very structures themselves? Thus, each side simply (if unconsciously) projects the assumption that there is no risk within history itself onto Hegel and so dismisses him cleanly out of hand, as if Hegel were a sacrifice to the gods of philosophy.

The impetus of this book revolts against this double-empty threat, for it is our belief that the principle reason why Hegel was dismissed is because it is his thought above all that gives us true risk, it gives us hope. Here we merely repeat Slavoj Žižek's thesis originally submitted in *Le plus sublime des hysteriques: Hegel passé*, namely, that Hegelian "dialectics is for Hegel a systematic notation of the failure of all such attempts—'absolute knowledge' denotes a subjective position which finally accepts 'contradiction' as an internal condition of every identity."[18] In other words, Hegelian "reconciliation" is not a pan-logicist sublation of all reality in the Concept but an affirmation of the fact that the Concept itself is "not-all" (to use this Lacanian term). Such an understanding of Hegel inevitably runs counter to the accepted notion of absolute knowledge as a monster of conceptual totality devouring every contingency.

This still-too-prevalent interpretation of Hegel, to continue quoting Žižek,

> simply *shoots too fast*, like the patrolling soldier of the well-known joke from Jaruzelski's Poland immediately after the military coup. At this time, military patrols had the right to shoot without warning at people walking on the street after curfew (ten-o'clock); one of the two soldiers on patrol sees somebody in a hurry at ten minutes to ten and shoots him immediately. When his colleague asks him why he shot when it was only ten to ten, he answers: "I knew the fellow—he lived far from here and in any case would not be able to reach his home in ten minutes, so to simplify matters, I shot him now. . . ." This is exactly how the critics of Hegel's presumed "panlogicism" proceed: they condemn absolute knowledge "before it is ten o'clock," or high noon, without reaching it—that is, they refute nothing with their criticism but their own prejudices about it.[19]

In short, Hegel needs to be reclaimed to overcome the death of thought that resulted from philosophy's linguistic turn in the twentieth century which ended up subverting the very core of philosophy's desire, namely, the pursuit of truth.[20]

As such this volume represents thinkers from both sides of this debate with the goal of not just presenting Hegel in a neutral fashion (for this stance never truly exists) but rather to continue to open up the debate about which Hegel is most viable for our time. The editors here side with Hegel's more radical side, which escapes the generic and misplaced boxes into which Hegel's thought simply doesn't fit, especially in light of the need to embody an ontology that resists being arrested by the death of metaphysics, neoliberalism, and capitalism, which together form a front that forecloses the possibility of truth alighting in the world.

Each of the chapters in various ways push Hegel beyond the stereotypical postmodern critique where Hegel represents the totalizing philosopher par excellence, whose system proceeds with a relentless accumulation that swallows up all difference and prevents any genuine change or becoming. In other words, this volume's thesis revolts against the process that returns back and only repeats the world's happening in the same terms as before. In this way, our thesis breaks with the mechanical logic of the world, which can be found in the very heart of Hegel's outlook—a virtue that twentieth-century philosophy has systematically overlooked. Each of the authors presents a genuine engagement with Hegel, whether as a serious Hegel scholar, a significant contemporary philosopher, or both, and these engagements are constructive and critical. Furthermore, the contributors consider various aspects of Hegel's philosophy in its religious and political implications, providing readers an opportunity to reassess Hegel's contemporary significance for considering important intersections of political and religious reflection.

In her essay "Is Confession the Accomplishment of Recognition," Catherine Malabou, the contemporary French philosopher, student of Jacques Derrida, and author of *The Future of Hegel: Plasticity, Temporality, Dialectic*, sets Hegel up with Rousseau and claims that Hegel's perspective in the *Phenomenology of Spirit* allows us to integrate Rousseau's political philosophy as expressed in *The Social Contract* with his autobiographical reflections in *The Confessions*. Hegel combines these two tendencies within Rousseau, but he also reverses Rousseau. For Hegel, the general will, understood as language, or a linguistic community, precedes the individual will and therefore the specific political community.

Malabou develops the motif of confession in relation to forgiveness, specifically in relation to Derrida's thought. Confession haunts modern nation-states, according to Derrida, and forgiveness works (when it does work) to reconcile the self with the broader community. A Hegelian perspective views the state as a sublation and reconciliation of the subject and the community. According to Malabou, God occupies the structural role of the overarching forgiver, as the absolute witness, who allows forgiveness to occur by confession and recognition, by confession as recognition of the need for and possibility of forgiveness. Just as religion is the penultimate step before absolute knowing in Hegel's *Phenomenology*, here religion subverts the essence and identity of the individual and the political community.

Malabou identifies three political languages: the language of contracts, the language of self-expression (confession), and finally a shadowy religious dimension of language as self-belief in oneself and one's testimony. This religious essence is a third that is situated between the particular and the universal. According to Malabou, the contemporary challenge is the political and literary reorientation of the philosophical concept of the religious meaning of the nonreligious. This means that we are forced to stretch the possibilities of our language and our politics to account for our accountability itself, which is one way to understand and articulate the Hegelian dialectic. Confession accomplishes recognition with religious language, which is not a substantial, essentialist language but rather the form of language in its drive for recognition, which is also a drive for forgiveness. Who and how do we forgive, and how does this forgiveness exceed the attempts of the state and the media to control political confession?

In chapter 2, "Rereading Hegel, The Philosopher of Right," the Italian philosopher Antonio Negri launches a profound critique of the *Philosophy of Right*, one that dialectically or antagonistically enables Negri to envision his own emancipatory political theory. According to Negri, Hegel's *Philosophy of Right* represents the assimilation of Right to the State, where the aim of the State is the social control of living labor. Hegel is not only a historical relic but also a contemporary author, because his theoretical achievement allows the command of labor by the State precisely by being mediated, subordinated, and universalized by Right as the form or scheme of the modern state. Because labor is always labor of and for the State, labor is controlled and commanded in a bourgeois and capitalist manner. In the twentieth century, the Hegelian dialectic is continued by Western political science, and even the socialist State is a form of control over labor that is a more subtle version of Hegelianism.

Negri's description of the Hegelian dialectic, "where it seems that everything is complete, everything is incomplete," can function as a slogan for the book. The apparent completeness of the Hegelian absolute is on second glance rendered absolutely incomplete, and Negri expresses in a more negative and polemical way what other authors, including Malabou and Pahl, express more positively. For Negri, the key to liberation from the control of the State beyond recuperation by the Hegelian bourgeois dialectic lies in the refusal of labor, which encompasses a refusal of the State. In practical terms, the refusal of labor brings about a crisis of the State that can only function by the command or control of labor. This State is being shaken by an almost unimaginable credit crisis, which threatens to overwhelm the enormous victory that global capitalism has "won" over labor across the globe.

The hope of liberation from the dialectic by refusing labor in service of the State constitutes a rejection of Hegel and a valorization of the particular over the mediating prison of the universal. Although Negri does not spell this out, we could characterize his hope for liberation as a religious or quasi-religious hope. Negri ends on a bitter note, affirming his hatred for Hegel's philosophy of right, but then he insists that this relation still contradictorily binds us to him. Negri's chapter sets the stage for a rereading of Hegel precisely because he does not try to evade or avoid the dialectic, but rather sets up a direct, antagonistic encounter with his thought.

John D. Caputo, arguably the foremost American Continental philosopher, also has an ambivalent reading of Hegel, although less hostile than Negri's. Caputo is able to value Hegel's significance for contemporary religion and politics by following Slavoj Žižek's lead and excising the perverse core of Hegelianism. In "The Perversity of the Absolute, the Perverse Core of Hegel, and the Possibility of Radical Theology," Caputo elaborates a radical theology out of the context of Hegel by affirming that Hegel is the first thinker to think theology without the metaphysics of a two-worlds mentality. Hegel opens up the possibility for radical theology, a thinking of God and the world not as two disparate entities, but together, with God in the world as the radical implication of the Christian idea of the Incarnation.

Caputo follows Hegel's lead, but also claims that Hegel fails to go far enough, that he is still tied to metaphysics insofar as he posits absolute Spirit as governing and directing the process of self-knowing. Hegel thinks the death of God, of God without God as an essential aspect of the worlding of the world; but here, where everything seems complete, everything in Hegel is still incomplete, and he needs to be pushed beyond himself. The radicalization of Hegel's radicalization of theology occurs by a perversion. Caputo thinks "perversatility," that is, the perversion of the straight path of Christian orthodoxy and the straightforward Hegelian progression from art to religion to its consummation in philosophy. This perverse core of Hegel animates radical theology and prevents Hegelian philosophy from its attempt at closure.

Caputo calls for a perversion of strength into weakness by rereading and recognizing the event as the work of God in and as the world. The task of a radical politics informed by a theology of the event is one of responsibility—to transform ourselves and make ourselves and our relationships worthy of the event. Political theory cannot simply disavow or do away with theology: Caputo follows Derrida in claiming that there is an unavowed theologism at work in all political philosophy. Radical theology consists of acknowledging that theologism and using it to think better and anew philosophy and politics and that insofar as we identify with the spirit of radical theology we are heirs of Hegel.

In his chapter "Hegel in America," Bruno Bosteels elaborates a critique of many of the en vogue finite readings of Hegel, some of which are represented in this volume, and insists on the irreducibility of the infinite character of the Hegelian dialectic. Bosteels, who has established himself as a brilliant interpreter of Badiou's dialectical materialism, as well as an important guide for contemporary Latin American thought, connects the dogmatic and narrow interpretation of Hegel, which became established in the twentieth century (especially in Continental philosophy) to the European colonialism that grew into the present day imperialism that is "America" (i.e., the United States of America). Bosteels exposes Hegel's lapse in thinking about America in his *Philosophy of History*, partly by reading him through the Spanish philosopher Ortega y Gasset, but then recuperates an understanding of Hegel with the work of the Mexican novelist, playwright, and self-taught philosopher José Revueltas to show how reading Hegel as a thinker of infinite act makes his philosophy relevant for radical Leftist politics.

Against a reading that inserts alterity and finitude at the heart of Hegelian philosophy, Bosteels shows how Revueltas's novel *Los errores* demonstrates that this interpretation cedes the ground of the political to a liberal philosophy and politics based on ethics. This liberal interpretation affirms human beings as erroneous beings, finite and erratic, whose every attempt to achieve the Good ends up accomplishing Evil. Against this understanding, Bosteels develops, in the context of a short story by Revueltas, "Hegel and I," the idea of a profane illumination that occurs in an immemorial act. This immemorial act is a profane and secular rather than a religious illumination, and it has important political consequences. The character Hegel in the story is a bank robber who takes his name from the street on which the bank lies, Hegel Street. "From this character, in fact," Bosteels asserts, "we obtain above all the outline for a provocative theory of the act—of what it means to reach consciousness in the act of theory." A theory of the infinite in Hegel provides resources for thinking such a political act in and for America.

Mark C. Taylor is one of the founders of American postmodern theology, and as an heir to Kierkegaard, he has done more than any other scholar to bring French deconstruction to an American theological audience. At the same time, Taylor has also become more and more Hegelian over the last decade or so, wrestling with the theoretical, religious, and cultural implications of computer technology, money and finance, and complexity theory. In his essay "Infinite Restlessness," Taylor argues that we need to think beyond the stereotypical image of Hegel as the representative of totality and totalitarianism, which was the major threat to political and intellectual life in the wake of World War II and during the Cold War. Today, the main threat to our global civilization is sectarianism, the impossibility of mediating and reconciling differences, and Hegel provides important tools for this urgent project. Rather than seeing Derrida's work as diametrically opposed to Hegel's and viewing Hegel as the culmination of the onto-theological tradition, we can engage in a productive double reading, reading Hegel through Derrida and also Derrida through Hegel. In doing so, we can come to view Hegel's absolute as a process of infinite restlessness.

Taylor develops his reading of Hegel by situating Hegel in relation to Kant and a post-Kantian problematic in Germany in the 1790s and early 1800s. In certain ways, the situations and problems then resemble ours today, and so does the solution. Kant sets up and tries to overcome binary oppositions in his critical philosophy, and this finds echoes in structuralism and poststructuralism in the late twentieth century. Although Kant wants his solution, freedom, to be grounded in the moral law, it is really the third critique, the *Critique of Judgment*, that offers the solution that then becomes elaborated in Hegel's philosophy. The third critique provides a figuring of the imagination in terms of a differential relationality, whereby the free play of imagination constitutes a groundless an-archy of freedom, which is an abyss that is called sublime by Kant. Taylor reads the figuring of imagination in terms of contemporary information theory, where imagination is an "information process" that is both constructive information and destabilizing noise.

To view Kant's conclusion in the *Critique of Judgment* from the standpoint of Kant's successors, including Hegel, is to grasp the very essence of reason, how the "formal identity-within-difference and difference-within-identity of subject and object make knowledge possible." This identity-within-difference and difference-within-identity is not a static situation, however, but a dynamic and unending process. Taylor claims that while the finite pervades and limits the infinite, the finite is infinitely disrupted by the infinite, which is an infinite restlessness. Taylor, like Edith Wyschogrod later in the book, focuses directly on art and indirectly on politics. This specific aesthetic primacy characterizes American postmodern theology as it emerged in the 1980s out of the encounter between French poststructuralism and deconstruction and American Death of God theologies. At the same time, the conclusion that art is the endless working of creative imagination and a productive process that achieves freedom, a productive freedom, is inherently political in its implications. Productive freedom is everywhere under siege in the onslaught of late capitalism, which is currently consuming the means of production itself—living human labor—in order to perpetuate itself. How can we preserve space for art and for thought and for freedom? Hegel again offers us crucial insights.

Just as Negri is driven to oppose Hegel in his drive for right, William Desmond is also highly critical of Hegel, but for different, more explicitly theological, reasons. In "Between Finitude and Infinity," Desmond follows Taylor in analyzing the relationship between finitude and infinity, but he argues that Hegel's dialectic domesticates the space between the infinite and the finite. The problem is the immanence of Hegel's God, the fact that the infinite becomes finite in a predictable, overdeterminate, and absolute way. Desmond calls the dialectical process that makes the passage between finite and infinite too easy and renders finitude and infinity as equivalence a "sublationary infinitism." Sublationary infinitism sees God as selving or self-othering in a process of infinitization of the finite that issues in a postreligious humanism. Sublationary infinitism completes the circle, closing the middle space between the finite and the infinite. Rather than surrender to this sublationary infinitism, on the one hand, or retreat to a Kantian dualism between finitude and infinity, on the other, Desmond wants to articulate a "metaxological agapeics." Metaxological agapeics allows a passage between infinity and finitude; it does not equate them, but it sustains a fragile and asymmetrical (im)balance between the two.

Before developing his own view, Desmond considers and rejects two alternatives to Hegel's sublationary infinitism, which he calls postulatory infinitism and postulatory finitism. Postulatory infinitism simply replaces Hegelian Spirit, *Geist*, with humanity as a whole. Feuerbach and Marx are seen as examples of this process, and this marks a "self-infinitization of finitude." Basically, rather than an absolute sublating the difference between the finite and the infinite, this humanism postulates an infinite self-becoming of finite humanity in an ongoing process. The alternative, postulatory finitism, is better associated with figures such as Nietzsche and Heidegger and results in the "self-laceration of finitude as such." Here is an attempt to think the infinite as finite and live as if there is nothing but the finite, which leads to a counterfeit infinitude, or a false infinity. Desmond is highly critical of the obsession with finitude that characterizes contemporary "Left-Nietzscheans," and this anti-Hegelianism is no better than the Hegelianism it opposes. In a less explicitly religious vein, we could consider Quentin Meillassoux's attempt to think the limits of finitude in his book *After Finitude*.

Desmond argues that there is a relation between finitude and infinity, but there is an important difference and heterogeneity as well. There exists a porosity between the two, but this connection cannot be captured in an immanent totality. Desmond invites us to think the God of the Between, as an overdetermined excess of divine infinity, a Between tilted toward infinity, but whose movement carries being beyond any and every whole. Signs of infinity include thematics such as the idiocy of being, an aesthetics of happening, an erotics of selving, and most significantly an agapeics of community. A religious community that stresses agapeic service maintains this distance between the finite and the infinite that Desmond values, and precisely such a vision of community is missing from Hegel. Furthermore, such an agapeic community founds a more vital politics, even if Desmond is very implicit on this point. In this sense, though, Hegel can still be viewed as the philosopher of totality and wholeness who cannot respect or value difference.

At the same time, using Negri's mantra, here where it seems that everything is complete, everything is incomplete. Why? Because Desmond, like Negri, continues to think and write against Hegel, and specifically he suggests a kind of reverse sublation, a reworking of the necessary progression from religion to philosophy. At the same time, thinkers like Malabou and Caputo, not to mention Slavoj Žižek, give us tools to think Hegel's philosophy itself as a kind of reverse sublation and push us to imagine alternative forms of social and political and religious community in light of this shift in perspective. Katrin Pahl's essay, "The Way of Despair," gives us further evidence that Hegel's narrative is not simply one of cumulative and sublationary progress.

According to Pahl, most twentieth-century readers of the *Phenomenology of Spirit* assume that it is a narrative of progress; readers prefer and presume a happy ending. On the other hand, Hegel declares in the introduction that spirit proceeds by way of despair. Rather than an accumulation of truth and self-knowledge, the *Phenomenology* plots a path of despair that crushes and fragments the subject, rendering it into something akin to rubber due to the subject's infinite elasticity. The conscious subject proceeds by way of despair, but proceeds ironically precisely by forgetting this despair and destruction and cheerfully starting anew. Pahl describes conscious spirit like a Weeble that keeps wobbling over but then always tipping up because it is unable to stay down.

Pahl develops her reading of Hegel by crossing the *Phenomenology* with the story *The Passion According to G. H.* by Clarice Lispector. Lispector describes an encounter of an upper-class Brazilian woman with a cockroach, and in crushing a cockroach and consuming its crushed whitish pulp, the woman experiences a kind of transformation—G. H. and the cockroach are each other, they eat each other and they give birth to each other. The cockroach represents an absolute nakedness and undivided divine being that then gets destroyed and consumed, whereas the woman G. H. possesses secrets, and she gives the gift of death to the cockroach. Paradoxically, ironically, this shared death becomes a mutual transformation: "I am the cockroach," she declares. Returning to Hegel, Pahl shows how eating is a way of thinking, and how furthermore human despair is not so different from animal despair. When the conscious subject has to change, to alter, to become different by consuming and being consumed, it does not simply transform itself, it goes blank, which is a comical moment on the path to despair. The conscious spirit or subject cannot take account of its despair; rather, it can only respond to it by naively starting anew. Pahl reads Hegel's stations of despair in the *Phenomenology* through the Christian Stations of the Cross and the Greek Eleusian mysteries or Dionysian initiation rites. In both cases spirit is born anew after being segmented and disjointed and having its body torn apart and reborn, and for Pahl this story possesses comic appeal. What is more, such lighthearted despair is sexy!

According to Adrian Johnston, a philosopher of psychoanalysis, Hegel read through Freud and Lacan gives resources for a more materialistic philosophy. In "The Weakness of Nature," Johnston argues against the idealistic, and apparently Hegelian, Lacanian opposition of a "bad" biological naturalism in Freud and a "good" Freud of the signifier. Contemporary investigations in genetics and the neurosciences offer support to a psychoanalytic naturalism in which the brain and body are material in nature but open and underdetermined by established codes. This materialist psychoanalysis then allows a more nuanced appropriation of German idealist philosophies of nature such as Hegel and Schelling.

Johnston affirms a materialist reading of Hegel and Lacan, supported by Malabou and Žižek, whereby the opposition between nature and antinature is internal to nature itself, which is what distinguishes his philosophy as materialist rather than idealist. Johnston attends less to Lacan's explicit use of Hegel, taken from Kojève, and more to what he calls the "unconscious Hegelianism" that appears in a session of Lacan's *Seminar IV* on "The Signifier and the Holy Spirit." According to Johnston, the natural Real is already denaturalized in Lacan, because the Real is riddled with negativity. The denaturalizing negativity of *Geist*, as the Other of nature, is immanent to disharmonious nature itself, and this reading of nature in Lacan mirrors the Hegelian reading of Christianity.

Johnston uses Hegel to think through Lacan and science more generally, while Edith Wyschogrod in one of her last essays offers us a meditation on art by juxtaposing Hegel and Vincent van Gogh on reason and madness. In "Disrupting Reason," Wyschogrod echoes Taylor's emphasis upon the liberating possibilities of aesthetics, while at the same time she complicates any simple progression from art to philosophy, or madness to rationality. She considers Hegel's theoretical discourse on insanity in his *Philosophy of Mind* and compares it with his letters to his sister Christianne, who had a mental breakdown in 1820 and was briefly committed to an asylum. Although Hegel seems to be a prototypical bourgeois gentleman scholar, Wyschogrod reveals intriguing parallels with van Gogh, as shown in his accounts of his mental states in his letters to his brother Theo.

In his philosophy, Hegel understands madness as a stage on the way to higher rationality, while in personal terms he describes it in his letters as a reversion to animal nature. Wyschogrod also considers Hegel's affair with an abandoned wife with whom Hegel had a son, Ludwig. Essentially, both Hegel and van Gogh strive for wholeness and rationality but both also succumb to erotic temptation and the risk of madness. Art and madness are linked in the conception of irrational or suprarational genius and both represent stages along the path of the development of Hegel's dialectic. The goal is the Idea's self-realization in freedom, but art, like religion, is a necessary stage but also a transitional step on the way to this destination. At the same time, van Gogh's life and art and Hegel's life suggest that we cannot neatly separate the penultimate from the ultimate, or the private life from the public sphere.

The passage from art to philosophy, like the passage from madness to reason, is contested and incomplete, especially where everything would need to appear perfectly rational and complete. Hegel wrestles with the conflicts between his inner life, which he characterizes as marked by Christian love (for his sister and his bastard son), his objective family life, and his ethical duty, which is also a responsibility of political life. This passage from the private to the public is also marked by resistance, subject to feelings that resist sublation and continue to erupt. This passage and transition, from art and religion and their attendant feelings that threaten madness to philosophical rationality and its serene acceptance of public duty, is a political passage and marks the very space of the political in modern life. Wyschogrod forces us back onto the irruption of irrational art as the disruption of the security of our public life by attending to Hegel's irrationality.

Thomas A. Lewis raises the issue of the consummation of Hegel's philosophy of religion, and, like many of the other contributors, he resists the reading of Hegel's system as a closed and totalizing one. Lewis argues that a shift from philosophy and the Concept back toward religion and *Vorstellung* helps to work against this suggestion of closure, while also raising the specter of Hegel's declaration of Christianity as the consummate form of religion. Rather than endorse this turn to *Vorstellung*, Lewis follows Robert Pippin and Terry Pinkard in emphasizing the spontaneous and social character of Hegel's thought. Lewis argues that one cannot fix conceptual relations, and this is Hegel's criticism of Kant, for these conceptual relations are themselves products and processes that spontaneously emerge out of the representations they represent. The idea of closure that Hegel evokes in the Notion or Concept is only a provisional or weak notion of closure.

Lewis considers Hegel's *Philosophy of Religion*, and he shows how, on the one hand, Hegel does privilege the culmination of religion in Christianity as the consummate form of religion. On the other hand, Lewis stresses that even Christianity is a revealed, positive religion that is still a representation of spirit presented in representational form. This form is open-ended, however, and open to further development as philosophers interpret the conceptual and rational meanings implicit in Christianity and other religious forms. The only completion of Hegel's system is the self-consciousness of the dynamism within all determinate concepts, religion and Christianity included. In conclusion, Lewis claims that Hegel's thought possesses important political implications insofar as he directs us to consider the civil religion of our collective life in whatever forms it takes, and this is a continuous, open-ended transformation. Hegel is not a totalizing, protototalitarian thinker who suppresses alterity or difference, but neither is he a simple relativist who abandons any standards of political and philosophical comparison and truth.

In Hegelian fashion, these essays progress dialectically through politics, theology, art, literature, philosophy, and science, weaving in and out of diverse cutting-edge theoretical discourses to show how Hegel continues to inhabit them, offering unexploited insights for thinking about religion and politics. We end up at the rear, and Žižek in characteristically provocative fashion offers us a meditation on

"Hegel and Shitting" as a work against constipation and the understanding of Hegel as a constipating thinker. Žižek works against the conventional reading of Hegel's system as a voracious eater that swallows up everything and then keeps it all within itself, which would produce the most incredible constipation. Žižek reads Hegel's dialectic as more genuinely evacuating, as being consumed by excrementation or release. Here Absolute knowing is a thoroughly empty subject, a subject reduced to the void or the empty form of self-relating negativity. The Idea lets itself go, just as God lets go of divinity, releasing itself into temporal existence. Žižek claims that this is a Hegelian form of *Gelassenheit*, the letting go of itself as the culmination of sublation. Shitting is part of the process of sublation itself.

According to Žižek, this releasing is at the same time absolute liberation or freedom. He explains that freedom is also radically materialist, in a way that echoes Malabou and Johnston: material reality is a sign of essential conceptual imperfection, such that necessity is nothing but a contingency (material form) elevated to the form of necessity (conceptual universality). This process, however, always leaves a mark or a stain, which testifies to the original status of necessity as radically contingent. Žižek says that universal form itself is marked by the irreducible stain of contingency. This means that the process of philosophical appropriation is always accompanied by excrementation. Eating later becomes shitting. The Idea is an abstract representation of this process, but Absolute knowing involves understanding the backward movement as well, the return to embodied existence, which has revolutionary political and religious implications. Here Žižek explains that this excrementation opens up a space for ecological awareness: Absolute knowing understands nature not as a threat to be controlled but a process that can be left to follow its inherent (albeit erratic) path. Hegelian dialectic is a radical version of a process without a controlling subject. Readers are invited to risk themselves in reading and open themselves up to a future beyond representational philosophy, trivialized religiosity, and representative liberal democratic capitalism in these essays.

NOTES

1. Charles Taylor, *Hegel* (Cambridge: Cambridge University Press, 1975), pp. 545–546.
2. Herman Nohl, *Hegels theologische Jugendschriften* (Tubingen: Mohr, 1907), pp. 73–136.
3. *On Christianity: Early Theological Writings by Friedrich Hegel*, trans. T. M. Knox (New York: Harper Torchbooks, 1948), p. 5.
4. Ibid., p. 78.
5. Ibid., p. 84.
6. These citations were lifted from Knox's gloss in his introduction to ibid., pp. 5–6.

7. See Alenka Zupančič's brilliant rehearsal of Hegel's move here in *The Odd One In: On Comedy* (Cambridge, Mass.: MIT Press, 2008).
8. Alain Badiou, "Lacan and the Pre-Socratics," in *Lacan: The Silent Partners*, ed. Slavoj Žižek (London: Verso, 2006), pp. 7–16.
9. Thanks to Richard Kearney and Mary-Jane Rubenstein for conversations about *Totality and Infinity*.
10. Emmanuel Levinas, *Totality and Infinity*, trans. Alphonso Lingis (Pittsburgh: Duquesne University Press, 1969), p. 296. Our emphasis.
11. Jacques Derrida, *Glas*, trans. John P. Leavey Jr. and Richard Rand (Lincoln: University of Nebraska Press, 1986).
12. Heinz Kimmerle, "On Derrida's Hegel Interpretation" in *Hegel After Derrida*, ed. Stuart Barnett (London: Routledge, 1998), p. 232.
13. Jacques Derrida, *Positions*, trans. Alan Bass (Chicago: University of Chicago Press, 1981), p. 44.
14. Jean-François Lyotard, *The Postmodern Condition: A Report on Knowledge*, trans. Geoff Bennington and Brian Massumi (Minneapolis: University of Minnesota Press, 1984), pp. 33–34.
15. Gilles Deleuze, *Difference and Repetition*, trans. Paul Patton (New York: Columbia University Press, 1994), p. 44.
16. Slavoj Žižek, "Deleuze and the Lacanian Real," http://www.lacan.com/zizrealac.htm (accessed June 19, 2009).
17. Alain Badiou, "The Desire of Philosophy," in *Infinite Thought: Truth and the Return to Philosophy* (London: Continuum, 2003).
18. Slavoj Žižek, *The Sublime Object of Ideology* (London: Verso, 1989), p. xxix.
19. Ibid., pp. xxix–xxx.
20. In this regard, we follow Alain Badiou.

1

IS CONFESSION THE ACCOMPLISHMENT OF RECOGNITION?

Rousseau and the Unthought of Religion in the *Phenomenology of Spirit*

CATHERINE MALABOU

Is confession the accomplishment of recognition? This is one of the fundamental political questions that traverse the *Phenomenology of Spirit*.[1] I have chosen to expand upon it here according to one of its possible lines of interpretation, which concerns the divided and contradictory character of the figure of Rousseau in Hegelian discourse. This dual character is due to the following: it is the same philosopher, Rousseau, who is the author of both *The Social Contract* and *The Confessions*. Not that these two works would be incompatible with regard to their content or style. Hegel is much too subtle a philosopher to pick out just any old separation between the philosophical and the literary. No. For Hegel, the dialectical tension that comes to be established between these two works indicates a properly political contradiction. This contradiction is related, eminently, to the motif of recognition. Rousseau has posed, following Hegel's reading, two possible types of recognition: contractual and personal. And these two types of recognition pass through two types of institutional form: the contract and literature.

Now, if there is a contradiction between these two forms—contradictory in themselves—this is not because the contract would have nothing to do with the literary institution. Quite the reverse, the contract has *everything* to do with the literary institution, insofar as it is the same question that sustains them both: *What is the language of recognition? In what language does one demand to be recognized? In what language does one accede to recognition?* Rousseau, according to Hegel, was never able to answer these questions because he constantly made use of two languages to approach the problem of language itself: the judicial and the fictional, thus producing a major political aporia.

This aporia, as Hegel will show in the last part of section VI ("Spirit That Is Certain of Itself. Morality": "Conscience. The 'Beautiful Soul,' Evil and Its Forgiveness") as well as in the last part of section VII ("The Revealed Religion"), only finds its resolution in the religious sphere of Spirit. Our initial question (is confession the accomplishment of recognition?) might imply that the social and political motif of recognition is dialectically sublated by a religious motif—confession. Surprisingly though, according to Hegel, recognition and confession both suffer, in their immediate forms, from the same excess of abstraction. *They both have to be confronted about their hidden and unconscious religious content to gain their genuine speculative meaning.* According to Hegel, Rousseau is in search of two main conceptual figures: that of the Witness (in confession) and that of Forgiveness (in politics), which both exceed the spheres of morality and contractual political philosophy.

In the first part of this essay, I would like to situate and clarify this problematic in order to show, subsequently, that it still has an effect on our contemporary philosophical and political scene. The dialectic of the recognition of consciousnesses is not only set out in the second section of the *Phenomenology*, "Self-Consciousness." The theme of recognition is treated throughout the work until the very end with the issue of reconciliation, which appears to be the dialectical transition from Religion to Absolute Knowledge. I will first linger over the role that recognition plays in the third part of the section of the work entitled "Spirit," in the chapter entitled "Spirit that is certain of itself. Morality." In this chapter, Hegel exposes the two central aspects of Rousseau's thought and introduces the reader to the split between the contract and the confession. In the global introduction to this section, Hegel demonstrates the teleological sense of all previous development by insisting on the diverse types of Self that have been met previously: the abstract person (in "Ethical Order"), the revolutionary citizen (in "Culture"), and finally the moral will (in "Morality"). During these three moments, the motif of recognition is present. This no longer concerns the encounter between two self-consciousnesses, but rather the political community. "The Ethical Order" exposes the recognition of the particular self that becomes politically "actual"; the second part, "Culture," which is the moment of the social contract as such, marks the emergence of the general will. "Through this process," Hegel writes, "the universal becomes united with [individual] existence in general."[2] The third and last development, "Morality," is the moment of self-certainty, that is, of singularity, of self-consciousness.

The motif of confession appears here. There is no self-certainty without confession. Rousseau plays an important role in the last two moments, which correspond to the drawing up, and then to the consequences, of the social contract: the emergence of the will to confess. Considering this development, we can see very clearly that confession, according to Hegel, is nothing private, secluded from the political sphere. On the contrary, it is a political achievement. Confession is the postcontractual expression of the will. In what sense? Through the drawing up of the contract, "the power of the individual conforms itself to its substance, externalizes its own self and thus establishes itself as substance that has an objective existence."[3] With the social contract, the individual "acquires an acknowledged, real existence."[4] However, this process of recognition lacks something essential. Each consciousness, writes Hegel, stays alien to itself.

Hegel insists upon the inherent contradiction in the principle of the social contract, which he had already raised in the *The Jena Lectures on the Philosophy of Spirit* of 1805–1806: "One imagines the constitution of the general will as if all the citizens gathered together and deliberated, as if the plurality of voices made the general will."[5] One imagines in this way the movement by which the individual ascends to the universal thanks to the negation of self. And yet, the general will appears to the individual as an alien will, not as an expression of her own. Why? "The general will must first of all constitute itself from the will of individuals and constitute itself as general, in such a way that the individual will appears to be the principle and the element, but it is on the contrary the general will which is the first term and the essence."[6] So if the general will appears first of all to the individual, not as a realization of her individual will, but as a foreign or alien will, it is because the individual as such is the result, and not the origin, of the general will, and this is why she does not recognize herself in it. She needs to invent herself. The confession, as the very form of this self-invention, constitutes in this sense the achievement of political recognition.

The motif of confession appears in the *Phenomenology of Spirit* with the evocation of Goethe's *Wilhelm Meister's Apprenticeship*, the "Confessions of a Beautiful Soul," and then with Rousseau's *Confessions*. This is the moment of the moral *consequences* of the social contract, where the individual who does not recognize herself in the general will firmly maintains her conviction, in the need to express her self-certainty: the self understands itself as well as it is understood by others. Again, the expression of this self-certainty is the confession, the accomplished form of the individual's self-recognition. I quote here a passage from Jean Hyppolite's commentary in *Genesis and Structure of Hegel's Phenomenology of Spirit*:

> How can one not think, before this text, of an entire literature which runs from the *Confessions* of Rousseau to the *Confessions of a Beautiful Soul*, passing by the *Sorrows of Young Werther*? What is important is not what the self has achieved, because this determined action is not necessarily recognized, but rather the assurance that he gives to have acted according to his conviction. "It is this self-assuredness within himself which in these *Confessions* or in these *Sorrows*, in all this literature of the self, shows through outwardly and becomes actual: It is this form which is to be established as

actual: it is the *self* which as such is actual in language, which declares itself to be the truth, and just by doing so acknowledges all other selves and is acknowledged by them."[7]

"What is important is not what the self has achieved": what the self has achieved is the contract. Hegel means to say that what is important here is no longer the act of deliberation and agreement by which the self commits itself contractually, but rather the feeling of having acted according to his or her conviction. How can we understand this? If it is true that the individual is not the origin but the result of the social contract, the product of the general will, if it is true that the general will precedes, in its truth, the individual will, then the abstract political recognition that takes place in and by the contract must be pursued, concluded, and accomplished, the truth of the individual must be produced and recognized, and it is the role of confession to allow this recognition. Confession appears as a social contract between self and self. If we follow Hegel on this point, then it is necessary to insist once again upon the fact that confession, that is, the act of producing oneself as truth, is a fundamental dimension of political life. Confession is even fundamentally caught up in public life, since it produces the private sense of the public, without which the public would be senseless.

How can Hegel carry out such an inversion: the general will *precedes* the individual will? Is this not a reversal which threatens to ruin Rousseau's entire theory for which there is no doubt that the general will is a product of the union of individual wills? To answer these questions, we have to examine the role of language in this process.

We are familiar with the Hegelian critique of the contract and contractual ideologies. But the essential reason for this critique is perhaps not always well understood, this being precisely that contract theory in general presents a relationship between the individual and the community that is not ordered in conformity with the concept, since this theory affirms that there are first individuals and then the social body. We know, moreover, the fact that, for Hegel, this general will is obtained in contract theory and, particularly in Rousseau, by the exchange of particular abstract wills, without substance, and that, therefore, the contract remains purely formal. The community that results remains, as we have seen, alien to itself.

Why this accusation of formalism? One of the more difficult problems that Hegel reproaches Rousseau for having left unresolved is that of knowing in which language the contract is worded. Rousseau neglects to specify the essential thing, that is, that the contract is first of all a linguistic act. Rousseau states the formula of the contract as if it were ready-made, issued straight from a universal philosophical language, beyond any particularities belonging to a nation-state, as if its idiomatic dimension were evaded from the outset. This is to say that what is hidden, passed over in silence, is the moment of the access to sense, the access of the general will, and consequently of the community, to its own sense.

The linguistic community precedes the political community. Language is always, originally, the expression of an impersonal social order that carries the individual beyond herself, meaning that language is the first social contract, preceding by right and in fact the second. But what Rousseau obscures is precisely the fact that the social contract is the doubling of an earlier contract. Sense is obtained from this doubling whose philosophical import Rousseau does not examine, except to say that the first language is metaphoric, then becomes literal at the time of the contract's stipulation.

If Hegel can affirm that the general will precedes individual wills, this is because the consciousnesses who are drafting the contract are speaking consciousnesses, already capable of distinguishing between the literal and the figurative. In this sense, they already no longer exist as singular individuals but are rather bound by the idiom that, as we know, always makes of the self a universal. To present, therefore, the contract as the process by which the individual accedes to its universal signification amounts to obscuring the existence of an earlier community, of an earlier ethos, which proves that the isolated individual never exists as such, or at least is not an origin.

Not *reflecting* its own language, the contract is therefore expressed in an alien language, that of *things* and of the *economy*. As though such a language could exist, neutral and without ambiguity, an idiom without idiomatism, a language whose phantasmic character Marx will later demonstrate. Hegel shows, in effect, that the contract makes *the alienation of property* the fundamental form of exchange between wills. The social contract effectively expresses the necessity of the "total surrender of each associate, along with all of his or her rights, to the entire community." The language that allows this clause to be formulated is also, by the same token, alienated, forced to speak another language: that of the exchange contract. Hegel shows that contracts bearing on property are the prototypes of political contracts, not the other way round. Contract theories take as their model the relationship between men and things, or between things themselves, and not the relationship of men among themselves.

The contract silences its own language at the very moment that it asserts itself as the expression of the will. The result of this silence is that the repressed and denied language will be *interiorized*, becoming thereby a secret. But in fact, it is the constitution of this secret that coincides with the birth of individuality. There is no individual before the secret in Hegel, that is, before the censure of a language, before the interdiction of an idiom. What is thus required henceforth to be recognized is indeed this language, the postcontractual sense of the singular individual.

This very special political moment, the postcontractual, gives rise, in the *Phenomenology of Spirit*, to the fine analyses of the relationship between politics and language in the section devoted to the *Aufklärung*.

In modern society, Hegel writes, "the self knows itself as actual only as sublated."[8] In fact, the individual, as we were saying earlier, does not recognize itself in the community that it is nevertheless supposed to have wanted. She is *nonrecognized* (non-reconnu) *by her own recognition*; she is outside herself, in an alien spirit. The individual is "alienated from itself."[9] The repression and interiorization of the secret becomes, therefore, the deepest fold of interiority and the birthplace of moral consciousness and its language. As Hegel asserts: "The content of the language of conscience is *the self that knows itself as essential being*. This alone is what is declared, and this declaration is the true actuality."[10] And as Hyppolite comments: "Whereas the self [*moi*] becomes alien to itself and is alienated from itself in the language of the seventeeth century, in this new language the *self* [*soi*] *states itself* in its *inner certainty*" as being the truth.[11]

This expression presupposes that consciousness recovers the lost language. And it is precisely the role of confession, which Hegel still calls the "aesthetic contemplation of self," to allow *the invention of the recovered language*. Modern confession becomes, therefore, the fictitious but effective site of the restoration of the political space that gives the individual subject its substance. Rousseau's *Confessions* are, in this sense, the accomplishment of *The Social Contract*. The philosopher cannot write about recognition, cannot make recognition his subject—as is the case in *The Social Contract*—without recognizing himself, without writing himself as just, as a recognized, singular individual. A confession has worth, not so much in virtue of its content—the facts that are recounted or owned up to—as in its political task, which is to let the individual accede to its own idiom, and by this to reintroduce her into the political community that had become alien to her. The subject must become the creator of its own history to experience, in language, "the majesty of absolute autarky, to bind and to loose," to be, at the same time, both within and outside the contractual community.[12]

This analysis of Hegel's, which sees in Rousseau's two major works both a *political* opposition and a *political* continuity, is fundamental. It brings to light one of the most difficult paradox that structures secretly the motif of recognition: is the political recognition of the subject a political movement or is it not always doomed to anchor itself in a nonpolitical realm, in the extraterritoriality of fiction for example?

To answer these issues, we now need to turn towards the last moment of "Morality," concerning Evil and Forgiveness, and to the following section entitled "Religion." The two spheres of culture and politics, in the way Rousseau has defined them, are too narrow to allow a solution to this contradiction. "The one who made the confession" is split between his interiority ("keeping himself to himself")[13] and community with others, which he repulses. In consequence, "in so far as the self-certain Spirit, as a 'beautiful soul,' does not possess the power to renounce the knowledge of itself which it keeps to itself, it cannot attain to an identity with the consciousness it has repulsed, nor therefore to a vision of the unity of itself in the other, cannot attain to an objective existence."[14] The two sides (self-conscious and objectively existent in the political community) need to be equalized. The "self" of confession must "renounce its separate being-for-self."[15] In other words, the "self" must *forgive* and must also *be forgiven* for staying secluded from the community. Forgiveness is "the work of reconciliation" as the subjectively *and* objectively "existent Spirit." The subject of confession opens himself to the substance of the community. In reverse, in order not to get lost or dissolved, the subject must find a *witness*, or a reminder, in the community itself. The two motifs of forgiveness and witnessing lead both the subject of the confession (singularity) and the subject of the contract (universal form of subjectivity) to the religious spiritual content of their selves. Hegel writes: "The reconciling *Yea*, in which the two 'I's let go their antithetical *existence*, is the *existence*, of the 'I' which has expanded into a duality, and therein remains identical with itself, and, in its complete externalization and opposite, possesses the certainty of itself: it is God manifested in the midst of those who know themselves in the form of pure knowledge."[16] Further, in "The Revealed Religion," Hegel adds: "The transcended immediate presence of the self-conscious essence has the form of universal consciousness."[17] The individual is reconciled with the community. This reconciliation once again excedes the limits of the moral and political sphere. It is God who forgives; it is God who is the witness. Rousseau would not really have exposed the necessary theologico-political dimension of recognition, and of language itself.

We can refer to Derrida on this point when he declares in *Faith and Knowledge*: "Without God, no absolute witness. No absolute witness to be taken as witness in testifying.... In the irrepressible invoking of a witness, God would remain then one *name of the witness*, he would be *called* as witness."[18] No forgiveness without God either. This does not mean that the resolution of the divorce exposed by Rousseau is "religious." Derrida adds: "with God, a God that is present, the existence of a third ... that is absolute, all attestation becomes superfluous, insignificant or secondary."[19] With and without God: such is the meaning of the philosophical sublation of religion accomplished by philosophy in the last moment of the *Phenomenology of Spirit*, Absolute Knowledge.

In *The Philosophy of Right*, Hegel provides us with a theory of political recognition that is supposed to put an end to the dilemma between confession, contract, and religion. He writes: "the principle of modern states has prodigious strength and depth because it allows the principle of subjectivity to progress to its culmination in the extreme of self-subsistent personal particularity, and yet at the same time brings it back to the substantive unity."[20] Recognition in modern States, therefore, has the sense, not only of a guarantee of universality, that of the citizen's existence, it is also related to *the singular individual's* social status. The singular individual thus demands to be recognized as well. He is, in the words of Sartre, "a being that is in question of its own being."[21]

The desire for recognition is this: the expectation of a response given to a being's concrete questioning of its own being. The expectation of a response given to an ontologico-political question, which consists in knowing what is becoming of the singular individual, was at first denied by the social contract. Recognition, in modern States, must therefore always be made up of an objective institutional component—the political community—and a subjective institutional component.

Hegel's particular contribution consists in developing a theory of the State that puts an end to Rousseau's vision of an individual divided between its situation as a political subject on the one hand and a self-certain individual on the other, between its juridical and its confessional language. In this way there appears at the end of *The Philosophy of Right*—as Sartre, once more, comments in *Life/Situations*[22]—the idea of a possible recognition of minorities *by the State* and not simply by a literary act (this question also appears in Sartre's preface to Frantz Fanon's book *The Wretched of the Earth*).[23] Hegel intends to show that a State which truly conforms to its concept does not require individuals to invent themselves, that is, to invent their language, that is, again, to invent their law through the intermediary of a narrative. The contradiction that exists between formal legal language and the secret idiom must therefore be dialectically sublated. The question of religion is inescapable on this point, which does not mean that religion, once again, is the ultimate solution to this problem. As Clayton Crockett declares, commenting on Slavoj Žižek's argument about the meaning of religion in Hegel: "the essence of politics repeats the founding gesture of Christianity and involves a 'kind of short circuit between the Universal and the Particular.'"[24] Rousseau would have stayed blind to this dialectic dimension of politics and of language in which the cultual community precedes the emergence of the individual.

Today, the entire question is that of knowing whether this contradiction between the private subject and the citizen has disappeared, and whether the religious dimension of the substance-subject is taken for granted. To bring this essay to a close, I would like to open up a series of questions with regard to this point. It seems to me that this contradiction has reappeared—that, perhaps, it has never even disappeared. I take as proof the political signification that a philosopher such as Derrida gives anew to confession, against Hegel in a sense, showing how this motif haunts modern States.

The text *Circumfession*[25] focuses on the motif of the struggle between the civil state and the "name hidden from the civil state," between public life and the secret life that is necessary to write, to which one must give one's language. The profoundly political aspect of confession, for which, according to Derrida, St. Augustine provides the foundation, stems from the fact that the political subject has to invent its own *facticity*. Facticity, as we have seen, never preexists the political community. And invention corresponds to the act that Derrida calls, taking up one of St. Augustine's expressions, "faire la vérité" (to make the truth). The facticity of "making" renders possible the facticity of "being."

What does "to make the truth" mean? As Derrida says, "To make the truth cannot simply mean 'to tell it,' if 'to tell the truth' presupposes 'information,' 'presentation,' a manner of 'bringing to knowledge' something that 'is.'"[26] Further on he says that one can "'speak truthfully' without 'bringing out the truth'";[27] or again: "one can always describe or note the truth without avowal."[28] This means that to confess is not to recount one's life, according to what would be a purely private gesture, but rather *to give life itself the political access to its own facticity*. To free, in and by writing, the structure of a recognition that forever escapes the civil state, that of the recognition of the minority, of the necessarily minoritarian character of every singular individual, the minoritarian character that Derrida names the *sentence*: "I have been seeking myself in a sentence," he says.[29]

This fissure between the life of the political subject and the life of the individual phrase is found again in the motif of forgiveness, whose decisive political signification Derrida, once again, has demonstrated. Forgiveness does not speak, no more than does the confession, the language of the civil state, and yet the State today lasts only if it forgives. We have already insisted upon the proximity of forgiveness and confession. Forgiveness consists in the mutual recognition of confessed singular individuals. The yes of forgiveness thus shatters the negativity of their isolation, but the movement is the same: "it is the same movement which was expressed in the consciousness that made confession of itself."[30] The confession, at once singular and collective, is therefore at work in political life as its paradoxical condition.

But here, once again, where Hegel envisaged a dialectical resolution of this contradiction, are we not on the contrary confronted with its return, a return without solution? Individuals, minorities, must they not always *show themselves, make themselves—in the sense both of the fictitious and the factical*—to exist politically? A politician today must be perceived as someone who is ready to confess his errors and, in so doing, accept responsibility for those errors. He must be willing to ask forgiveness in his own name for the wrongs of the entire nation. The media thus becomes the site of political confession where power creates an individual figure.[31]

Every citizen would thus have to give, as Judith Butler says, an account or a narrative of herself or of himself. In her book *Giving an Account of Oneself*, Butler insists upon the aporetical intrication of the private and the public meaning of the "I": "When the 'I' seeks to give an account of itself, it can start with itself, but it will find that this self is already implicated in a social temporality that exceeds its own capacities for narration; indeed, when the 'I' seeks to give an account of itself, an account that must include the conditions of its own emergence, it must, as a matter of necessity, become a social theorist."[32] This transcendence of the self has also and inevitably a religious dimension because of the very structure of the *address* of the narrative. The "account of oneself" can be interpreted as a pure act of faith: faith in oneself and faith in the other.

The dilemma today would thus no longer be between man and citizen, the dilemma or schism whose fallacious character Marx has shown, but between three types of political languages. First, there is, again, the language of contracts, which are multiplying in the social sphere—one may think here of the increasingly differentiated character of work contracts. Second, there is the language of self-expression, which allows the subject of these contracts to make or form herself as a genuine individual through the medium of the "account"—a new form of the confession. Third, there is the religious dimension of this belief in oneself and in the value of this self-testimony. Three heterogeneous idiomatic systems working together. This would relaunch the problem of the religious essence, in the Hegelian sense, of the relationship between the individual and the political community. This religious essence seems currently to be separated from its content, appearing as a third term, not as a synthesis, between the particular and the universal. The double challenge of Rousseau by Hegel and of Hegel by contemporary Continental philosophers would then inform, without providing us with any dogmatic answer, a political and literary reorientation of the philosophical concept of the religious meaning of the nonreligious.

NOTES

1. G. W. F. Hegel, *Phenomenology of Spirit*, trans. A. V. Miller (Oxford: Clarendon Press, 1977).
2. Ibid., p. 306.
3. Ibid., p. 299.
4. Ibid.
5. *Hegel and the Human Spirit: A Translation of the Jena Lectures on the Philosophy of Spirit (1805–1806) with Commentary by Leo Rauch* (Detroit: Wayne State University Press, 1983), trans. from G. W. F. Hegel, *Gesammelte Werke*, vol. 8, *Jenaer Systementwürfe* III [also known as *Realphilosophie* II, first published 1931, section II, B, "The Contract"].

6. Ibid.
7. Jean Hyppolite, *Genesis and Structure of Hegel's Phenomenology of Spirit*, trans. Samuel Cherniak and John Heckman (Evanston, Ill.: Northwestern University Press, 1974), p. 512.
8. Hegel, *Phenomenology of Spirit*, p. 299.
9. Ibid., p. 306.
10. Ibid., p. 396.
11. Hyppolite, *Genesis and Structure of Hegel's Phenomenology of Spirit*, p. 512.
12. Hegel, *Phenomenology of Spirit*, p. 393.
13. Ibid., p. 405.
14. Ibid., p. 406.
15. Ibid.
16. Ibid., p. 409.
17. Ibid., p. 471.
18. Jacques Derrida, "Faith and Knowledge," in *Acts of Religion*, ed. Gil Anidjar (New York: Routledge, 2002), p. 65.
19. Ibid., p. 65.
20. "and so maintains this unity in the principle of subjectivity itself" (G. W. F. Hegel, *Philosophy of Right*, trans. T. M. Knox [Oxford: Clarendon Press, 1967], §260).
21. Jean-Paul Sartre, *Being and Nothingness*, trans. Hazel E. Barnes (New York: Philosophical Library, 1948), p. 52.
22. Jean-Paul Sartre, *Life/Situations: Essays Written and Spoken*, trans. Paul Auster and Lydia Davis (New York: Pantheon, 1977).
23. Frantz Fanon, *The Wretched of the Earth*, trans. Constance Farrington (New York: Grove Press, 1965).
24. Clayton Crockett, *Interstices of the Sublime* (New York: Fordham University Press, 2007), p. 152.
25. Jacques Derrida, "Circumfessions," in Geoffrey Bennington and Jacques Derrida, *Jacques Derrida*, trans. Geoffrey Bennington (Chicago: University of Chicago Press, 1999).
26. Ibid., p. 48.
27. Ibid., p. 56.
28. Ibid., p. 99.
29. Ibid., p. 14.
30. Hegel, *Phenomenology of Spirit*, p. 407.
31. Even though he refused to talk about his personal life in the beginning, Nicolas Sarkozy eventually wrote *Witness*, a book that presents his political convictions in the form of a confession: "As far as I can remember, I always wanted to achieve in the political realm. Politics was not part of my family's tradition. In fact, I probably should have stayed away from it: I had neither connections nor wealth, I was not a bureaucrat, and my name, since it sounds foreign, would have been enough for someone other than myself to descend into anonymity. I like to build, to move, to resolve problems. I think that the effort is always worth it, and in the end, it always pays off. Those are my values. That is why

I am a politician. That is what I am here to tell you" (my translation from *Témoignage* [Paris: Editions XO, 2006], back cover)

It is impossible here not to think of the very beginning of Rousseau's *Confessions*: "I will present myself, whenever the last trumpet shall sound, before the Sovereign Judge with this book in my hand, and loudly proclaim, 'Thus have I acted; these were my thoughts; such was I'" (Jean-Jacques Rousseau, *Confessions*, trans. W. Conyngham Mallory [New York: Tudor, 1928], §3).

32. Judith Butler, *Giving an Account of Oneself* (New York: Fordham University Press, 2005), p. 8.

2

REREADING HEGEL

The Philosopher of Right

ANTONIO NEGRI

TRANSLATED FROM THE ITALIAN BY PETER THOMAS

I

1. The theoretical and political problem of the State and Right seems to be focused today on the theme of the social control of living labor, or rather on the theme of the legal control of social labor. This is to say that if the contemporary State is becoming ever more socialized, if its action has become ever more diffuse, and if this is due to the extreme importance that the movements of the world of labor have progressively assumed, then it follows that the juridical essence of the contemporary State tends at its limit to merge with the form of the social organization of labor. The planned State, both in the case in which the fiction of the private property relation is still admitted and the case in which it is negated (social State and socialist State), thus really establishes its legitimacy in the entire context of the nexuses of coercion and consensus that it lays out and with which it forms the mode of social production. To the extent that organized labor has become the exclusive foundation of social wealth, it has become, to the same extent, the foundation of constitutions, that is, the material condition of legality. The contemporary State is above all command of social labor, the organization of living labor.

To reread today a philosopher of Right with the claim to affirm his contemporaneity—in the sense that the problems he treated can be objectively translated for the contemporary reader—means to place him in front of the problems we have mentioned, to ask him how he thinks of the command of social labor, to consider to what extent this type of problem distinguishes his thought. The history of the philosophy of Right begins to be interesting only at the point where it is manifested as the philosophy of the organization of social labor.

※ ※ ※

2. Hegel's *Philosophy of Right* is perhaps the first philosophical text of modernity for which such an approach can be valid—and valid in an exclusive manner. Hegel, the philosopher of Right, is from this point of view an entirely contemporary author.

Right is the organization of and command over social labor, the form in which civilization [*civiltà*] is constituted via labor. This is a recurring and fundamental concept:

> *Education* [*Bildung*],[1] in its absolute determination, is therefore *liberation* and *work* toward a higher liberation; it is the absolute transition to the infinitely subjective substantiality of ethical life [*Sittlichkeit*], which is no longer immediate and natural, but spiritual and at the same time raised to the shape of universality [*Allgemeinheit*]. Within the subject, this liberation is the *hard work* of opposing mere subjectivity of conduct, of opposing the immediacy of desire as well as the subjective vanity of feeling [*Empfindung*] and the arbitrariness of caprice.
>
> [Certainly,] the fact that it is such hard work accounts for some of the disfavor that it incurs. But it is through this work of education that the subjective will attains *objectivity* even within itself, that objectivity in which it alone is for its part worthy and capable of being the *actuality* [*Wirklichkeit*] of the Idea.[2]

Substance, therefore, is the entire labor of civilization as the rational organization of the Idea, as the objectivity of the Idea and its new necessity of an ethical universe. Right is completely contained in this self-objectification—via labor—of the Idea: "The system of Right is the realm of actualized freedom, the world of spirit produced out of itself as a second nature."[3] It is a nature that is not found but radically constructed by the social activity of men, who are all included in the profound necessity of the labor of the Idea. The hard labor of individuals is included and contained in the design of the absolute labor of Spirit. Labor is the substance of the spiritual world [*mondo spirituale*].[4]

※ ※ ※

3. Now, this substantiality of labor as the foundation of the civil world [*mondo civile*] that Hegel assumes in the *Philosophy of Right* is stated even more explicitly in the early writings in which Hegel's thought was developed, particularly in the early philosophico-juridical writings.

Between Frankfurt and Jena, through economic analysis and with explicit reference to the classics of English economic thought, labor (as the source of value) and wealth (as the result of labor) are integrated into the narrative of Spirit and considered as terms of positive qualification of objectivity. Society is constituted as a totality by the demanding synthesis of material motivations, by the valorization of the determinateness of total human labor. The previous youthful image of the ethical community in which individuality and rationality harmoniously and classically converged, and on which his first investigations were based, is dissolved by the Hegel of Jena into a process traversed by the stages of human industriousness from need to the interdependence of needs, from labor to the social collectivities that manage total labor. Here he depicts the rationality of the entire picture: "physical needs and pleasures . . . posited for themselves in the totality, obey in their infinite intertwinings a necessity and constitute the system of general mutual interdependence with a view to the physical needs and the labor and the accumulation of the same [needs and labor] and—considering this as science—the system of so-called political economy."⁵

From this point, however, the picture is further deepened. The deepening is perfected until it finds in individual labor the substantial origin of ethical value in its universality. In the *Phenomenology of Spirit* a few years later, Hegel will say:

> The *labor* of the individual for his own needs is just as much a satisfaction of those of others as of himself, and he attains the satisfaction of his own only through the labour of others. As the individual [*der Einzelne*] in his own particular [*in seiner einzelnen*] work *ipso facto* accomplishes *unconsciously* a universal [*allgemeine*] work, so again he also performs the universal task as his *conscious* object. The whole becomes *in its entirety* [*als Ganzes*] his work, for which he sacrifices himself, and precisely by that means receives back his own self from it.⁶

※ ※ ※

4. Substantiality of labor is therefore the foundation of human civilization [*civiltà*]. Nevertheless, "need and labor, raised to this universality, constitute for themselves . . . an extensive system of commonality and reciprocal dependence, a life of that which is dead that moves in itself, that is agitated in its movement blindly and in an elementary way in one sense or in another, and that like a wild ferocious animal needs to be constantly tamed and domesticated."⁷

Here is the point at which Hegel's thought assumes, even more expressly, a contemporary figure. The recuperation of the positivity of labor to the life of Spirit, labors's very deep involvement [*inerenza*] and its very fundamental nature, cannot be given as such. Civilization [*civiltà*] isn't simply labor but regulated, organized, and controlled labor. Labor, without Right, without the State, becomes chaos, the life of a dead body, particularity that arrogates universality for itself. Labor, on the other hand, can and must be universal: but only in the mediation of the State. The fundamental nature of labor is dialecticized, subsumed, sublimated. The involvement [*inerenza*] of the economic in the entire development of ethical life is subordinated already in Jena to the necessity of labor's regulation. Rather, the regulation is slowly abstracted from the content to which it is applied: the economic and the juridical are born together, among the elementary processes of socialization of need and enjoyment, through the system of needs. However, this proceeding together lasts until the "second State", that is, until the acquisitive class; then Right is emancipated. It can regulate this process only by negating its commonality with the process of the socialization of labor. Thus, it definitively declares the substantiality of labor to the human world. Right is contract, punitive justice, institution: here it is still mixed up with the direct necessity of the economic. But then it becomes constitution, State, government; that is, regulative and at the same exalting the reality of that regulated world. From now on, labor will appear in the command of the State.

※ ※ ※

5. The picture that the *Philosophy of Right* presents is that of the complete hegemony of Right over labor—which is nevertheless the substance of the ethical world. Command over social labor here ends up constituting the schema of the State itself: the assumption of labor in the Absolute occurs in the form of command, in the form of the statal articulation of social labor—as articulation for social classes. The division of labor has here a figure immediately functional to command over labor. The capitalist mode of production in the phase of primitive accumulation is sanctified and assumed as the substance of the general social relation. Within it command the political forces that are the guarantors of this phase of development. Idealism triumphs over economic analysis, exalting into spirituality the forces that in economic reality exercise command.

Here in the *Philosophy of Right*, the system of needs, though conceived in the wealth of its internal dialectic ("In this dependence and reciprocity of work and the satisfaction of needs, *subjective selfishness* turns into a *contribution toward the satisfaction of the needs of everyone else*. By a dialectical movement, the particular is mediated by the universal so that each individual, in earning, producing, and enjoying on his own account [*für sich*], thereby earns and produces for the enjoyment of others")[8] is immediately submitted to the dialectics of capitalist "participation" in wealth:

> The *possibility of sharing* in the universal resources—that is, holding particular resources—is, however, *conditional* upon one's own immediate basic assets (i.e., capital)

on the one hand, and upon one's skill on the other; the latter in turn is itself conditioned by the former, but also by contingent circumstances whose variety gives rise to *differences* in the *development* of natural physical and mental [*geistigen*] aptitudes which are already unequal in themselves [*für sich*]. In this sphere of particularity, these differences manifest themselves in every direction and at every level, and, in conjunction with other contingent and arbitrary circumstances, necessarily result in *inequalities in the resources and skills* of individuals.[9]

Nor is participation that is different from wealth an individual fact, an exception of singularity: the universality of the process equally has to express the diversity in "universal masses" [*allgemeinen Massen*],[10] in different collectivities of participation and command over social living labor.

Thus Right is superimposed over the living community of social cooperation in the organization of wealth.

※ ※ ※

6. The nexus of unity and division, of cooperation and subordination proposed by the capitalist organization of social living labor thus ends up constituting also the interior nexus of the Hegelian conception of Right.

Right is in fact presented in the *Philosophy of Right* in three figures: It is abstract Right, norm and prohibition, the moment of negative protection of personality, element conditioning the constitution of the society as such; but it is also, in the second place, immediately, subjective Right, claim—the person becomes subject, will conforms positively as action. The auroreal life of Right is constituted in this intertwining in a form completely analogous to the self-constitution of social cooperation in the productive world. Right confers here to particularity the capacity and the possibility "of developing and moving on all levels."[11] It is the liberty of action that particularity develops in the world as the collective intention of determined sociality: "the particular reflected in itself is in general well-being."[12] That is, it is the collective growth of labor from the system of needs to the production of wealth. Labor, as constructed world and as forming force, as second nature, as produced objectivity, therefore constitutes the base on which both society and Right develop at the same time.

But Right is presented in the *Philosophy of Right* also in a third, definitive figure: as organic nexus of the ethical world, as ethical institution, as the determined articulation of the entire social world. Now, the emergence of that which for Hegel is the real Spirit, the passing from particularities to universality, from the finite to the infinite, produces the fact that the entire process of the definition of Right is modified and that the nexus that united Right and social cooperation is completed and sublimated in the nexus that sees cooperation in subordination. Liberty, in becoming "substantial liberty," subordinates completely—almost sends back to the background of an unattainable negativity—the world already seen as a human construction, as the collective undertaking of liberty. Cooperation and its dialectics of the positive production of the collective are dissolved inside a context that sees it completely enclosed in the subordination of their process to the absolute—to an absolute that is before any process of any type: "this idea is the being, eternal in itself and for itself and necessary, of Spirit."[13]

Certainly,

> in relation to the spheres of civil law [*Privatrecht*] and private welfare, the spheres of the family and civil society, the State is on the one hand an *external* necessity and the higher power to whose nature their laws and interests are subordinate and on which they depend. But on the other hand, it is their *immanent* end, and its strength consists in the unity of its universal and ultimate end with the particular interest of individuals, in the fact that they have *duties* [*Pflichten*] towards the State to the same extent as they also have Rights.[14]

But this duplicity of the relation between civil society and State, according to which the State would be at the same time negation and the becoming truth of civil society, is duplicity only in appearance, because the becoming truth consists in subordination, and the process is real only in negation. Thus the system of social labor assumed inside the system of Right to constitute its reality can exercise definitively its substantial function and can continue to be its (the system of Right's) condition only by subordinating itself completely to the State. The State is in the last instance the true ethical reality: society and the world of cooperation assume reality only in the act of subordinating themselves to it. Subordination penetrates the very process of cooperation, giving it its own sign. Subordination, the reality of the State, is ontologically immanent to the dialectical process that constitutes it, and it is present in the moment of social cooperation that gives it its determinate being. Labor is the foundation of the State, it is the foundation of the entirety of legality insofar as it is the material of the control of the State. The control of social living labor is the labor of the State.

II

1. The thought of Right and of the State as the thought of labor and its organization is therefore completely explicit in the *Philosophy of Right*. It is a thought of labor and its determinate organization: bourgeois and capitalist.

This is immediately evident in the presuppositions of Hegel's analysis, conditioned to an extreme by the Smithian and Ricardian conception of the foundations of political economy. Value is thus indeed assumed in its laborist origin;[15] however, it is also certainly translated, on that basis, into the universality of exchange value:

> A thing [*Sache*] in use is an individual thing, determined in quantity and quality and related to a specific need. But its specific utility, as *quantitatively* determined, is at the same time *comparable* with other things of the same utility, just as the specific need which it serves is at the same time *need in general*. . . . This *universality*, whose simple determinacy arises out of the thing's particularity [*Partikularität*] in such a way that it is at the same time abstracted from this specific quality, is the thing's value, in which its true substantiality is *determined* and is an object [*Gegenstand*] of consciousness.[16]

In the second place, the bourgeois and capitalist determinateness of the Hegelian discourse on labor and its organization results from the assumption of inequality as a fundamental term in defining the subjects of the labor process. This is not simple naturalistic inequality[17] but exaltation (that is, posed in terms of having to be so) of the diverse functions of the productive process: association necessitates subordination, laboring cooperation necessitates differentiation in the process of valorization, and labor necessitates command, capital.[18]

Third, and consequently, the same Hegelian conception of civil man sees the rule of exchange as predominant: the citizen, as "bourgeois,"[19] is the encounter of the necessity of counting as abstract interchangeable need (all men are, in society, before anything else commodities) and of the possibility of playing a determinant role—and collective as class—in the mechanism of the whole social subordination.

Hegel, therefore, the philosopher of Right, is the philosopher of the bourgeois and capitalist organization of labor.

※ ※ ※

2. In Hegel, however, there is not only the theorization—and the justification—of the given situation of the capitalist process. There is not only the recuperation of the theoretical intuition of classical economy between Smith and Ricardo. Beyond these, there is the utopia of capital, the perfect definition of the transcendental and driving relation of two propositions: the reality of the rational and the rationality of the real. If the reality of the rational is the apotheosis of the state of fact, the absolute immanentism of the pacification of the idea and of the real, determinateness conquered as pacification, and capital thus functions as absolute ordering in the bourgeois determinations that Hegel was able to comprehend, then, besides

this, there is also the completely dialectical affirmation of the rationality of the real. The revolutionary passion of the Enlightenment is thus consciously subordinated to the necessity of capital.

The State is the reality of ethical life, the reality of labor: it is above all the driving rationality of this absolute identity. The world, in which what is rational is given and justified is shaken by the tension that emanates from the interior essence of rationality. A sort of unsatisfied will of understanding, of domination through doing and the intelligence of doing, thus traverses the entire picture. Where it seems that everything is complete, everything is incomplete. Where it seems that determinateness triumphs, the margins of the real's practicability are revealed to be unlimited. But all of this occurs in the measure of a control and of a management of development that cannot but find its own definitive condition in the realized ethical Idea, in the State. It is the essence of the State, it is the essence of capital as the completeness of the subordination of the world of labor: all of that is the absolute, autonomous and self-moving. The immobile of the abstract ethical Idea rediscovers itself as motor of the real. And if the real is labor, if the rational order is "capital," if the relation between cooperation and subordination and between particular and universal is the State, then, we have here the State as development, as capital in necessary development. The State as capital is the State as development. Power is exercised in development, by development. The State is a dynamic institution that sees Right developing as determinate action within the context of society bringing back every social action to the total determinations of the given rational order.

At this point, the rediscovery of universality in the discontinuous seriality of events, the connection of actions in a coherent universe of interior experiences, the fixation of a necessary nexus between individual meanings and overall meaning becomes a task that will find a response. Science is filled and satisfied by this process that feels in itself the absolute: in operating, it is justified, it is always reproposed as objective, though being in every moment result. The equilibrium of all triumphs over the tension of the parts and, vice versa, the determinateness of the parts is placed harmoniously in the movement of all. The capitalist urgency of exalting the world, dissolving it into its parts, reconstructing it, dominating it completely—never any rest, always a firm command: this urgency is translated by Hegelianism into science. From Giovanni Gentile to Carl Schmitt, the European intellectual *entre deux guerres* has learned that this is its apologetic mission.

※ ※ ※

3. The enduring fortune, bourgeois and capitalist, of Hegelianism consists in this image of a rationality that is both given and continually transcendent, incomplete

as development and complete as State. Nothing corresponds more to the image that capital produces of itself than this image, in the perpetual alternation of development and crisis, of reformism and repression, which its existence determines. And in no place is this total and dynamic projection of the State of capital offered better than in the *Philosophy of Right*. Neither Hegelian aesthetics nor logic, even less the philosophy of religion or of history, manage to produce this completeness of image. In the *Philosophy of Right*, the conciliation of positivity and the Idea are given without incoherencies: neither the indeterminateness of religious intuition, nor the coarseness of historical typology, nor the instability of the aesthetic vision, nor the formalism of the logical process are able to upset the picture. In fact, in the *Philosophy of Right*, neither the mere positivity of Right nor the merely statal normative are valorized more than the Idea; rather, here the complete positivity of social production through labor is at play. This compact social reality, unitarily assumed and resolved in the process of the Idea, is the measure of the dynamic positivity that the universal configuration of the *Philosophy of Right* manages to attain. It is an image that interprets the rigidity of the social structures that it reads as positive, an image that interprets the necessity that emanates from the same social structures as dynamic, in order to comprehend, ever more profoundly and rationally, this determinate world of capital within which contemporary man is completely contained.

※ ※ ※

4. This interior completeness of the *Philosophy of Right* has nourished and at the same time imprisoned the philosophical and political thought of the nineteenth and twentieth centuries. It is a generously positive prison when one thinks of the continuous self-critical initiative that the living nexus of rationality and positivity imposed on bourgeois thought. The nineteenth-century conception of progress in positivity closely linked to this (and with this eighteenth-century rationalism was overcome); historicist optimism; the great wave of scientific thought itself: all that is perhaps incomprehensible if it is not linked to the intuition that the real can be moved from the inside without thus losing its positive composition. For the first time in the history of man, in an Hegelian fashion order has become progressivist and power has become reformist. The bourgeoisie, in the name of Hegelianism, had the possibility of renewing an old, revolutionary demand of the Renaissance—the nostalgia for which it had perhaps never lost until now.

But a prison is always a prison, even when it is gilded—above all, if it comprehends bourgeois thought only in the way that it subordinates and crushes the society of labor, only in the way that the bourgeois apology of development in order is posited on the exploitation of total social living labor. Development, domination, wealth: but these are "confronted with a material which offers infinite resistance, i.e., with external means whose particular character is that they are the property of the free will [of others] and are therefore absolutely unyielding."[20] Here the cage of the absolute wavers, it really finds its antithesis. The "absolutely unyielding" does not accept the composition of the plan of reason, of the State.

※ ※ ※

5. When bourgeois thought feels all of this, as a crisis in the entrails of the absolute in which it reposes, it nevertheless does not manage to liberate itself. The prison that Hegelian thought imposes here is not gilded anymore; rather, it is dramatic. An "irresolute determinateness and absolutely unyielding" lived, received, suffered; yet the cage of the absolute, cannot, must not, and does not want to be shattered. After the nineteenth-century apotheosis of Hegelianism, here is the twentieth-century nemesis of the scheme of reference, of the absolute as the project of reason, which the most lucid bourgeois theory has inherited from Hegel. This new hard-won determinateness cannot be subordinated. A new dialectic, within and against the Hegelian absolute, is opened: no longer triumphal, but from time to time mystical or ascetic, always tragic, always more negative.

Here, in fact, the totality of the Hegelian process of reason cannot manage to constitute itself anymore, the process is given as interrupted: and yet it wants to constitute itself. Philosophical science moves from the determined, it wants to reconstitute the determined in the perspective of the absolute: but by now the absolutely unyielding, the reality of an irreducible conflictuality, has been shown. The demand of totality is uncoupled and takes distance from the recompositive mechanism; process and result are not able to attain identity. Here it is that totality is pursued with the rhythm of an unresolved dualism: it will be the ascesis of a functioning intentionality that repeats the models of the transcendental schematism but with a charge of phenomenological heaviness that does not permit the apprehension of the absolute. It will be, inversely, the acceptance of a world of meanings, historically given, which will be held on to in the absence of an overall and ontologically convincing meaning: here the absolute becomes convention, the given is mystically confirmed with stupor and submission to its power that cannot be broken. It will be, finally, the awareness that the nexus between meanings and sense of the ontological event cannot be resolved, that the relation between determinateness and totality is not concluded: "the whole is the untruth." But what a terrible destiny lies behind this discovery! The negation is painfully qualified by the nostalgia of the absolute content on which it is exercised. Hegelian phenomenology is completely relived in inversion: not in the process that carries it to the height of the capitalist composition of the *Philosophy of Right*, but inversely, beginning from the critique of it, within the series of contradictions that constitute the process—a series of contradictions that are today irresolvable, but evermore deepened. The Hegelian totality is dissolved in the contradictions that constituted it without the possibility of triumphing over them. The "tragedy in the ethical" is not the condition of the totality anymore but rather the result of the process.

III

1. The trajectory of Hegel's thought on the State and on Right is not merely bourgeois and capitalist: the Hegelian impact is so complex that it reverberates and is also valid in very, or at least potentially, contradictory locations.

If it is in fact true that the insubordinate determinateness of labor is felt on the development of bourgeois philosophy such as to induce in it desperate results, then it is so much more true that this particularity, really, historically, rises against the general capitalist interest that is supposed to be represented in the figure of the Hegelian State. When, beginning in 1848, and then in the great revolutionary undertakings of the working class in 1870 and in 1917, the particular worker is qualified as subject, proposing and undertaking the rupture of the machines of statal domination over subordinate labor, it seems that the Hegelian ideology of the State has closed its account with history:

> Capital stands on one side and labour on the other, both as independent forms relative to each other; both hence also alien to one another. The labour which stands opposite capital is *alien [fremde]* labour, and the capital which stands opposite labour is *alien* capital. The extremes which stand opposite one another are *specifically* different.[21]

Still, that is not verified; or it is only verified in the form of utopia, of revolutionary hope. In effect, the real experience of realized socialism verifies the continuity—paradoxal continuity, we will see—of a Hegelianizing practice of the State. The revolution is reorganized as capitalist institution; socialism takes the figure of the State. The militant cooperation of the revolutionary workers sees and poses in the first place the necessity of a phasal displacement between an egalitarian participation in the structure of the State and a subordinate participation, according to the urgencies and the positivity of the productive functions, in the structure of the economic process. Slowly—within this historical context—the same free participation in education and in the management of political will is destroyed and subordinated to the necessities of the economic mechanism. Socialism is given in the form of the Hegelian State: the particular worker's interest, its "obstinacy," is therefore not able to free itself from the general interest, from the plan of general subordination. Still, Marx had already noted in the *Grundrisse* that "the demand that wage labour be continued but capital suspended is self-contradictory, self-dissolving."[22]

※ ※ ※

2. Certainly, something has changed. Right and the State do not have here, as in the development of Hegel's thought, as in that crucial phase of the construction of the contemporary capitalist State, the necessity of transcending the world of labor—even if at the end of the dialectical process, in those pages of the *Philosophy of Right* that see the transition from civil society to the State or that of the second acquisitive class to the general class. Here labor is extended to the circle of the general class, but only to discover in itself that dialectic of cooperation and subordination, the continuity of which Hegel interrupted at this point, exalting—exterior to the labor process—its political autonomy and sublimation. In this new experience—which wants to be of negation—Hegelianism paradoxically subsists; it finds a more intimate coherence. The absolute does not need to cut its roots in labor, the order does not need to disengage from the dialectic that proposes and constitutes it: realized socialism gives us the continuity of the formative scheme of the State entirely within labor. Labor and Right, cooperation and subordination, society and State, occur together in an integrated and close community and at all levels of dialectical development.

The prison of the *Philosophy of Right* is thus extended here also to one of its potential negations. It triumphs over it. It triumphs over it at the point that negation, rather than proposing doubt, deepens the coherence of the context. What seems to be an overturning appears as a radical confirmation. The State, menaced, is reposed as the substance of the ethical idea, the solution of the particularity of the general nexus of Spirit. Certainly, it is a *Spirit* "that works." But wasn't the *Philosophy of Right* supposed to be from the beginning the "hard labor of the highest freedom"?

※ ※ ※

3. Does this extreme solution of insurgent and unsubordinated particularity, within the scheme of the Hegelian statal conciliation, really have the capacity to resolve its problem? Or doesn't it rather happen that the unresolved opposition finds here—after this extreme attempt of conclusion—the appropriate terrain on which to deepen itself? No longer, therefore, against Right, no longer merely against the State, but against labor, which the last solution has shown as universally comprehensive substance and the keystone of the relation between cooperation and subordination?

The impetuous advancing of the movement of insubordinate particularity, well beyond the limits imposed by the Hegelian prison of socialism, shows that the road to liberation is precisely that of the struggle against labor—and it shows that it cannot be contained in the Hegelian project of the absolute. As praxis and science, the revolution liberates itself from Hegelianism: the productivity of Spirit is shown to be a prison in the same way as the productivity of labor—this final contemporary divinity of the composition of exploitation with development, of labor with the enlightenment utopia of capitalist progress. The mass refusal of labor as general condition, of the insubordinate attitude fundamentally attacks the Hegelian composition (both in its capitalist and in its socialist figure) of cooperation and of subordination. For the first time, cooperation is dissociated, is turned against subordination, discovering itself in subordination "as object, as absolute misery," reflecting on itself instead—as cooperation—"as general possibility of wealth as subject and as activity." "Labour not as an object, but as activity; not as itself value, but as the living source of value. [Namely, it is] general wealth (in contrast to capital in which it exists objectively, as reality) as the general possibility of the same, which proves itself as such in action."[23] For the first time, labor breaks the substantialist definition that tied it to the State: in the refusal of itself it steps forward at the same time as refusal of the State, it asserts itself as the collective undertaking of liberty. The organization of social living labor is thus entrusted to the general human proposal of happiness and wealth, developing itself as such, against any moment of subordination.

※ ※ ※

4. The rupture of the nexus cooperation and subordination in the social practice of the refusal of labor recovers the obstinacy of particularity; it makes it true as acting particularity, as subject. An alternative world, a really constructed "second nature," opens as a very rich possibility beginning from the activity of the particular. But, critically, what should be emphasized above all is as follows: that the refusal of labor, the exaltation of the obstinacy of particularity inheres as negation at the deepest point, in the most radical dimension of the Hegelian process of the absolute. The shattering of the universe of the *Philosophy of Right* takes place at its sources: going beyond the necessity of Right and of the State, which are not however originary, attaining to the true nucleus of the necessity of the process of objectification, which is the necessity of the capitalist organization of labor. Here there is not some particular content of the dialectic that is placed in discussion; here the formalist business of the neo-Hegelian reform of the dialectic is not repeated: it is the dialectical process itself that is refuted as an adequate form of a specific content, the capitalist organization of labor. The refusal of labor deepens until appearing as the refusal of the dialectic, as the radical dissolution of the composition of the subject

of labor with the necessity of subordination, as the radical affirmation of the irreducibility of the collective reality of particular obstinacy.

From here on, the process is given only as the capacity of rupture, as a series of struggles: particularity shows itself to be in itself, as activity, as permanent struggle, more general that any possible absolute. There is no necessity of recomposition because the obstinacy of the particular does not recognize others than itself to exploit, to recomprehend in a unity of opposites: there is only the deepening of the particular in itself, the discovery of a new universe by a turning back, and an excavation of the collective particular into itself. Reality is not dialectical but partial, autonomous, singular. Reality is not universal but radically unilateral: it is praxis that anticipates and risks itself by constructing itself as a particular power.

Finally outside the dialectic, outside any compositive process that is only a process of mystification, outside of labor as the synthesis of oppositions, outside of philosophy as the terrain of the ideal usurpation of the real, of the particular, the refusal of labor thus draws the consequences of the discovery of the *Philosophy of Right* as the supreme index of bourgeois ideology and the capitalist practice of the organization of exploitation. Here the thought of the particular, liberating itself of the dialectic of labor, liberates itself from philosophy as the nocturnal apparition of an apologetic comprehension of the real: the owl of Minerva disappears from our evening.

※ ※ ※

5. On the two-hundredth anniversary of his birth, our homage to Hegel, to the great thinker of the *Philosophy of Right*, is bitter—as it should be when we recognize in his reflection the massive base, continually renewed, of an ideology that desires the exploitation of man over man, that imprisons, though recognizing it, the hope of liberation. The historical awareness of the necessity of that thought, necessary to the beginning of the nineteenth century and of the development of mature capitalism, is attenuated and changes, when faced with the warning of the mystifying importance, of the significance of the suffocating impact of the Hegelian philosophy on a century and a half of the history of thought. The mystification, the political deformation of revolutionary demands: all of that has referred to Hegel. Let's move this formidable obstacle out of our way! Let's liberate our praxis and our thought from its fascination! Maybe only hate, as the expression of the insubordinate particularity in which our thought grows, can still define the quality of a relation with Hegel.

And yet, nevertheless, precisely this sentiment, with its intensity, still contradictorily binds us to him.

NOTES

1. [Translator's note: The Italian translation of *Die Grundlinien der Philosophie des Rechts* cited by Negri (*La filosofia del diritto*, ed. F. Messineo and A. Plebe [Laterza: Bari, 1965]) translates the German *Bildung* with the Italian *civiltà*. For Hegel, *Bildung* refers to a process of intellectual or "spiritual" [*geistig*] formation whose meaning is only approximated by the English "education" or the Italian *civiltà* (or *formazione*, the term used to translate *Bildung* in reference to, for example, academic, humanistic education). In the interest of fidelity to both Negri's and Hegel's texts, the original terms are provided to enable the reader to note the constellation of meanings operative in these passages.]
2. PR §187n. [Translator's note: References to the *Philosophy of Right* are given according to paragraph number of what has now become the "standard" edition, indicated by the symbol "§" while "n" refers to a note. The German edition consulted is G. W. F. Hegel, *Grundlinien der Philosophie des Rechts*, in *Werke*, vol. 7, *Auf der Grundlage der Werke von 1832–1845 neu edierte Ausgabe*, ed. Eva Moldenhauer and Karl Markus Michel (Frankfurt: Suhrkamp, 1979).]
3. PR §4.
4. [Translator's note: The adjective *spirituale* derives from the established Italian translation of Hegel's *Geist* with *Spirito*. "Spiritual world" in this context could thus equally well be translated as "intellectual world" in its specific Hegelian meaning.]
5. G. W. F. Hegel, *Ueber die wissenschaftlichen Behandungsarten des Naturrechts: Seine Stelle in der praktischen Philosophie und sein Verhältnis zu den positiven Rechtswissenschaften*, in *Werke*, vol. 2, *Auf der Grundlage der Werke von 1832–1845 neu edierte Ausgabe*, ed. Eva Moldenhauer and Karl Markus Michel (Frankfurt: Suhrkamp, 1979), p. 482.
6. G. W. F. Hegel, *Werke*, vol. 3, *Auf der Grundlage der Werke von 1832–1845 neu edierte Ausgabe*, ed. Eva Moldenhauer and Karl Markus Michel (Frankfurt: Suhrkamp, 1979), p. 265.
7. G. W. F. Hegel, *Jenenser Realphilosophie*, ed. J. Hoffmeister (Leipzig, 1932), vol. 1, p. 239.
8. PR §199.
9. PR §200.
10. PR §201.
11. PR §184.
12. *Anmerkung* [Remark] on PR §113.
13. PR §258n.
14. PR §261.
15. PR §189ff.
16. PR §63.
17. PR §57ff.
18. PR §196ff.
19. PR §190.

20. PR §195.
21. Karl Marx, *Grundrisse*, trans. Martin Nicolaus (Harmondsworth: Penguin, 1975), p. 266.
22. Ibid., p. 309.
23. Ibid., p. 296.

3

THE PERVERSITY OF THE ABSOLUTE, THE PERVERSE CORE OF HEGEL, AND THE POSSIBILITY OF RADICAL THEOLOGY

JOHN D. CAPUTO

Orthodox Christianity offers a formula for triumph over death but the purchase price is high, the theory of two worlds: one here below, the other up above; the one up front, the other behind the scenes; the one in time, the other in eternity. By "radical theology" I mean among other things a theology that has been bold enough to pull up this venerable root and to treat it as so much alienation or self-estrangement, to take it as a kind of modified gnosticism. The two worlds theory is the basis of supernaturalism and superstition, of magic and thaumaturgy, in which we are called upon to enter into mysterious commerce with an otherworldly being in order to stay in his good graces. Radical theology has other advice to offer, like saying that death is part of the rhythm of things, albeit a divine rhythm. That uprooting of theology and subsequent transplanting onto more worldly soil got its most prestigious and powerful boost from Hegel, whose speculative tour de force left nothing afterward unchanged. But inasmuch as Hegel started something (radical theology) he did not quite finish, my tribute to Hegel will be perverse. I will treat him as a hero of "perversatility," by which I mean his success in introducing a felicitous and productive perversion—or if you prefer a "paradigm shift"—into the very nature of the absolute (if there is one), one that left Kierkegaard crying out for relief. In so doing, he opened the door for a radical theology and, as I hope to sketch here, for a new vision in political theology. I thus propose, in this very contrarian and perversatile spirit, to seek out the "perverse core" of Hegel and indeed of the absolute itself, to borrow the phrase Slavoj Žižek used of Christianity.[1] This will mean following Hegel where he did not mean to lead, marching to a drum he did not quite beat, taking up a cause he did not quite advocate, and so to pursue Hegelian perversatility to its felicitous end. I propose, as Heidegger would have said, that we "repeat" Hegel, repeat not what Hegel actually said, which has already been said by Hegel, but repeat the possible in Hegel, the possibilities Hegel opened up for us, repeating what is unfinished and still becoming in what Hegel said about becoming, repeating him, to be sure, in what is hopefully a perversely productive way, in the likeness of his own prodigious perversatility.

I treat Hegel as the springboard to radical theology precisely because he proposes a way to continue to think theologically even after laying to rest the metaphysics and metaphorics of the two worlds, which then as today might have been mistaken for the very essence of theology, but is in fact an elemental figure of a pre-Copernican imagination and of mythological thinking. Like Hegel and Heidegger, like Nietzsche and like Levinas, I have lost my patience with the "world behind the scenes" of mythology and classical metaphysics. Hegel thinks theologically by taking the world as a horizon and by thinking God *in* the world, thereby radicalizing the Christian doctrine of Incarnation. But let me say at the start that the relationship of God to the world defended by Hegel himself—that of being-in-itself externalizing or expressing itself in being-for-itself and returning home in the spirit as being-in-and-for-itself—is for me a no less extravagant flower in the garden of metaphysics. It will be replaced in these remarks by the relationship of the "event" to the "world," which is a more descriptive way to look at things. Very simply put, the event is not what happens but what is going on *in* what happens, while the world is everything that happens. The event is what is astir in the world, the root (as in "radical") of the restlessness and impatience of the world with what happens, with its present configurations. A radical theology is a theology of the root, of the event. In this view the world—what is being called in this volume the "secular" order—arises as a provisional and imperfect solution, a kind of makeshift, to a problem posed to it by the name of God, or rather by the event that is stirring in the name of God, as a temporary configuration patched together under the impact of a kind of divine eventiveness. The world, I hope to show, is everywhere marked by patches of the "sacred" and the "holy," which are streaks and traces of divine events. That is why it makes no more sense to oppose the "secular" to the "sacred" or to the "holy" than to oppose a question to its answer or a problem to its solution.

My aim is thus to embrace this figure of perversity as a way to reconfigure the relationship of the secular order to the sacred and the holy and to suggest a new constellation, to introduce another figure or framework, a more chiasmic one in which the two intertwine, interact, interbreed so closely that it is misleading to speak of "two." In this new configuration certain restless forces, certain impatient powers and potentialities, seek expression, and this expression is called the world (the secular order). The world trembles with possibilities, is rocked by immemorial memories, grieves and rejoices in forces still unformed, giving form and expression to such forces only to become in turn undone and to stand in need of further reform, of still new forms, of realizing still more hidden potentialities which give it life in the first place. Such possibilities are the stuff politics and ethics are made of, they being arts of the possible or, more precisely, of the possibility of the impossible. On this view the world is made to tremble by certain divine forces or intensities, certain events harbored in the name of God, which beat like the heart of a heartless world.[2] Thus it would make no sense to speak of keeping such forces out of politics—for that would be to keep our dreams of peace and justice out of politics—although it will be of the utmost importance to rethink and reconceive the "divine" and the "theological," not to mention the political. I treat these events or forces as a new post-Hegelian version, or perversion, of the absolute, whose perversity is such that the absolute is not exactly absolute but pure, where what is pure is not exactly being but becoming, where what is becoming, pure and simple, is the world, and the world is not simply what happens but what is inwardly disturbed by the event that is going on in what happens.

On this post-Hegelian accounting theology belongs to the world as an ingredient in and constitutive of our cultural imagination, which means of the world's imagination. Theology dreams the dreams of the gods, dreams hitherto undreamt, hopes against hope for what is coming, even as it remembers the dead who shall not have died in vain. Such dreams are the stuff of the Hegelian triumvirate of "Religion, Art, and Philosophy," the core of the life of the absolute Spirit. But on my telling, a theological imagination is as much a part of culture as is artistic or conceptual imagination, with which it is inextricably related. So I propose to pervert this Hegelian schema by reproducing it without the hegemony and the hierarchy exercised by the metaphysical Concept (*Begriff*) or absolute knowledge (by which it itself is perverted). I take religion, art, and philosophy as three forms of a pluriform imaginative life—not so much a *Vorstellung* as a *Darstellung*, a presentation or exhibition of inner forces—giving multiple forms and shapes to a restlessness within the world, within ourselves, and within the things themselves. If there is any "concept" at all, it is that of the event, where the concept does not "grasp" anything but points, like a finger pointing to the moon, making for a concept of an inconceivable excess of things that it indicates but does not conceive. I number theology among the several discourses—and there are more than three—that suspect an inner restlessness in things and feel called upon to give it voice.

THE PERVERSE CORE OF CHRISTIANITY

In borrowing the trope of perversity from the subtitle of Slavoj Žižek's *The Puppet and the Dwarf*, I want to draw attention to the provocative ambiguity by which it is beset. Does Žižek mean that the "perverse core of Christianity" lies in the way that Christianity, while supposed to give us the freedom of the children of God, the new being, the life of grace which liberates us from the law, is actually perversely reinscribed within the economy of sacrifice and death, where the infinite debt of sin gets paid off by Christ's sacrificial death? This perversity of Christianity would then mean, as Žižek says, that God's "'free' gift is aimed at putting you in a position of permanent debt."³ While that may seem to be its most likely meaning, the "perverse core" really lies in exactly the opposite direction—now that sounds like Žižek!—that the death of Jesus on the cross is the death of God, the last gasp of that transcendent and separate being whom we can count on to keep general watch over mundane affairs here below and to bail us out when the going gets rough. Christianity thus turns out to be like psychoanalysis:

> Contrary to all appearances, this is what happens in psychoanalysis: the treatment is over when the patient accepts the nonexistence of the big Other. The ideal addressee of our speech, the ideal listener, is the psychoanalyst, the very opposite of the Master-figure that guarantees meaning . . . the patient accepts the absence of such a guarantee.⁴

And further, contrary to all appearances, that is also the "very core of Christianity," a Christianity for which "My God, my God, why have you forsaken me?" (Matthew 27:46) has become the watchword:

> The "Holy Spirit" is the community deprived of its support in the big Other. The point of Christianity as the religion of atheism is not the vulgar humanist one that the becoming-man-of-God reveals that man is the secret of God (Feuerbach et al.); rather, it attacks the religious hard core that survives even in humanism, even up to Stalinism, with its belief in History as the "big Other" that decides on the "objective meaning" of our deeds. . . . That is the ultimate heroic gesture that awaits Christianity: in order to save its treasure, it has to sacrifice itself—like Christ, who had to die so that Christianity could emerge.⁵

If Christianity is the beginning of the end of the big Other, and if this was recognized first by Hegel and the young Hegelians' critique of religion, psychoanalysis is its *consummatum est*. I cannot resist pointing out that in *Erring: An A/theology* Mark C. Taylor made pretty much the same argument on behalf of deconstruction,⁶ when he said that *"deconstruction is the 'hermeneutic' of the death of God."* For by deconstructing the "transcendental signified," it has deconstructed not only the old God but any big contenders for the place vacated by the old God—Subject or

Object, History or the Book, Structuralism or Humanism, Science or Psychoanalysis (as a strong version of the big all-knowing Listener). The name of God here is the name of anything that pretends to provide abiding and centered presence, which is the "theological gesture" par excellence. In deconstruction, or in psychoanalysis (à la Žižek), "Man" is not the secret of God. The secret is, to paraphrase Derrida, there is no Secret, no big Other who has the Secret.[7] Deconstruction is the deconstruction of the theological "place," the very place of the big Other, of the very taking place of theology. On this point, whatever his rhetorical sallies, Žižek is serving up vintage deconstruction.

The perverse core of Christianity is thus to be the perversion of a perversion. But we should resist concluding that this sets things straight—since the "straight," the *orthe* in orthodoxy, is tied up with the two worlds theory. It is better to say that this sends this perversity off in a more productive and inventive direction, like a productive misreading, a fertile and seminal heresy. The death of God is the death of death (of the big Other), where a perversion means that the native forces and energies of a thing are turned against itself, are alienated and become destructive, so that what is meant to liberate binds us up, what is meant to empower enervates us. But to pervert a perversity it is not a matter of a simple negation, where the negation of a negation returns us to an affirmation, for dialectics, too, is a distortion of the event, an attempt to repress and rule the event. Perversatility requires that we reinhabit and redescribe and redirect the perversity to reform it from within in order to release its elemental forces, its anarchic energies, its chaosmic tendencies. The perversion of a perversion requires working through it, reinterpreting it, "repeating" it so that what has all been recorded in the register of death and repression may now be replayed, repossessed, reenacted in the register of life, of free play, of the gift, of the grace of the event. I endorse Žižek's insistence that with "Christianity" nothing is finished, that nothing more than a transition will have been marked, because the future stretches before us as a task to be achieved in which we bear the responsibility to fill up what is lacking in the body of God. That is the basis of a productive theo-politics, in my view. This means that the messianic postures of Judaism and Christianity are different but overlapping. In Judaism, we are called upon to expect and make ready for the Messianic age. In Christianity, the Messiah has *already* come, but that means that *we* ourselves are called to carry out the messianic event, to bring it to completion, to occupy the messianic position, and to make ready a *second* coming, where everything turns on what is coming. That represents a very powerful perversion of the messianic event, which might be compared to the one that has been marked off by Benjamin's reversal of the messianic age—where we are the ones in the messianic position, the ones the dead have been waiting for to remedy the evil that has been done to them.

THE PERVERSITY OF POWER AND THE WEAKNESS OF THE ABSOLUTE

The perversity introduced by Christianity is, as Žižek says, that God has entered into his own creation so as to expose himself to all its contingencies and vagaries. But if that is so, then in what sense is this absolute still an absolute? In what sense is God still God? In one sense, in more than one sense, it is not, which is why Spinoza was attacked as an atheist. That is the "radical" in radical theology, the perversity of it all, and what I am calling here the perversity of the absolute. The absolute is not the absolutely transcendent and sovereign being of classical theology, nor is it the deeper law of nature (Spinoza), nor the ground of being in Tillich's theology of culture, which steers all things wisely and mightily, albeit immanently and mediately, into a good dialectical outcome. The absolute is neither Absolute Transcendence nor Absolute Transcendence-in-Immanence, neither a supreme being nor Being In and For Itself, nor Being as the ground of beings. Nor is it "beyond" or "without" being in the sense of mystical theology, for the *hyper* in *hyperousios* is another more resourceful attempt to preserve the transcendence of the absolute, although its felicitous tropes and gestures elicit widespread admiration and awaken another possibility that I am not exploring here.

The difficulty with all these versions of the metaphysics of the absolute is that they take the absolute to be a strong force not a weak one. That perversion of strength into weakness, the perversatility of the weakness of God which is greater than the strength of the world, is a crucial motif for me, the motif of the cross itself, the very perversity of the cross. On my accounting—and I would like to see this as a long-range effect or by-product of Hegel—the great perversity of classical theology is to treat God as an effective force, either an actual and entitative power, as in the *deus omnipotens* of classical creation theology, or as an ontologically effective force, as in Spinoza's *natura naturans* and in Hegel and Tillich, which exercises its power mediately in the world. In classical theism, God is the supremely powerful and transcendent creator of heaven and earth, where the main thing that baffles us about a being so powerful, wise, and beneficent is how the world God made could have turned out so badly for so many. Hegel took the revolutionary step of divesting this supreme entity of its separate transcendence and harnessed all this power to driving the forces of history and culture. God is not a supreme and separate actuality, not actually absolute, but an absolute becoming or becoming absolute, a process unfolding not only *in* history, a figure that still preserves the transcendence implied by the figure of "incarnation," but more important *as* history, in and as history itself. God is the becoming absolute of the absolute, the actualization of the absolute, through the laws of its dialectical unfolding. But the proximity of Hegel to classical theism shows up in the way that Hegel is exposed to exactly the same objection as classical theism, for how could history as the becoming absolute of the absolute have run such a bloody course? What sort of perversity is it, what sort of blasphemy or obscenity against life is it, to say that the absolute mounts its progress on the bodies of the dead, that many an innocent flower is trampled along the way of the absolute's itinerary? As Lyotard has shown, there is no excuse today for even asking what divine wisdom was served by such merciless slaughters.[8] It was to Tillich's credit that he saw this as a problem and for that reason had recourse to Schelling's *Ungrund*, which at least allows him to inscribe a certain undecidability in the absolute in virtue of which it can occasionally go over to the dark side, not to another place, but to its own dark side, the underside of its own nature.

In any version of this metaphysics of the absolute, the assumption is that God is an effective force which influences the flow of things on earth—either a direct, supernatural, or magical force, as in classical theism, or an indirect and mediated one immersed in nature and history, over whose actualization God exercises effective force, as in Hegel and Tillich. But suppose this assumption is questioned, suppose this perverse power of metaphysical theology is perverted? Suppose there is a flow of time and expanse of space over which God exerts no effective force or power, whether as a supreme being or being itself? Suppose God is not an actual power but a "weak" force? Suppose the only power of God is the power of powerlessness, because God, or the event that transpires in this name, belongs to another order than the order of actual or effective power? Suppose God does not belong to the order of effective power at all, neither transcendent nor immanent, but to another order, that of the event, as a kind of teeming of the event, or boiling of the virtual? Suppose perversely that God is a certain play of virtualities, whose actual effects, outcomes, instantiations, or actualizations form a complex of time, chance, and circumstance, for better and for worse, issuing in irregular and unpredictable combinations of human malice and benignity, natural abundance and scarcity, in times and places good and bad, in ecstasies both joyous and horrifying, in circumstances that constrict and strangle no less than in ones that liberate and open up? Suppose that God makes both his rain and his sun to shine on both the righteous and the unrighteous? Suppose that God is a kind of infinite reservoir of virtualities seeking actualization?

DELEUZE AND THEOLOGY

I am in part drawing upon the framework proposed by Deleuze's philosophy of the event to imagine God, but not uncritically. The limitation of Deleuze is the limits of his imagination when it comes to God, whose escape from classical theology he rarely plots. For the most part the name of God for Deleuze represents the rule of identity over difference, of hierarchy over freedom, of necessity over chance, of what he calls the "analogy of being," where all things are proportioned and distributed according to the standards and measure set by God. So when Deleuze marks off a "fixed" distribution, where each thing has a predefined place to which it is assigned, once and for all, where individuals are monitored so that Being is distributed across them according to the rule of "categories" and "sedentary proportionality,"[9] he decides to call that an orderly and a "divine" distribution. This is distinguished from *nomadic* distribution which happens across borders, in open space, in an errant or delirious distribution, which he calls "demonic" because it operates in the intervals between the fields marked off by the gods, upsetting their sedentary structures, producing a "crowned anarchy."[10]

While I support and understand the strategic value of these designations vis-à-vis the old onto-theologic, it is long overdue to ask whether there is not another view of the divine. Is not Deleuze criticizing a very literal reproduction of the old theology rather than its genuine theological repetition? For example, is this not a very shortsighted view of the distribution of bodies in the New Testament, which is marked precisely by upsetting such sedentary structures, overthrowing its temple tables, violating its rules of ritual purity and separation, trafficking among the lame and lepers, the prostitutes and the poor, and by feasts where the outsiders are in and the insiders are out? Is this not a very shortsighted view to take of the prophets of the Jewish Scriptures, dressed in sackcloth, railing against the powers that be, who end up losing their life for their troubles? Is there no way to think the name of God as associated precisely with the unequal, different, impure, the disturbing and anarchical? Might not the royalty of God be a crowned anarchy? Might there not be a divine disturbance, a precious perversity, let us say a "sacred anarchy" that is a counterpart to this crowned anarchy?[11] What is more perverse than the reversals and paradoxes that the figure of Jesus puts into effect in the order of temple authority? The same point may be made in reference to the early use of the word "theology" in Derrida, for whom the "book" exercises the "encyclopedic protection of theology and logocentrism against the disruption of writing, against its aphoristic energy, and, as I shall specify later, against difference in general."[12] But what if everything about the name of God were to suggest that this name belongs precisely on the side of aphoristic energies and difference, of what disrupts encyclopedic projects? Then theology would go on, this time reinscribed within difference.

To be sure, there are times when Deleuze himself recognizes this—as does Derrida later on—moments when he says that what is actual is like the solution to a problem whereas problems are of the order of the event, which function "like the dreams of the gods," singular points of virtuality distributed throughout real things. Events are the dreams of the gods that the world wants to make come true. The world is a game of divine dice,[13] of the chance of grace, of the grace of a chance. That is to associate God not with the actual but the virtual, not with order but with chance, not with what is finished or finalized but what is still to come, not with what is but with what is coming or becoming, which is why Deleuze thinks that even the "dissolved"—or fragmented—"self still sings the glory of God."[14] At these moments, it has to be said, Deleuze is thinking with Nietzsche of the Greek gods, the "pagan" gods, of what we can call the "sacred," but without Levinas's sneer. We in turn are duty bound to recover what Levinas obscures, that the Jewish and Christian Scriptures are packed with praise for the glory of the world that God has created—the imagery of Jesus in speaking of the kingdom of God is drawn almost completely from the natural world—even as they do indeed highlight what Levinas, breathing easier now, calls the "holy," the face of the neighbor and the stranger. But there is no need to choose among the multiple play of divine effects, to choose between the sacred and the holy, for both the lilies of the field and the widow and the orphan bear the glory of the Lord, both instantiate, actualize, embody the events that stir in the name of God. Deleuze's logic of sense is thus implicitly a theo-logic of the event without being an onto-theology. It is a logic of divine events, of the "sense" of God, but not of some supreme and powerful entity or underlying being. The world is a set of provisional solutions to the question put to it by the name of God, by the singularities that circulate, combine, and recombine in unforeseeable ways in the name of God. Such divine events are the salt that gives taste to the food of the world, the yeast that leavens the bread of the world, the "absolute" that is astir in the multiple forms of "Spirit." That is why there ought to be no war, no contest, between the "sacred" and the "secular," between the events that stir within the name of God and the multiform and plurivocal world that rises up in response to a divine provocation. That is why, as I will point out below, it is not a question of keeping theology out of politics but of rethinking the radical theology that drives a more radical politics.

In this theology more radically conceived, the name of God harbors an infinite reservoir of virtualities, like a great divine gathering place or *khora*. It proceeds on the assumption that the name of God is a signal of a vast depository of every actuality gone by, of the potentiality to which they return, of an infinite sea or endless ensemble of potentialities from which things arise and in return to which all things actual come and go in a great cosmic inhalation and exhalation, like the rising and sinking of a huge divine breast. The name of God is a marker of the uncontainable, irrepressible excess things contain, or cannot quite contain, like a buoy on the surface of the water alerting us to a dangerous swirl below.

THE PERVERSE CORE OF HEGEL, OR HOW TO SAVE GOD

The perversity of Hegel's rereading of Christian theology as the death of God, and as the death of this death, and hence his radical perversion of the figure of Incarnation—which sent Kierkegaard into spasms—opens the door to radical theology today.[15] The grievances Kierkegaard brought against Hegel opens the divide between the Neo-Orthodoxy of Barth and the correlational theology of Tillich, who is the grandfather of radical theology. Hegel launched the task of thinking God without God. He perverted the vertical and separate transcendence of a being presiding over this world from his station in another, higher one behind the scenes. Hegel launched the project of the radicalization of the Incarnation and of the theme of "God with us," proposing to take it all the way to the end, which means to bring it back into this world. He proposed thinking God reconciled with the worlding of the world, with the pain and death that is woven into the world, reconciling God with time and history and culture. When he said that the absolute is both subject and substance,[16] he was acknowledging his antecedents in this risky business—Spinoza, on the one hand, whose famous *deus sive natura* had boldly charted a part of the path Hegel was following, and Fichte, on the other hand. He was saying that the world is the body of the absolute, its embodiment and palpability, even as the absolute is the inner subjective and spiritual life of the world. Hegel's limitation was to do all this while remaining in the thralls of metaphysics—the metaphysics of substance and subject, as well as a metaphysics of history over which the absolute presided as its immanent teleological force. The perverse core of Hegel lay in being a liminal figure, the lining surface that on one side is the absolute consummation of metaphysics, where metaphysics tries to contain the uncontainable force of the event, while on the other side simultaneously showing the way out of such perversity.

It is clear that the perversion launched by Hegel is incomplete and that it needs to be pushed beyond itself, that the perversatility of Hegel has not yet been fully tapped. We are in search of another Hegel, a perverse core in Hegel, beyond the Hegel who thinks the Absolute makes its cunning way by subtly steering the passions of human beings who are but bearers of its absolute force. Žižek has recently offered another way to look at Hegel, elaborating the proposals made in *The Puppet and the Dwarf*, which deserves our attention. Žižek wants us to treat the orthodox Hegel as a cliché about Hegel and proposes a more productive perversion of Hegel's "Spirit." Žižek follows the standard reading of Hegel that the Incarnation is the death of God as Father, as a separate and transcendent being, and that the Crucifixion is the death of the Son, the break up of the empirical being of Jesus in order to make way for the coming of the Spirit. But the new twist he introduces is to revise our understanding of the Spirit. The last words on the Cross, "My God, my God, why have you abandoned me?" represent the expiration not only of the orthodox version of Spirit in Nicene Christianity but of the standard reading of Hegel, where the Spirit is the transcendence-in-immanence of the Absolute that makes use of individuals and their passions:

> The point this reading misses is the ultimate lesson to be learned from the divine Incarnation: the finite existence of mortal humans is the only site of the Spirit, the site where Spirit achieves its actuality.... Spirit is a *virtual* entity in the sense that its status is that of a subjective presupposition: it exists only insofar as subjects *act as if it exists*. Its status is similar to that of an ideological cause like Communism or Nation: it is the substance of the individuals who recognize themselves in it, the ground of their entire existence, the point of reference which provides the ultimate horizon of meaning to their lives, something for which these individuals are ready to give their lives, yet the only thing that really exists are these individuals and their activity, so this substance is actual only insofar as individuals believe in it and act accordingly. The crucial mistake to be avoided is therefore to grasp the Hegelian Spirit as a kind of meta-Subject, a Mind, much larger than an individual human mind, aware of itself: once we do this, Hegel has to appear as a ridiculous spiritualist obscurantist, claiming that there is a kind of mega-Spirit controlling our history.... This holds especially for the Holy Spirit: our awareness, the (self)consciousness of finite humans, is its only actual site ... although God is the substance of our (human) entire being, he is impotent without us, he acts only in and through us, he is posited through our activity as its presupposition.[17]

By claiming that the Spirit is a *virtual* entity, and by recognizing the *impotence* of God as an actual entity, Žižek comes very close to the view I am here advancing and have advanced in *The Weakness of God*, but with one important difference. Žižek's view of "virtuality" is too much turned to the subject and its belief systems and not enough turned to *the event itself*. The virtuality of the event is expressed in subjective beliefs even as it is actualized in things, but it is not reducible to subjective beliefs. Subjective beliefs arise in response to events, give words to events, and are translated into deeds and institutions by believing subjects. They are *responses* to the events that precede them, not simply sustained in the thin air of subjectivity itself by the subject's ability to suspend its disbelief in a fictive "as if."

To put my concern in Hegelian terms, we might say that Žižek fails to do justice to the claims of the virtualities of "substance," for the event is no less instantiated in things (substance) than it is expressed by the names that galvanize the beliefs of the subject. From Hegel's point of view, Žižek's view of virtuality is one-sided. The name of God, or of the Spirit of God, arises as a response to events; it gives words to powers that overtake the subject, that lay claim to it. If the "Spirit" is the name of a "subjective presupposition," that is only because it is first of all the name of something that prepossesses the subject and calls it forth, something by which the subject is constituted in the first place. The virtuality of the event is felt in both the beliefs of subjects and the energies of things, and it shows up in both names and things. The virtual includes not only what is named by our names but what is worlding in the world, the thinging-of-the-thing in Heidegger's play on *Be-ding-ung*. The virtual is both substance and subject, realized in things and named by subjects.

But to be more precise, or more perverse, the perverse core of Hegel is to conceive a world in which the absolute would be *neither substance nor subject*, or in which "substance" and "subject" would only be provisional nominal effects, stand-ins for more nameless and boundless virtualities, for virtualities still unnamed. By the same token, history would be a radically immanent movement without the steadying hand of teleology at its wheel. That is what it means to say there is no big Other. Hegel relocated the absolute, but he himself left its classical attributes in place. But what if—and this is the perversatility of Hegel—history is really history, really has the teeth and eventiveness of history, only as a radically a-telic and contingent process, where its outcome or *Resultat* is radically unforeseeable, where there is no one identifiable and overarching result but only so many fortuitous effects? What if instead of a teleological movement history is marked by the vagaries of change, the fortuitousness of little graces, and fortunes variously good or bad? What if events are not contained by a *telos* guaranteeing their direction and good outcome? What if the event is but a promise that provokes us and stirs our heart, or a memory of the dead that haunts us? What if instead of teleology there is only or at most the promise still unkept lodged in events still unsaid? What if substance and subject are nothing more than a certain shorthand we have devised for the play of events? What if, instead of the absolute steering all, we are thrown back on ourselves, made radically responsible for responding to the address that comes to us from events? If it is events that call, it is we who are made responsible. Hegel argued that nothing in the realm of ideas, of the concept, or meaning, nothing even about God himself, can be a real and effective actuality unless it becomes what it is in space and time. But the becoming effective of the absolute is our responsibility, just as Paul said that it is we who are expected to fill up what is lacking in the body of Christ (Colossians 1:24).

What if the absolute were not a matter of a *logos* at all, of a wisdom and a power that steers things wisely and well to their appointed *telos*, but a kind of a-logical "sense" that we can call the "intensity" of existence? What if the force that is harbored by the word "divine" is not "providence" or "omniscience" but excitation, exaltation, exultation, rejoicing in the moments when the flow is intensified, concentrated, when it shines bright with the splendor of becoming, when it resonates with the clamor of becoming? What if existence were a matter of awakening to the flow within, sensitizing ourselves to its impulses, rejoicing in its joys, suffering with its sorrows? What if the "absolute" is found not in treating all suffering as for the better, as belonging to a deeper divine calculation and foreknowledge that sees it all to a happy conclusion? What if, instead, suffering were a sigh from the depths of becoming, the intensity of a divine sigh, a divine lamentation, that asks everything of us, that demands our response, our redress? What if it is the divine becoming itself that suffers and that asks not to be abandoned? The perversatile result would be not that it is God who brings relief but that it is we who are asked to relieve the suffering of God, to answer the divine lamentation, to hold out a hand to those who are laid low by the shifting tides of becoming.

What if the name of God is not the name of the *telos*, *logos*, and *nomos* that hover protectively over becoming, but of events astir within becoming itself that leave their trace in the absolute intensities of becoming? Life is not justified because there is some divine watchman overseeing it from afar in a distant heaven, nor even, as in Hegel himself, when this watchman or logos is restationed within becoming itself. Life is justified by life itself. If you ask life, why do you live, Meister Eckhart said, it would answer, "I live because I live."[18] Life is justified by the intensities of life, by movements of intense joy or compassion, by movements of authentic intensity, by the intensity of the most quotidian events, by events both sacred and holy, by the event of intensity, which is life itself. Then everything is redeemed—which is not to say that it was ever fallen or lost—by being made into an affirmation, even though we suffer daily from a sea of troubles and outrageous fortune. The world is not fallen, but the world is a challenge, a task; the world is not lost, but it is risky business.

Events are not philosophical objects that suffer from the lack of a philosophical *logos* that works like a rule to stabilize them or a key to unlock their secret, even as life is not a game in which we are asked to guess the secret word. Life is an incomparable and unencompassable flow in which we are swept up that offers us the occasional chance of intermittent grace, the passing opening of momentary glory, moments that give life its passion, its intensity. It is not a matter of the rationalization or the justification of events but of their intensification, not of finding the logos of becoming but of undergoing its pathos, its passion, the passion of existence. Life is a flow by which we are carried and the passion of life is the passion of the flow. Our passion is to awaken to and feel life's pulse, our task is to let life pass through our bodies so that we tremble with joy, even as it is no less our task to reach out to those whom life has laid low. We are called upon to let the sparks of becoming fly up in all their unpredictable and immeasurable chance, to let the dance of becoming, the grace of life flow freely. Without turning life into a preexistent and autonomous force of which individuals are merely bearers—that is exactly why Levinas thought that Bergson is a "pantheist"[19]—it is still true that life passes through our bodies and minds, our hearts and souls, with all the force of a wind-swept beach, with all the lightness and grace of a gentle breeze.

Hegel labored under the classical metaphysical assumption that becoming is a process to be interpreted, not a process to be intensified, magnified, and made more elastic and electric. By reinscribing God in the world, Hegel sent theology down a radical path. But the perverse core of Hegel is that, by saying that the absolute is the substance and the subject of the world, Hegel opened the door to seeing God as the body and the soul of the world. To say the world is made in the image of God means the world is God's body or flesh. From the standpoint of religion—the terms are different in art or philosophy—the world beats with the heart of God, pulsates under a divine impulse, breathes with God's breath. What Marx said of religion, that it is the heart of a heartless world, he might better have said of God. The ecstasies of joy and sorrow are the sighing and heaving of God. The lamentation of the wretched, the shouts of exaltation, what the Catholic rosary calls the "joyful, sorrowful, and glorious mysteries," are the groaning of the Spirit, exclamations of the divine impulse with which things tremble.

What then of human responsibility? By his redescription of God, Hegel prepared the way for the insight that just as God is not a being that steers things from above, neither is God some immanent guiding force situated here below. Rather God is the name of events that call upon us to complete what is missing in the body of God, to rush to the aid of God's suffering flesh, to rejoice in the joy that surges through God's limbs, to sanctify what is holy and what is sacred, to remedy the divine travail, to bring relief wherever his lamentations can be heard. The upshot of Hegel's revolutionary paradigm shift is not that we become instruments of the cunning of Reason but that we become responsible. Extending Benjamin's perversatile interpretation of the Messiah, we are prepared to say that we are the ones whom God has been waiting for. We are not waiting for God or Godot, but God has been waiting for us. The weakness of God goes hand in hand with the responsibility of humankind. The name of God is the name of the beating of the world's heart, of the event that simmers in what happens, and we are asked to respond to it, to preserve the sacredness of earth and sky, to honor the holiness of the face. For the absolute is both the sacredness of the substance and the sanctity of the subject, both the face of the mountain and the flesh of the face. The heart of the absolute—by which I mean the events that stir restlessly with things—beats in both, chiasmically, for the mountain is both flesh and face, and the face is both invisible and visible incarnation, vulnerability, materiality. All things are chiasmically substance and subject, both sacred and holy, and we are asked to be both poets of the sacred and prophets of the holy no less than prophets of the sacred and poets of the holy. The perverse core of what religion calls salvation lies here, for it is not God who saves us but we who are asked to save God, to save the name of God, to save the event that stirs in the name of God. We are asked to make ourselves worthy of what happens to us,[20] where God is what happens to us. The Incarnation means that we are asked to assist at his birth in the world, to let the event happen and thereby to save God, to save the event that stirs in the name of God. We are called upon to let the event happen in us, with us, through us, to let the flow of events, the absolute becoming of the flow, pass through our bodies and pass into the world. By virtue of the virtuality of the event, we are called to assist in the realization of God, of the event that is harbored in the name of God, to make ourselves worthy of events, both sacred and holy.

THE POLITICS OF PERVERSATILITY

The politics of perversatility is the politics of responsibility, which is why this radical theology is also a radical politics. This shift from the powerless power of the event that stirs in the name of God to the responsibility we bear to respond to the event is at the same time a shift to the ethical and political order, which is the order of making ourselves worthy of the event. For the political order has for too long been organized around a theology of power which Deleuze describes as the "fixed distribution" of the "analogy of being," the top-down hierarchical order in which all power flows from above, around a "theological" order of God over the world, man over woman, animal, and earth. That is what we have described as the perversity of trying to forcibly contain the forces that things contain, to forcibly contain the uncontainable. The politics of sovereign power turns on what Derrida calls the "unavowed theologism" of the sovereignty of God.[21] Just so, the interest we have in perverting this political order by what Deleuze calls the "nomadic distribution" of a "crowned anarchy," and by what Derrida calls a radical "democracy to come," are not best served by repudiating theology but by rethinking theology from within, by thinking theology through to a more radical theology, of the sort that we have been describing under the trope of perversatility, of the perversion of an already perverted order.

We will never be done with theology and just when we think we are, theology will be more profoundly at work on us than ever before as the blind spot that is working on us from behind, as the part of our text that we do not command, bleeding into our assumptions with all the force of the "unavowed." That is why it is necessary not to jettison theology and exclude it from politics, but to rethink theology and allow it have a voice in rethinking politics. Apart from and opposed to the fixed distribution of power exercised by what Kierkegaard liked to mock as "Christendom," which is a power of this world, the Hebrew prophets and the New Testament propose to us a power of an entirely different sort. There we find the paradoxical "rule" (*arche*) of the an-archic, of the one lost sheep, not the ninety-nine; of children, not adults; of those who were not invited to the feast; of sinners, not the righteous; of the prodigal son, not the loyal one; of the lepers and ritually impure, not the pure; of the weak, not the strong; of everyone who is summed in Paul's ringing articulation of the perversatility of God:

> God chose what is foolish in the world to shame the wise; God what is weak in the world to shame the strong; God chose what is low and despised in the world, things that are not [*ta me onta*], to reduce to nothing things that are. (1 Corinthians 1:27–28)

I propose a sacred anarchy that is in every case the counterpart to the crowned anarchy of Deleuze, which places the crown of divine preference upon the brow of the nomadic and the immigrant, of the outsider, the marginalized, the disempowered, of the least among us, which is sharply put by Paul when he says that "the weakness of God is stronger than human strength" (1 Corinthians 1:25). The name of God is the name of weakness, or of a weak force, not the name of a physical or metaphysical force that can magically intervene and supervene upon the forces of nature or of history. The name of God is not well served by a powerful institution that enforces its own will under the cover of the name of God, as when the Church authorizes itself by placing the words "thou are Peter and upon this rock I will build my church" on the lips of Jesus. That is autocrowning of the strong with real power and goes hand in hand with its secular counterpart, the sovereignty of the nation, to whom power is transferred in modernity. That does not reflect the sacred anarchy of Jesus, who exercised only the power of powerlessness, who embodied the weakness of God, who practiced not the sword, but the power of forgiveness and of loving his enemies, even unto death.

What would a nation look like that renounced sovereignty, that flexed the muscles not of military strength but of forgiveness, that organized a foreign policy around hospitality to the dispossessed and impoverished, that opened its borders to the widow, the orphan, and the stranger, that took the food out of its own mouth and shared its wealth, that placed the crown of privilege upon what Paul called *ta me onta*, "the nothings and the nobodies of this world"? That is the politics of perversatility called for by the event harbored in the name of God, the most perverse possible politics and the interruption of the business as usual of brutal power.

To be sure, these images from the New Testament and the prophets of the Jewish Scriptures are fantastic, imaginative leaps. But that is ever the function of literature, to give sensible and imaginative form to the event, to let the event come into word, image, and sound, all so many ways to respond to the address issued by the event. They are indeed dreams, the dreams of the gods, God's dreams, dreaming of the messianic age, of messianic justice, and of such dreams is politics made, lest it become something less than itself. Unless there is an excess in politics, something more than politics in politics—and the name of God is the name of excess—then politics will fail to be itself. Unless it dreams of the impossible, it will be content with a compromised and brutal realpolitik of the possible. It is theology's function, the function of a radical theology, to dream, to pray, and to weep over the excess of the event that keep political orders open-ended and dreaming of what is coming.

CONCLUSION

When we say that God is not above being but within, neither as a first being nor the being of beings, we stand in Hegel's debt. When we say that the name of God is the name of an event that pulsates throughout being, an inner beating that rises to excess from time to time and from place to place, we enter a space cleared by Hegel. God is everywhere as the excess that things contain, the promise that they hold, the deep deposit of the memory of the dead. The lamentations of the wretched of the earth, the cries of pain and injustice, are God's pain. This is not because God associates Godself with them in a movement of divine empathy, as happens in the various world religions, which is not to be taken lightly, as it remains one of religion's most powerful figures. Rather, and more radically, it is because bodies in pain embody the pain that expresses God's life, the excess that rises up and breaks through the tranquil surface of existence and elicits the name of "God" as a cry for justice, peace, joy. As the excess of the event, God is expressed in both exultation and abjection, joy and sorrow, glory and misery. "God" is the name we give to events that have increased their velocity to infinity, that glow white hot in intensity, to the flow of events that exceed the speed limits of a mediocre life and break through the surface in times and places of excess—of excessive joy or sorrow, beauty or horror. God is not the source of beauty or horror, like some first being or uncaused cause, but horror is a wound in the body of God that requires our redress, even as beauty is a jewel adorning the body of God that calls for our celebration.

When we says that God belongs to another order, to the ordering order of events that call for a response, that call and recall, that have a certain power which is not that of effective forces, we pursue a path Hegel made possible, which hears the name of God as an event occurring in matter, space, and time. What Hegel called "Idealism" we have redescribed as the power of an event that calls, which is the power of powerlessness. The Idea is not an effective force, but a call. Calls can go unanswered or unheeded, calls can be declined or rejected, calls can be refused or ignored. Calls lay claim to us but we can always resist their claim. Calls solicit, but we can turn away the solicitor. Calls enjoin, but we can always refuse or disobey. The responsibility of the response is ours—that is what we can call "Materialism," which means turning the virtual event into material actuality. Idealism solicits, materialism answers. Materialism means that we are the hearers of the call, the one laid claim to, solicited, visited, invited, enjoined to materialize events, to make them happen materially, which is why Levinas says that faced with the hunger of the other "there is no bad materialism other than our own."[22]

On such a view, one might even say that in a theology of the event, there is a remarkable transmutation and perverse reversal that has so far gone unremarked—namely, a perversatility of prayer. For materialism is the answer to God's prayers. By this I mean that if it is God who calls and we are the ones called upon, then it is God who solicits us, who thus prays to us and seeks our aid and succor. But insofar as we also pray, for we are woven of prayers and tears, we in turn pray for the heart to respond, to make ourselves worthy of the event. We pray for peace, long for justice, dream of the messianic age, call for the democracy to come, pray and weep over what is missing in the body of God. These are God's dreams, God's prayers, and ours, with the result that we and God together form a common bond and are both praying for the messianic age, for the coming of the Messiah. Here is another parallax for Žižek: our prayers to God are but God's prayers to us, from another point of view. But of course the messianic age will never come, for its being is its becoming, its to-come. Its being is the various intensities of becoming, the becoming of events, the events of becoming. The figure of messianic peace and joy floats like a cloud—which Plato called "Ideas" and Kant called "Ideals" and Hegel called the Absolute—giving suggestive form to our imaginative life, sparking the flow of philosophical questioning, giving heart and mind to the great religious traditions, taking shape in the work of the work of art in all its variations. The powerless power of events is the power of appeal, and the name of God harbors events of the most excessive and provocative appeal, eliciting the most powerful invitations, summoning up what is best in us, appealing to the better angels of our nature to make ourselves worthy of what happens to us, to make ourselves worthy of the event.

To say all this is to step into a place that was first opened up by Hegel.

NOTES

1. Slavoj Žižek, *The Puppet and the Dwarf: The Perverse Core of Christianity* (Cambridge, Mass.: MIT Press, 2003), p. 130.
2. Karl Marx, introduction to *A Contribution to a Critique of Hegel's Philosophy of Right*, http://www.marxists.org/archive/marx/works/1843/critique-hpr/intro.htm.
3. Žižek, *Puppet and the Dwarf*, p. 171.
4. Ibid., pp. 169–170.
5. Ibid., p. 171.
6. Mark C. Taylor, *Erring: A Postmodern A/theology* (Chicago: University of Chicago Press, 1984), p. 6.
7. Jacques Derrida, *On the Name*, ed. Thomas Dutoit (Stanford, Calif.: Stanford University Press, 1995), pp. 29–30.
8. Jean-François Lyotard, "Result," in *The Differend: Phrases in Dispute*, trans. Georges Van Den Abbeele (Minneapolis: University of Minnesota Press, 1988).
9. Gilles Deleuze, *Difference and Repetition*, trans. Paul Patton (New York: Columbia University Press, 1994), p. 284.
10. Ibid., pp. 36–37.
11. I have elaborated the notion of a sacred anarchy in greater detail in *The Weakness of God: A Theology of the Event* (Bloomington: Indiana University Press, 2006).
12. Jacques Derrida, *Of Grammatology*, corrected ed., trans. Gayatri Chakravorty Spivak (Baltimore: Johns Hopkins University Press, 1997), p. 18.
13. Deleuze, *Difference and Repetition*, pp. 283–284.
14. Ibid., p. 79.
15. See Hegel's presentation of the three elements of "consummate religion"—the religion of the Father; the religion of the Son, who had to perish in his empirical reality; and the religion of the Spirit, of the historical community that bears and is borne by the Spirit—in G. W. F. Hegel, *Lectures on the Philosophy of Religion: The Lectures of 1827*, ed. Peter C. Hodgson, trans. R. F. Brown, P. C. Hodgson, and J. M. Stewart (Oxford: Clarendon Press, 2006), pp. 389–489.
16. G. W. F. Hegel, *Phenomenology of Spirit*, trans. A. V. Miller (Oxford: Clarendon Press, 1977), pp. 9–10.
17. Slavoj Žižek, "From Job to Christ: A Paulinian Reading of Chesterton," in *St. Paul Among the Philosophers*, ed. John D. Caputo and Linda Martín Alcoff (Bloomington: Indiana University Press, 2009).
18. Raymond Blakney, *Meister Eckhart: A Modern Translation* (New York: Harper & Row, 1941), p. 127.

19. Emmanuel Levinas, *Time and the Other*, trans. Richard Cohen (Pittsburgh: Duquesne University Press, 1987), pp. 91–92.
20. Gilles Deleuze, *The Logic of Sense*, trans. Mark Lester with Charles Stivale, ed. Constantin V. Boundas (New York: Columbia University Press, 1969), p. 149.
21. Jacques Derrida, *Rogues: Two Essays on Reason*, trans. Pascale-Anne Brault and Michael Naas (Stanford, Calif.: Stanford University Press, 2005), p. 110.
22. Emmanuel Levinas, *Difficult Freedom*, trans. Sean Hand (Baltimore: Johns Hopkins University Press, 1990), p. xiv.

4

HEGEL IN AMERICA

BRUNO BOSTEELS

HEGEL WITH HERGÉ

The expression "Hegel in America" should resound with something of the comic incongruence associated with titles such as *Tintin in America*, not to mention *Tintin in the Congo*, which allowed their author Hergé, at the time of Belgium's infamous enterprise in Africa, to give vent to his colonial unconscious. The element of incongruence ought to be even more striking if we take "America" to mean "Latin America," which we should not forget includes a large portion of "North America," that is, modern-day Mexico. Lighting up his words across an empty outline of the United States on a giant computerized billboard, Chilean-born artist Alfredo Jaar still felt the need not so long ago to remind passersby in Times Square in New York City, in a geopolitical diversion or *détournement* of that verbal-visual pun of another Belgian pipe smoker, the surrealist René Magritte: "This is not America." The real question, however, is whether such comic effects still have the power to jolt us out of the new dogmatic slumber that, with the themes of finitude, restlessness, and plasticity, now seems to have overcome many of the most illustrious heads in the family of Hegel scholars—a family still prone to perceiving itself as based exclusively in Western Europe and the United States of America.

In fact, a nearly identical formulation, "Hegel and America," already exists as the title of an essay by José Ortega y Gasset, no doubt the foremost philosopher to have emerged from the "generation of '98," named after the so-called disaster of Spain's loss of its last colonies, Cuba, Puerto Rico, and the Philippines, upon defeat in the Spanish-American War of 1898.[1] Ortega y Gasset carefully crafts his text so as to tease his reader for several pages until the grand finale in which he quotes the now well-known passage at the start of Hegel's *Lectures on the Philosophy of History* where the German philosopher excludes America from the purview of both history and philosophy, all the while designating the continent as "the land of the future" in what can only be called a giddy overcompensation for the guilt incurred in this very exclusion. Ortega y Gasset laconically quotes the following words from Hegel, without further comment, as the final lines of his own essay:

> America is therefore the land of the future, where, in the ages that lie before us, the burden of the World's History shall reveal itself—perhaps in a contest between North and South America. It is a land of desire for all those who are weary of the historical lumber-room of old Europe. Napoleon is reported to have said: "*Cette vieille Europe m'ennuie.*" It is for America to abandon the ground on which hitherto the History of the World has developed itself. What *has* taken place in the New World up to the present time is only an echo of the Old World—the expression of a foreign Life; and as a Land of the Future, it has no interest for us here, for, as regards *History*, our concern must be with that which has been and that which is. In regard to *Philosophy*, on the other hand, we have to do with that which (strictly speaking) is neither past nor future, but with that which *is*, which has an eternal existence—with Reason; and this is quite sufficient to occupy us.[2]

Actually, as Enrique Dussel among others was to insist many years after Ortega y Gasset, Hegel does not so much dismiss as conceal the determining role of the discovery and conquest of the New World for the historical emergence of that Old Europe which today seems to bore the likes of Donald Rumsfeld almost as much as yesteryear it did the otherwise incomparable Napoleon. America, then, is not the land of the future so much as it is the necessary past of a geopolitical present, the one ciphered in the shorthand notation of "1492," whose subsequent erasure from historical memory is ultimately what allows for the self-affirmation of Europe, henceforth endowed with "an eternal existence" that alone would be worthy of philosophical speculation.

Ortega y Gasset argues that this treatment of America reveals a fundamental paradox in Hegel's entire philosophy of history. In the latter, there simply is no place to put America—except, precisely, in and as a place: in geography. Without wishing to enter into the sour discussion over whether such treatment is actually better or worse than the one given to Asia, as part of "unhistorical History," we should not forget that Hegel relegates America together with Africa to a prior section in his *Philosophy of History*, "Geographical Basis of History."[3] More importantly, the ambiguity of the very expression of "the land of the future" to designate America sums up a pivotal vacillation on Hegel's part, as though he were not altogether certain that the continent in question could not also open up a vista onto the spirit's future, including a future that would lie in wait for Old Europe itself. This last dimension of futurity, which would anticipate the possibility of an end to the end of history as envisaged in Hegel's apology for the Prussian State, for this same reason cannot find its way into the main body of *The Philosophy of History*. When Hegel says about the United States, for example, that they are insufficiently advanced to feel the need for a monarchy, he is unable to envision for them any future other than a repetition of the trajectory already followed in Europe: "The idea that Prussia might, over time, come to shake its monarchy as one shakes off a nightmare must not have crossed Hegel's mind."[4] Were such an idea actually allowed to cross his mind, America would cancel out, perhaps even without sublation, the eternal present of Hegel's Europe.

America may well contain a vast expanse of land, but it must remain just that: a continent whose content cannot be allowed to leak back onto the Old World. This is the paradox that lies revealed in Hegel's treatment of America:

> Here we touch in a concrete point upon the enormous limitation of Hegelian thought: its blindness for the future. The future to come upsets him because it is what is truly irrational and, thus, what a philosopher esteems the most when he puts the frenetic appetite for truth before the imperialistic drive of a system. Hegel makes himself hermetic to the tomorrow, he becomes agitated and restless when he comes upon some dawn, he loses his serenity and dogmatically closes the windows so that no objections come flying in with new and luminous possibilities.[5]

By pushing back the future into a section on geography prior to history, Hegel in one fell swoop limits the scope of his entire endeavor to the past (history) and the present (philosophy)—without a future relevant enough to speak of in the main body of the text. "The case of Hegel clearly reveals the error that consists in equating what is historical with the past," writes Ortega y Gasset: "Thus it happens that this philosophy of history has no future, no escape. Therein lies the peculiar interest of studying how Hegel deals with America, which, if anything, is certainly something future."[6]

By anticipating such skepticism, Ortega y Gasset can be read as having set the tone for subsequent interrogations of the limits and blind spots in Hegel's philosophy of history, particularly as seen from the global South—including, in this case, from the privileged vantage point of post-1898 Spain. Indeed, what is ciphered in the so-called disaster of 1898 gives us a retrospective glimpse into the truth of 1492 that hits home with a vengeance as Spain definitively loses its status as a colonial world power.[7] "Hegel and America," in this sense, is nothing if not premonitory of the kinds of reading that would be produced in the latter half of the twentieth century, once the providential history of the world-spirit qua theodicy is set against the backdrop of the dilemmas of colonialism, dependency, and underdevelopment that since then have become unavoidable even for some of Hegel's most admiring readers in the global South.

It is then perhaps ironic that Catherine Malabou, in her otherwise stunning book on *The Future of Hegel*, does not consider for one moment that which for Hegel himself constitutes the land of the future, that is, America. Then again, Malabou pays only scant attention to *The Philosophy of History*. Aside from briefly mentioning the possibility that there might be something "clumsy" about Hegel's approach, which "cuts abruptly across centuries and speculative moments," she is quick to add that "history and philosophy intersect, an intersection that immediately justifies this approach."[8] In fact, she seems to feel no need to distance herself from the overarching structure of Hegel's study of the history of the world-spirit as centered on the advent of Christianity and raised up from abstract "personality" or "ego" among the Greeks to the higher principle of "freedom" in Hegel's own philosophy: "Given its form by Descartes, radicalized in its significance by Kant, the subject will henceforth appear as an independent principle and as the absolute autonomy of thought."[9] Similarly, in discussing the striking possibility of a "history of the future," Malabou reduces the available options to two fundamental moments, the Greek and the modern, without for a moment pausing to consider the role of Asia, Africa, or America—not to mention the enormous lapse of the Middle Ages—in the movement from one to the other: "Subjectivity comes itself (*advient*) in two fundamental moments: *the Greek moment and the modern moment*, which prove to be, both in their logical unity and in their chronological succession, 'subject as substance' and 'substance as subject.'"[10] Thus, even if Malabou argues that the dimension of futurity is actually a crucial component of Hegel's philosophy, this insight does not significantly alter the latter's view of world history and of the place of America in it or, as the case may be, outside of it.

As for the element of comedy, it comes into play when what at first sight may seem merely clumsy or odd turns out to be an essential part of the most abstract speculative movement of the concept itself. Ortega y Gasset understands this when he quotes the following description from *The Philosophy of History* in which Hegel highlights the inferiority not only of the human inhabitants but also of the fauna of the New World:

> In the very animals one notes an inferiority equal to that of the people. Animal life includes lions, tigers, crocodiles, etc., but these wild creatures, although they are notably similar to types of the old world, are, nonetheless, in all senses smaller, weaker, more impotent. They swear that edible animals in the New World are not as nutri-

tious as those of the old. In America there are huge herds of cattle; but European beef is considered to be an exquisite mouthful there.[11]

From this observation Ortega y Gasset goes on to infer a general interpretive principle for the reading of Hegel. Indeed, immediately after explaining how "we see that the great errors in his work do not stem from his speculative method but rather from the limitations from which all empirical knowledge suffers," he continues as if to rescue the element of error as the principal charm of Hegel's philosophy of history:

> The *gaucheries* of old photographs are, at the same time, their greatest charm. These, and not the elements that appear correct and contemporary, tear us away from the present and transfer us with voluptuous historical magic to that time now past. It seems we now similarly regard Hegel, in his great Muscovite cap, reading in his office a story of travels through America where it is noted that European *beefsteak* is preferred in America to the indigenous beef.[12]

Hegel's truth would lie in the clumsy and incongruent details of his untruth. "His philosophy is imperial, Caesarean, Genghis-Khanesque. And so it happened that, finally, he dominated politically the Prussian state, dictatorially, from his university professorship," but this does not mean that there is not also a moment of truth in the failures of this imperial ambition: "And yet, and yet . . . Hegel never comes off completely empty. In his mistakes, like the lion with his bites of flesh, he always carries between his teeth a good chunk of palpitating truth."[13]

PROVINCIALIZING HEGEL

When looked at from the vantage point of Latin America, the commonplace or downright hackneyed objections against Hegel—against his panlogicism, against his view of history as theodicy, against his apology for the inherent ethical order of the State—are further compounded and given their proper world-historical stage, so to speak, where they seem to have to represent the same play over and over again, now as tragedy and then as farce. The most frequently rehearsed criticism of Hegel's thought in Latin American circles indeed does not apply in the first place to his dialectical method or to his inveterate idealism but rather and inseparably to his philosophy of history with its pivotal concept of the world-spirit driving home the identity of the real and the rational. Even commentaries on Hegel's *Logic* or his *Phenomenology of Spirit* always must undergo the retroactive effects of a gaze that is unable to stop staring at those remarkable opening pages from *The Philosophy of History*.

José Pablo Feinmann, writing in the wake of dependency theory and anti-imperial struggles throughout the continent, devotes several pages of his *Philosophy and Nation* to a "Brief (Very Brief) Social and Political History of European Philosophy: From Descartes to Hegel."[14] Feinmann boldly moves through this particular part in the history of modern European philosophy by reading it as the expression, in thinking, of the history of Western imperialism. Thus, whereas with Descartes the *res cogitans* necessarily still confronts the inertia of the *res extensa*, for Kant reason begins to dictate its own laws to nature, following the insights of his Copernican revolution. Even for this thinker of the Enlightenment, however, the thing-in-itself continues to confront the powers of reason as an unknowable. It is not until Hegel that the in-itself will become sublated and pass over into the for-itself of reason: "There is no more in-itself, nor are there any regions of being forbidden to reason. Reason now possesses being and has engraved its own teleology on it: *being, thus, has transformed itself into reason*," Feinmann writes: "In Hegel, indeed, the process of the overpowering of the *in-itself* by the subject reaches its culmination."[15]

Feinmann claims that there is nothing mechanical or reductive about reading the history of European expansionism into the history of philosophy and vice versa. "The transformation of substance into subject expresses, *philosophically*, the appropriation of history on behalf of European humanity. There is no reductionism in affirming that, in Hegelian philosophy, the development of the spirit is identified with that of European history," insofar as Europe names this very process of appropriation or overpowerment itself: "Now the magnificent scaffolding of Hegelian logic can unfold itself: the laws of thinking are the laws of being, there is a profound unity between logic and ontology, the method is not exterior to the object, for if knowledge is conceived of as different from its object, then neither can knowledge know of the absolute nor can the absolute come to know itself."[16] It will not do, therefore, merely to separate Hegel's method from his system or his politics, as though one—the dialectical method—could emerge unscathed from its separation from the other, from the reactionary political premises behind the system identified, in Hegel's day, with the Prussian State. Seen from Latin America, Hegel's dialectical method and his world-historical system would appear for what they are, namely, provincial self-legitimations of Europe's colonial ambitions.

Based in Mexico, Enrique Dussel seems to reiterate several of the points made by Feinmann. In his recent *Politics of Liberation*, he too refers to the way in which Hegel, in paragraphs 246–247 from *The Philosophy of Right* already quoted at length by Ortega y Gasset, legitimates the experience of colonialism by pointing at the need for European civil society to reach out and expand into peripheral territories:

> As in no other philosopher, and this could not have happened before, the global hegemony of *mature modernity*, thanks to the impact of the industrial revolution, allowed Europe to experience for the first time that it was the "center" of planetary history. This it had never been! Hegel had an acute philosophical-historical instinct and he captured this *recent* experience—just a few decades old—of European supremacy. He is the first Eurocentric philosopher who celebrates with optimism the hypothesis that "the History of the World travels from East to West, for Europe is absolutely the end of History" and, again, "Europe is absolutely the center and end of universal history." Moreover, the "Southern Europe" has ceased to be the "bearer" (*Träger*) of the Spirit, a function which in this final stage of history corresponds only to "the heart of Europe," the Germano-Anglo-Saxon Europe of the North. These pseudoscientific "inventions" in history allow Hegel to reconstruct world history by projecting hegemonic Europe, after the industrial revolution (an event not quite fifty years old), onto the origin of Greek culture and Judeo-Christianity (both phenomena dislodged from their purely "oriental" context) with pretenses of world-historical explanation.[17]

This backward projection of European hegemony onto its supposed Greek and Judeo-Christian origins is precisely what leads to the occlusion of perhaps the most decisive fact for the history of that much-vaunted discourse of modernity, namely, the discovery of the New World.

In his famous Frankfurt Lectures, originally delivered in 1992, Dussel had made very much the same point by playing on the words *descubrimiento* (discovery) and *encubrimiento* (cover-up):

> The possibility of modernity originated in the free cities of medieval Europe, which were centers of enormous creativity. But modernity as such was "born" when Europe was in a position to pose itself against an other, when, in other words, Europe could constitute itself as a unified ego exploring, conquering, colonizing an alterity that gave back its image of itself. This other, in other words, was not "dis-covered" (*descubierto*) or admitted, as such, but concealed, or "covered-up" (*encubierto*), as the same as what Europe assumed it had always been. So, if 1492 is the moment of the "birth" of modernity as a concept, the moment of origin of a very particular myth of sacrificial violence, it also marks the origin of a process of concealment or misrecognition of the non-European.[18]

From Hegel to Habermas, most European philosophers participate in this trend, which consists in defining modernity on the basis of the Enlightenment or the

French Revolution. What remains hidden in all such accounts, with their customary leaps from ancient Greece to modern Christianity, is the violent process of primitive accumulation and imperial expansion without which the so-called movement of world history from East to West would never have reached its end point in Europe.

Both Dussel and Feinmann seem to want to give Hegel and his European followers a guilty or bad conscience. The question then becomes whether there are not also elements within Hegel's method and system, no doubt starting with the very notion of bad conscience as unhappy consciousness, that would enable the recognition of the non-European. Even the project of a universal history might not be beyond salvage. "If the historical facts about freedom can be ripped out of the narratives told by the victors and salvaged for our own time, then the project of universal freedom does not need to be discarded but, rather, redeemed and reconstituted on a different basis," as Susan Buck-Morss suggests in her groundbreaking essay "Hegel and Haiti."[19] If Hegel's philosophy of history is ever to allow that its hidden and undisciplined stories be told, then the task cannot consist only in providing more empirical evidence of those revolts and uprisings whose rumble can be heard beneath the loud trumpets of theodicy, but the question is also one of principle, including at the level of philosophical logic proper.

Indeed, if the culmination of world history reveals the necessary backward projection of the identity of being and thinking, then should we not look for elements of truth in traces of nonidentity or in instances where there is a lack of adequation between the two? Would this not require that we raise the irreducibility of error, of failure, and of alienation into a new speculative principle—not least of all because its opposite, the unerring authenticity of a correct line, is inaccessible to us other than as a fiction? As Gayatri Chakravorty Spivak observes in her own reading of Hegel in India: "Indeed, there *can* be no correct scholarly model for this type of reading. It is, strictly speaking, 'mistaken,' for it attempts to transform into a reading-position the site of the 'native informant' in anthropology, a site that can only *be* read, by definition, for the production of definitive descriptions. It is an (im)possible perspective."[20] Whoever seeks to incorporate the non-European by way of a moralizing corrective into the Hegelian logic of history must come to terms with the fact that these figures not only do not ever appear as subjects but, even as objects for an anthropological gaze, are always originally lost. If ever the subaltern is going to be refigured into an alternative world history, the latter will have to start from the limit where it resists being retrofitted into logic. As Spivak writes elsewhere: "The historian must persist in *his* efforts in this awareness, that the subaltern is necessarily the absolute limit of the place where history is narrativized into logic. It is a hard lesson to learn, but not to learn it is merely to nominate elegant solutions to be correct theoretical practice."[21]

Then again, is this not precisely the elegant lesson to be learned from the new consensus regarding Hegel's legacy, namely, that far from confirming the identity of thinking and being in a supremely metaphysical panlogicism, he is actually already a thinker of nonidentity, or even of alterity, albeit in spite of himself; that instead of subsuming the particular under an empty universal, his is actually a thinking of pure singularity, of the event, and of the encounter; and that far from affirming the status quo of what is with the positivity of the infinite, his dialectic actually invites us to throw ourselves into the most extreme experience of self-divestiture?

In short, if we were to update Theodor W. Adorno's *The Jargon of Authenticity*, which targeted mostly Heidegger and his lesser imitators, could we not capture the essence of the new consensus surrounding Hegel's legacy today by referring to the jargon of finitude?[22] Philosophically, this means going behind Hegel's back and reading him against the grain so as to retrieve a principle that Heidegger was one of the first to attribute systematically to Kant but that others might associate already with Descartes: "Cartesian reason and Kantian reason offer plenty of differences and even stark oppositions between them, but they find one point of coincidence: the finitude of reason."[23]

THE JARGON OF FINITUDE

Through the narrow gates of the finite, we could certainly glimpse the hollow presence of the problematic brought to the surface in our quest for Hegel in America. Even if this reemphasizing of all things finite is becoming a new dogma that actually might turn out to be more pernicious than advantageous from a political point of view, it is no exaggeration to state that from Kojève to Malabou there exists a consensus to place the concern with finitude squarely at the center of Hegel's thought.

Adorno for a number of reasons constitutes somewhat of an exception in this regard. Not only does *The Jargon of Authenticity* put us on the right track toward a critique of the jargon of finitude, but even where Adorno draws attention to the truth that lies revealed in Hegel's errors, blemishes, or weak spots, as he repeatedly does in *Hegel: Three Studies*, he never fails to add that this faltering dimension of mortality always appears as though in spite of Hegel himself: "For all his emphasis on negativity, division, and nonidentity, Hegel actually takes cognizance of that dimension only for the sake of identity, only as an instrument of identity. The nonidentities are heavily stressed, but not acknowledged, precisely because they are so charged with speculation."[24] In other words, if Hegel indeed needs rescuing, it is precisely because he does not do the job of self-divestiture himself, at least not willingly.

Putting into practice his own principle of reading against the grain, starting from Hegel's blind spots, Adorno is also one of the few to concentrate on the notion of world-spirit, most notably in "An Excursion to Hegel" in *Negative Dialectics*, though this was already a major stake in *Hegel: Three Studies*. Here, the history of the world-spirit in an immanent critique is shown to be true after all: "Satanically, the world as grasped by the Hegelian system has only now, a hundred and fifty years later, proved itself to be a system in the literal sense, namely that of a radically societalized society."[25] The global integration of the world under capitalism thus verifies even the most outrageous claims about the identity of the real and the rational, whose nonidentity cannot fail to show through the cracks: "Hence the locus of Hegel's truth is not outside the system; rather, it is as inherent in the system as his untruth. For this untruth is none other than the untruth of the system of the society that constitutes the substratum of his philosophy."[26] In the end, perhaps not surprisingly, such an immanent critique in the same gesture enables an otherwise extremely rare acknowledgment of the importance of the conquest of America: "Even the Spanish conquests of old Mexico and Peru, which have been felt there like invasions from another planet—even those, irrationally for the Aztecs and Incas, rendered bloody assistance to the spread of bourgeois rational society, all the way to the conception of 'one world' that is teleologically inherent in that society's principle."[27] Little if anything from this reading of the world-spirit will survive once the dialectic, purged of its historical substratum, becomes equated with an analytic of finitude that is ultimately as antidialectical as it claims to be radically antitotalitarian.

Slavoj Žižek also cannot—or can no longer—be considered the epitome of the argument for a finitist reading of Hegel. True: for years Žižek has argued that Hegel's logic is the very opposite of banal panlogicism but also and at the same time that it is identical to the logic of difference with which Jacques Derrida, among others, sought to outwit Hegel. More recently, however, both Žižek and his colleagues in Ljubljana, especially Alenka Zupančič, have been actively pursuing the infinite as part of a critique of the finitist argument. Both Žižek and Zupančič, finally, perform these criticisms of finitude—which may very well amount to self-criticisms—by way of a renewed appreciation of comedy. Thus, in *The Odd One In: On Comedy*, Zupančič argues in favor of the "physics of the infinite" over against the "metaphysics of the finite."[28]

Perhaps the most eloquent and didactic overview of Hegel as a thinker of finitude can be found in Jean-Luc Nancy's *Hegel: The Restlessness of the Negative*. Each subheading in this little gem of a book—from "Restlessness" through "Logic" and "Trembling" all the way to "We"—could serve as a separate entry in a dictionary of finitude. What emerges is a renewed appreciation of spirit, of subject, and of philosophy itself in terms of the pure effectuation of self-relating negativity. The Hegelian subject is far from being the absolute master of the process of going out of itself and coming home to itself. Instead, it is what undoes every determination and exposes every position. "In a word: the Hegelian subject is in no way the *self all to itself*. It is, to the contrary, and it is essentially, what (or the one who) dissolves all substance—every instance already given, supposed first or last, founding or final, capable of coming to rest in itself and taking undivided enjoyment in its mastery and property."[29] The stage for the subject's activity is still the stage of world history, but now the relation between subject and substance is not one of appropriation or overpowerment but rather of expropriation and passing: "The *subject* is what it *does*, it is its act, and its doing is the experience of the consciousness of the negativity of substance, as the concrete experience and consciousness of the modern history of the world—that is, also, of the passage of the world through its own negativity."[30] Even the history of the world-spirit can appear as the manifestation of the absolute *as* self-liberation, now understood as the absolution *from* any given self.

Philosophy here does not come full circle by ending with a speculative return to the beginning, now raised to a higher level. Instead, it does nothing more, but also nothing less, than expose the restlessness of being itself in its pure immanence. If there is an infinite, it is only the infinite exposure of finitude to itself—without either a stable beginning or a transcendent end:

> Hegel neither begins nor ends; he is the first philosopher for whom there is, explicitly, neither beginning nor end, but only the full and complete actuality of the infinite that traverses, works, and transforms the finite. Which means: negativity, hollow, gap, the difference of being that relates to itself through this very difference, and which *is* thus, in all its essence and all its energy, the infinite act of relating itself to itself, and thus the power of the negative.[31]

At the level of logic, this means that we find ourselves at the opposite extreme of any presupposition of identity. "Hegel is the first to take thought out of the realm of identity and subjectivity," Nancy writes: "The Hegelian world is the world in which no generality subsists, only infinite singularities."[32] Thought does not at all operate according to the impoverished dialectic of particularity and generality. The notion of singularity, negating both of these poles, emerges as the epitome of the speculative "concept" or "grasp," Hegel's *Begriff*:

> Grasp is thus the grasping of the singular in its singularity, that is, in what is unique and unexchangeable about it, and therefore at the point where this unicity is the unicity of a desire and a recognition of the other, in all the others. The ones and the oth-

ers—the ones who are all others for each other—are among themselves equals in desire.[33]

Nevertheless, the question immediately arises whether this view of the Hegelian logic is really any better equipped to acknowledge not just alterity in general but the concrete other that is the non-European. For all the stress on the labor of the concept as the power to delink the self from all given attachments, this perspective does not fail to corroborate the fundamental gesture that equates the movement of history with the manifestation of absolute liberty: "Hegel names this manifestation 'the spirit of the world.'"[34] Is this truly liberty for all those others whose unexchangeable singularity the movement of spirit is supposed to expose? More importantly, is the renewed emphasis on alterity and finitude not bound to introduce a point of blockage in any contemporary attempt to put this philosopher to good political use for the Left? Should we not look for an alternative to this profoundly Kantian reading of Hegel? Finally, should we not acknowledge the historical circumstances that explain why there is such a strong desire today to rescue Hegel from the tainted image of him as a "dogmatic" and perhaps even "proto-totalitarian" thinker, presented by his *Philosophy of Right* or his *Philosophy of History*?

Not so long ago, for example in his polemic with Jacques Derrida and Rodolphe Gasché in *For They Know Not What They Do*, Slavoj Žižek could still convincingly take aim at the "typical deconstructivist" portrayal of Hegel as a thinker of an all-absorbing Absolute, to which he then opposes, with help from Lacan's logic of the signifier, the "elementary" Hegelian dialectic of the not-All and the lack in the Other. Even the notion of an unavoidable excess or remainder would not be able to avoid the profound misunderstanding involved in the deconstructivist reading with its altogether commonsensical attempt to free heterogeneity from identity. For Žižek, the only true alternative is to experience how the difference supposed to be sublated never existed but was always already a lost cause: "The dialectical 'sublation' is thus always a kind of retroactive 'unmaking' [*Ungeschehen-machen*]; the point is not to overcome the obstacle to Unity but to experience how the obstacle *never was one*; how the appearance of an 'obstacle' was due only to our wrong, 'finite' perspective."[35] Today, with Derrideans and Heideggerians such as Nancy or Malabou turning to Hegel for positive inspiration and not merely for a straw man argument, the same rebuttal is no longer possible. Hegel, who once stood for the textbook platitudes of absolute reason, now posits alterity and plasticity as such—and not even as a concession but as his first and last contribution to philosophizing proper.

Nancy barely hints at the historical circumstances behind this strange anamorphosis within a broadly understood deconstructive tradition, preferring instead—

almost as a simple matter of fact—to free Hegel of the charges of being a circular, foundational, or metaphysical thinker, since he neither begins nor ends nor grounds nor completes anything: "In these two ways—absence of beginning and absence of end, absence of foundation and absence of completion—Hegel is the opposite of a 'totalitarian' thinker."[36] So what exactly has happened? How can the horizon of expectation have shifted so dramatically to begin with, to the point where even Hegel's *Aufhebung* begins to read as a quasi synonym for a Heideggerian-inspired *Ereignis* as the event of appropriation without which there would be no historicity and, therefore, no history? In short, what are the political conditions that enable the reading of Hegel as the first full-fledged thinker of a finitist ontology to emerge as a crucial component in the recent history and theory of the Left? Only if we begin to formulate answers to these questions will we also know whether the language of finitude actually constitutes a jargon, or whether it is not perhaps, in the very manner of Hegel's phenomenological attitude, the exposition of the real itself.

DID SOMEBODY SAY LEFT-WING COMMUNISM?

To answer some of these questions, I want to turn to the work of the Mexican novelist, playwright, and self-taught philosopher José Revueltas. In his 1964 novel *Los errores*, this author gives us important insights into the potential destiny of the whole jargon of finitude when combined with an antitotalitarian, Left-wing revisionist reading of Hegel. In fact, his novel can serve as a pivotal transition between Lenin's orthodox view, in *Left-Wing Communism as an Infantile Disease*, and the view of the New Left, exemplified in Daniel and Gabriel Cohn-Bendit's *Leftism as the Remedy for the Senile Disease of Communism*.[37]

Aside from its melodramatic plot line that pits the lumpenproletariat of prostitutes and pimps against the fascistoid anticommunists, *Los errores* presents a narrativized judgment regarding the dogmatic excesses of Stalinism, including in the Mexican Communist Party. In this sense, the novel participates in a larger self-evaluation of the twentieth century in which we could also include Alain Badiou's *The Century* or, closer to Revueltas's home, Bolívar Echeverría's *Vuelta de siglo*.[38] Revueltas is concerned above all with the interpretation that history has in store for the great events in the international expansion and perversion of communism. Its main problem is addressed in an odd parenthesis, in which the narrator's voice seems indistinguishable from the author's:

(One cannot escape the necessity of a *free and heterodox* reflection about the meaning of the "Moscow trials" and the place they occupy in the definition of our age, of our twentieth century, because we true communists—whether members of the party or not—are shouldering the terrible, overwhelming task of being the ones who bring history face to face with the disjunctive of having to decide whether this age, this perplexing century, will be designated as *the century of the Moscow trials* or as *the century of the October revolution*.)[39]

Revueltas leaves us no clear verdict in this regard. Was the twentieth century criminal or revolutionary? The disjunctive remains open throughout *Los errores*, since there is also no single character capable of occupying the organizing center of consciousness that we might attribute to its author. Critics such as Christopher Domínguez Michael, after expressing their dismay at Revueltas's "far-fetched and immoral" hypothesis regarding the trials, are quick to add how much they lament the fact that Revueltas could have suggested some kind of dialectical justification of sacrifice and terror: "Revueltas takes the liberties of a novelist with regard to history and, in his enthusiasm for the Hegelian triads, he converts Bukharin's tortured mind into a precise and chilling dialectical synthesis."[40] In reality, the text is far more ambiguous.

Thus, we find examples of an analysis of the corrupting nature of power with regard to historical truth. Other arguments leave open the possibility that it may be too early to judge the situation in the Soviet Union. That humanity, being still too alienated or else—metaphysically speaking—being merely mortal, cannot exclude the future vindication of sacrifice. Precisely to the extent in which truth must inscribe itself concretely in the time and space of a specific situation, there exists no absolute vantage point from where it could be judged once and for all. Finally, there is a moment for the justification of a heroic outlook in history:

> Tomorrow history will vindicate these heroes, in spite of the errors, vacillations and weaknesses of their lives; these human beings who were able and knew how to accept the defamating stigma before the whole world, whose names are Bukharin, Piatakov, Rykov, Krestinski, Ter-Vaganyan, Smirnov, Sokolnikov, Zinoviev, Kamenev, Muralov and so many others.[41]

All these interpretations are not mutually exclusive nor do they present a clear-cut picture of the ideological debate surrounding the Moscow trials. They sometimes invade the mind of a single character, dividing his inner sense with a terrifying uncertainty. This is the case of the communist intellectual Jacobo Ponce, who is on the verge of being expulsed from the PCM:

> The other part of his self, the other part of his atrociously divided spirit, replied to him: no, these concrete truths are only small and isolate lies in the process of a general

reality that will continue its course, despite and above everything. The miseries, dirty tricks, and crimes of Stalin and his cohorts will be seen by tomorrow's communist society as an obscure and sinister disease of humanity from our time, from the tormented and delirious twentieth century that, all in all, will have been the century of the greatest and inconceivable historical premonitions of humanity.[42]

From such ruminations, it is difficult to draw the simplistic conclusion that history, understood dialectically, would justify every possible means in the name of the communist end. Moreover, only a melodramatic imagination would define communism as a cause that is "pure and untouched by evil," to speak the novel's language, but this does not mean that we should move to the opposite extreme of the ideological spectrum so as to interpret evil as the profound truth of all militancy, a sure way if ever there was one to refute beforehand any future for the communist project.

In the final instance, as the novel's title indicates, everything revolves around the status of errors: is there or not sublation of the errors committed by history, in the sense of a dialectical *Aufhebung*? For those who reproach Revueltas for his blind confidence in the Hegelian dialectic, it seems that the sheer idea of finding some sense or relevance in such errors only aggravates their criminal nature to the point of justifying terror and totalitarianism. But this view leads to a position outside or beyond the history of communism, by defending liberal democracy as the only remedy against the repetition of radical Evil—that is, against the threat of so-called totalitarianism with its twin faces of Hitler and Stalin.

For Revueltas, the task consists in thinking the crimes from within the politics of communism, not the other way around, not to ratify the facts with the stamp of historical inevitability but to formulate an immanent critique that at the same time would avoid the simple abandonment of communism as such. What seems to be happening today, however, is a tendency to interrupt in anticipation any radical emancipatory project in the name of a new moral imperative that obliges us above all to avoid the repetition of the crime. With *Los errores* Revueltas may have become the unwitting accomplice of contemporary nihilism, which consists precisely in defining the Good only negatively by way of the necessity to avoid Evil.[43] In particular, there are two aspects in the novel that run the risk of contributing to this complicity: the ethical role attributed to the party and the metaphysical speculation about "man" as an erroneous being. Both of these themes are presented with the hope of serving as possible correctives to the reining dogmatism, but they could easily invite an ideological conclusion that runs counter to its intended effect.

Revueltas, on one hand, lets Jacobo Ponce devote most of his energy to the task of an ethical reflection about the party's authority. "The party [serves] as an ethical notion," against the orthodoxy of the party vanguard of the proletariat: "The party [is] a superior moral notion, not only in its role as political instrument but also as human consciousness, as the reappropriation of consciousness."[44] At the end of the novel, in the "Blind Knot" that serves as its epilogue, Ismael reaches the same conclusion as Jacobo: "The conclusion to be derived from this, if we introduce into our study of the problem the concepts of a humanist ethics, the concepts that stem from an ethical development of Marxism, can only be the most overwhelming and terrible conclusion, especially considering the parties that come into power."[45] The exercise of dogmatism, with its "consoling tautology" that "*the party is the party*," in reality involves "the most absolute ethical nihilism, the negation of all ethics, ciphered in the concept: *to us everything is permitted.*"[46]

If, on the other hand, "thought and practice ... are identified as twin brothers in metaphysics and in dogma," then it is understandable that Jacobo would propose a philosophico-anthropological reflection about "man as erroneous being."[47] This reflection is part of the "essay" in which Jacobo has inverted "close to three months of conscientious and patient labor," no doubt similar to the labor it would take Revueltas to write his own essay, *Dialectic of Consciousness*, a few years later. Jacobo reads from this text:

> Man is an erroneous being—he began to read with his eyes, in silence; a being that never finishes by establishing itself anywhere; therein lies precisely his revolutionary and tragic, unpacifiable condition. He does not aspire to realize himself to another degree, and this is to say, in this he finds his supreme realization, to another degree—he repeated to himself—beyond what can have the thickness of a hair, that is, this space that for eternal eternity, and without their being a power capable of remedying this, will leave uncovered the maximum coincidence of the concept with the conceived, of the idea with its object: to reduce the error to a hair's breadth thus constitutes, at the most, the highest victory that he can obtain; nothing and nobody will be able to grant him exactitude.[48]

What Jacobo proposes can be read as a new metaphysics—or antimetaphysics—of error and equivocity, over against dogma and exactitude. If the identity of being and thinking defines the basic premise of all metaphysical dogmatism, human conscience or consciousness (*conciencia* in Spanish means both) can avoid dogmatism only by accepting an infinitesimal distance between the concept and the thing conceived.

Revueltas accepts the need for a revision of the Hegelian dialectic in ways that are similar to what Adorno around the same time proposes with his negative dialectics, according to which no concept ever completely covers its content without leaving behind some leftover, or some remnant of nonidentity. Much of Revueltas's intellectual work as a novelist and a theorist during the sixties and seventies is devoted to such a reformulation of the dialectic, as the conception of the nonconceptual. In the case of *Los errores*, though, it is not difficult to guess where the ethics of the party and the metaphysics of error will end up. Both arguments in fact could be invoked in order to stop, interrupt, or prohibit any attempt to organize politics as well as any project to approach the truth of consciousness. Not only would all organizational matters then be displaced onto moral issues, but this could even lead to a position for which the knowledge of our essential nature as "erroneous beings" would always be morally superior and theoretically more radical than any given action, which in comparison cannot but appear "dogmatic" and "totalitarian." In full melodramatic mode, we would end up with the attitude of the "beautiful soul" from Hegel's *Phenomenology*. The history of the 1970s and 1980s, with its peremptory declarations of the "end of ideology," the "death" of Marxism, and the "ethical turn," would end up confirming the extent to which the defense of liberal democracy against communism also adopted some of the features of this same "beautiful soul" who at least knows that its inactivity protects it from the Evil incurred by anyone intent upon imposing, here and now, some Good. "Politics is subordinated to ethics, to the single perspective that really matters in this conception of things: the sympathetic and indignant judgement of the spectator of the circumstances," writes Badiou: "Such is the accusation so often repeated over the last fifteen years: every revolutionary project stigmatized as 'utopian' turns, we are told, into totalitarian nightmare. Every will to inscribe an idea of justice or equality turns bad. Every collective will to the Good creates Evil."[49]

Hegel's finitude should be revisited from the point of view of this outcome. The premise of the irreducibility of error and of the necessary inadequacy between concept and being indeed runs through the entire finitist tradition of reading Hegel. Thus, central to the Kojève's claim that Hegel is the first to attempt a complete atheist and finitist philosophy, we find the idea that this requires a view of "man" as an essentially erroneous being:

> Being which *is* (in the Present) can be "conceived of" or revealed by the Concept. Or, more exactly, Being *is* conceived of at "each instant" of its being. Or else, again: Being is not only Being, but also *Truth*—that is, the adequation of the Concept and Being. This is simple. The whole question is to know where *error* comes from. In order that error be possible, the Concept must be *detached* from Being and *opposed* to it. It is Man who does this; and more exactly, Man *is* the Concept detached from Being; or better yet, he is the *act* of detaching the Concept from Being.[50]

The ability of human errors to survive, in fact, is what distinguishes man from nature:

Only the errors committed by man *endure* indefinitely and are propagated at a distance, thanks to language. And man could be defined as an error that is preserved in existence, that *endures* within reality. Now, since *error* means *disagreement* with the real; since what is *other* than what is, is *false*, one can also say that the man who errs is a Nothingness that nihilates in Being, or an "ideal" that is present in the real.[51]

It is only thanks to our essentially human tendency to err that truth is possible as well. Otherwise, being would be mute facticity: "Therefore, there is really a *truth* only where there *has been* an error. But error exists really only in the form of human discourse."[52] To use Hegel's own words in one of Adorno's favorite formulations: "Only out of this error does the truth arise. In this fact lies the reconciliation with error and with finitude."[53]

For Kojève, true wisdom famously will bring about the perfect adequation of being and concept in the figure of the sage or wise man at the end of history. By contrast, in the absence of any ultimate reconciliation, philosophy survives only in and through error, through the gap between the concept and its object, a gap that is thus not merely temporary or accidental but constitutive. And yet, if finitude today constitutes a new dogma that blocks all action to avoid the trappings of radical evil, should we not also invert this conclusion regarding the irreducibility of error by reaffirming the identity of being and thinking with Parmenides? Revueltas explores this possibility through his own notion of the act in "*Hegel* and I."

THE FUTURE OF PARMENIDES

A remarkably enigmatic short story, "*Hegel* y yo" was first published in 1973 as the planned onset for a future novel on the same subject that would never see the light. The text represents a culminating moment in the long trajectory of Revueltas as a narrator and a thinker. "*Hegel* and I," in fact, seems to take up and to try to solve some of the deadlocks present in Revueltas's strictly theoretical writings from the same period, most of which have been published posthumously in volumes such as *Dialéctica de la conciencia* and *México 68: Juventud y revolución*.

In *Dialectic of Consciousness*, Revueltas had proposed to himself various projects at once: a critique of the contemporary "compass madness" of the Left, symptomatically expressed in the proliferation of groupuscles of all kinds; a genealogical reconstruction to understand the true causes of the "crisis" of Marxism, by way of a return to the historical moment when Marx's thought splits off from the double tradition of Kant and Hegel; and, finally, through a series of ingenious "cognitive anecdotes," the elaboration of a subjective dialectic, or a dialectic of consciousness, as opposed to the excesses of the dialectic of nature. Though greeted by Henri Lefebvre in his preface as an effort comparable to that of contemporary figures such as Adorno, Revueltas's project does not give us much more than a glimpse of what it would mean to rescue and reappropriate, through the act of consciousness, the gigantic memory of human rebellion and defeat against alienation.[54]

Revueltas develops the notion of a "profane illumination" that takes place whenever an emergent consciousness is on the verge of breaking through the monumental obliteration of generic human labor. More specifically, he describes such moments in terms of "acts" that change the paradigms of existing knowledge in light of a truth that is historical yet part of an immemorial past that runs through, and sometimes interrupts, the continuum of human history.

History, seen in this light, is not an accumulation of cultural riches so much as the large-scale vanishing of misery into the unconscious of humanity's constitutive prehistory. How, then, does humanity escape from the almost mystical slumber of its general intellect and unconscious memory? Here, like Walter Benjamin, Revueltas seems to have been inspired by a letter from Marx to Arnold Ruge. "Our election cry must be: Reform of consciousness not through dogmas, but through the analysis of mystical consciousness that is unclear to itself, whether it appears in a religious or a political form," Marx had written to his friend: "Then people will see that the world has long possessed the dream of a thing—and that it only needs to possess the consciousness of this thing in order really to possess it."[55] Benjamin turns this election cry into the cornerstone of his dialectical method. "The realization of dream elements in the course of waking up is the canon of dialectics," he writes in *The Arcades Project*: "Is awakening perhaps the synthesis of dream consciousness (as thesis) and waking consciousness (as antithesis)? Then the moment of awakening would be identical with the 'now of recognizability,' in which things put on their true—surrealist—face."[56] This view of awakening in as "a supremely dialectical point of rupture" or "flash" is reminiscent of the moment when consciousness suddenly is "on the verge" of forming itself and bursting into our field of visibility, according to Revueltas. The latter proposes to see the activity of thought as a secular, or profane, illumination: "Consciousness, freed and bared of all divinity—in virtue as much as in vice—puts things on their feet that were standing on their head, it illuminates them, and it profanes them."[57] It is this kind of illumination that shines through "*Hegel* and I."

Hegel, in the story, is the nickname for a prisoner, a paraplegic who from his wheelchair exchanges anecdotes and philosophical musings with his cellmate, a thinly disguised alter ego of Revueltas himself. "It is a questioning of Hegelian philosophy, referred to the prison," the author explains in an interview: "A character who arrives in prison is a bank robber called *Hegel* because he robbed a bank on Hegel Street. Everyone calls him *Hegel*. From there the narrator takes up the positions of Hegel in order to demonstrate that the prison is the State."[58] From this character, in fact, we obtain above all the outline for a provocative theory of the act—of what it means to reach consciousness in the act of theory.

True acts have no witnesses in history. They belong to the silent reserve of an unconscious recollection. "The profound act lies within you, lurking and prepared to jump up from the bottom of your memory: from that memory of the nonevent [*lo no-ocurrido*]," Hegel says, and the narrator approves: "He's right: our acts, our profound acts as he says, constitute that part of memory that does not accept remembering, for which it does not matter whether there are witnesses or not. Nobody is witness to nobody and nothing, each one carries his or her own recollection of the unseen, or the unheard-of, without testimonies."[59] Without memory, without testimony, yet recorded in the blank pages of a collective unconscious, profound acts are those acts that define not only a subject's emergent consciousness but this very subject as well. "You," or "I," in this version of "*Hegel* and I," are but the result of the profound acts of history, whether in 1968 or in 1917, in 1905 or in 1871, acts that forever will have changed the conditions of politics in history. This is not a blind, voluntaristic account of the subject's capacity for action and intervention, since it is not the subject but the act that is first:

> Thus, insofar as you are here (I mean, here in prison or wherever you are, it doesn't matter), insofar as you stand in and are a certain site, you have something to do with this act. It is inscribed in your ancient memory, in the strangest part of your memory, in your *estranged* memory, unsaid and unwritten, unthought, never felt, which is that which moves you in the direction of such an act. So strange that it is a memory without language, lacking all proper signs, a memory that has to find its own way by means of the most unexpected of all means. Thus, this memory repeats, without our being aware of it, all the frustrations prior to its occurrence, until it succeeds in lucking again upon the original profound act which, for this reason alone, is yours. But only for this reason, because it is yours without belonging to you. The opposite is the case: you are the one who belongs to the act, by which, in the end, you cease to belong to yourself.[60]

The act not only constitutes the brief occurrence of an identity of thinking and being but also redeems past errors and failures. Through the notion of a repetition of the memory of *lo no-ocurrido*, that is, literally "the unhappened" or "the nonoccurred," Revueltas is inverting the logic of Hegel's sublation, which, as Žižek frequently reminds us, amounts to a kind of *Ungeschehen-machen*, incidentally the same German term that Freud uses in his understanding of denegation.[61] For Revueltas, however, the aim of the profound acts of history is not symbolically to *unmake* what *did* happen but rather to allow that what *did not* happen be *made* to happen.

Insofar as it repeats not the actual events of the past but the repetition of their halo of lack, the act proper has no beginning or end. "Where the devil did these things begin?" the narrator in "*Hegel* and I" asks himself: "It is not the things themselves that I recall but their halo, their periphery, that which lies beyond what circumscribes and defines them."[62] It is only afterward that historians—and perhaps philosophers of history as well—can name, date, and interpret the events that are repeated but not registered in such an immemorial act:

> It is an act that accepts all forms: committing it, perpetrating it, consummating it, realizing it. It simply is beyond all moral qualification. Qualifying it is left to those who annotate it and date it, that is, to the journalists and the historians, who must then necessarily adjust it to a determinate critical norm that is in force, whereby they only erase its traces and falsify it, erecting it into a Myth that is more or less valid and acceptable during a certain period of time: Landru, Ghengis Khan, Galileo, Napoleon, the Marquis de Sade, or Jesus Christ or Lenin, it's all the same.[63]

Revueltas himself, thus, responds to the acts and events of 1968 in particular with the demand for a theory of the act that would be able to account for the process by which the frustrated acts of the past—acts of rebellion such as the railworkers' strike of 1958 in Mexico—are woken up from their slumber and brought to realization. As prolonged theoretical acts in their own right, though, events cannot be seized without also sacrificing their nature, unless the interpretive framework is attuned to reflect this very event-like nature itself. To his fellow militants of May 1968 in France, for example, Revueltas sends a public letter with the following message: "Your massive action, which immediately turns into historical praxis, from the first moment on, possesses the peculiar nature of being at the same time a great theoretical leap, a radical subversion of the theory mediated, deformed, fetishized by the epigones of Stalin."[64] This radical subversion in turn must be theorized without losing its subversiveness in the no man's land of a theory without practice. Writing from his cell in the Lecumberri prison, Revueltas asks nothing less from his fellow Mexicans. "I believe," he writes against all odds in 1976 in a collection of essays about the massacre in Tlatelolco, "that the experience of 1968 is a highly positive one, and one that will bring enormous benefits, provided that we know how to theorize the phenomenon."[65] It is this attempt at theory that urges us to return to a certain shadowy presence of Hegel in America.

NOTES

1. José Ortega y Gasset, "Hegel y América," *El Espectador* 7–8 (1966): 11–27. There exists an English translation that I have consulted for this chapter: "Hegel and America," trans. Luanne Buchanan and Michael H. Hoffheimer, *Clio* 25, no. 1 (1995): 69–81.
2. G. W. F. Hegel, *The Philosophy of History*, trans. J. Sibree (Buffalo, N.Y.: Prometheus Books, 1991), pp. 86–87.
3. Hegel, "Geographical Basis of History," in *Philosophy of History*, pp. 79–102.
4. Ortega y Gasset, "Hegel y América," p. 23.
5. Ibid.
6. Ibid., p. 15.
7. Roberto Fernández Retamar, "Modernismo, noventiocho, subdesarrollo," in *Para una teoría de la literatura hispanoamericana* (Havana: Pueblo y Educación, 1984), p. 76.
8. Catherine Malabou, *The Future of Hegel: Plasticity, Temporality and Dialectic*, trans. Lisabeth During (London: Routledge, 2005), p. 79.
9. Ibid.
10. Ibid., p. 16.
11. Quoted in Ortega y Gasset, "Hegel y América," p. 20.
12. Ibid. Since I began by mentioning René Magritte's "This is not a pipe," I might add the odd detail that according to Buffon there were no crocodiles but only caimans and alligators in Latin America. This has led the contemporary Colombian artist José Alejandro Restrepo to play off Hegel and Alexander von Humboldt in the installation titled "Humboldt's Crocodile Is Not Hegel's" (originally presented in 1994). See Erna von der Walde, "'Ceci n'est pas un crocodile': Variations on the Theme of American Nature and the Writing of History," *Journal of Latin American Cultural Studies* 15, no. 2 (2006): 231–249.
13. Ortega y Gasset, "Hegel y América," pp. 11, 23.
14. José Pablo Feinmann, *Filosofía y nación: Estudios sobre el pensamiento argentino* (Buenos Aires: Ariel, 1996), pp. 149–164.
15. Ibid., p. 155.
16. Ibid., p. 157.
17. Enrique Dussel, *Política de la liberación: Historia mundial y crítica* (Madrid: Trotta, 2007), p. 380.
18. Enrique Dussel, "Eurocentrism and Modernity (Introduction to the Frankfurt Lectures)," in *The Postmodernism Debate in Latin America*, ed. John Beverley, José Oviedo, and Michael Aronna (Durham, N.C.: Duke University Press, 1995), p. 66.
19. Susan Buck-Morss, "Hegel and Haiti," *Critical Inquiry* 26, no. 4 (2000): 865.
20. Gayatri Chakravorty Spivak, *A Critique of Postcolonial Reason: Toward a History of the Vanishing Present* (Cambridge, Mass.: Harvard University Press, 1999), p. 49.
21. Gayatri Chakravorty Spivak, "Subaltern Studies: Deconstructing Historiography," in *Selected Subaltern Studies*, ed. Ranajit Guha and Gayatri Chakravorty Spivak (Oxford: Oxford University Press, 1988), p. 16.

22. Theodor W. Adorno, *The Jargon of Authenticity*, trans. Knut Tarnowski and Frederic Will (Evanston, Ill.: Northwestern University Press, 1973).
23. Feinmann, *Filosofía y nación*, p. 180.
24. Theodor W. Adorno, *Hegel: Three Studies*, trans. Shierry Weber Nicholsen (Cambridge, Mass.: MIT Press, 1994), pp. 13, 16.
25. Ibid., p. 27.
26. Ibid., pp. 31–32.
27. Theodor W. Adorno, *Negative Dialectics*, trans. E. B. Ashton (New York: Continuum, 1973), p. 302.
28. Alenka Zupančič, *The Odd One In: On Comedy* (Cambridge, Mass.: MIT Press, 2008), pp. 43–60.
29. Jean-Luc Nancy, *Hegel: The Restlessness of the Negative*, trans. Jason Smith and Steven Miller (Minneapolis: University of Minnesota Press, 2002), p. 5.
30. Ibid.
31. Ibid., p. 9.
32. Ibid., pp. 55, 22.
33. Ibid., p. 66.
34. Nancy, *Hegel*, p. 37.
35. Slavoj Žižek, *For They Know Not What They Do: Enjoyment as a Political Factor*, 2nd ed. (London: Verso, 2002), pp. 62–63.
36. Nancy, *Hegel*, p. 8.
37. Daniel Cohn-Bendit and Gabriel Cohn-Bendit, *Obsolete Communism: The Left-Wing Alternative*, trans. Arnold Pomerans (New York: McGraw-Hill, 1968).
38. Alain Badiou, *The Century*, trans. Alberto Toscano (Malden, Mass.: Polity Press, 2007); Bolívar Echeverría, *Vuelta de siglo* (Mexico City: Era, 2007).
39. José Revueltas, *Los errores* (Mexico City: Era, 1979), pp. 222–223. In the following two sections, I borrow and translate long segments from two previously published studies: Bruno Bosteels, "Una arqueología del porvenir: Acto, memoria, dialéctica," *La Palabra y el Hombre* 134 (2005): 161–171; and "Marxismo y melodrama: Reflexiones sobre *Los errores* de José Revueltas," in *El terreno de los días: Homenaje a José Revueltas*, ed. Francisco Ramírez Santacruz and Martín Oyata (Mexico City: Miguel Angel Porrúa/Benemérita Universidad Autónoma de Puebla, 2007).
40. Christopher Domínguez Michael, "Lepra y utopía," in *Nocturno en que todo se oye: José Revueltas ante la crítica*, ed. Edith Negrín (Mexico City: Era, 1999), p. 65.
41. Revueltas, *Los errores*, p. 198.
42. Ibid., pp. 197–198.
43. Alain Badiou, *Ethics: An Essay on the Understanding of Evil*, trans. Peter Hallward (London: Verso, 2001), pp. 9, 30 (trans. modified).
44. Revueltas, *Los errores*, p. 88.
45. Ibid., p. 271
46. Ibid., p. 272.
47. Ibid., p. 67.

48. Ibid., pp. 67–68
49. Ibid., pp. 9, 13.
50. Alexandre Kojève, *Introduction to the Reading of Hegel: Lectures on the Phenomenology of Spirit Assembled by Raymond Queneau*, ed. Allan Bloom, trans. James H. Nichols Jr. (New York: Basic Books, 1969), p. 144n.34. I have also consulted the French edition in *Introduction à la lecture de Hegel* (Paris: Gallimard, 1947). I am much indebted to Evodio Escalante for first putting me on the track of Kojève's Hegel in the context of my reading of *Los errores*.
51. Kojève, *Introduction to the Reading of Hegel*, p. 187.
52. Ibid., p. 188. We should note that there are actually two types of error in Hegel for Kojève: the inevitable erring that is part of our human condition and error as mistake or superable defect, as when Hegel's posits the dialecticity not only of History but also of Nature.
53. Quoted in Adorno, *Hegel*, p. 93.
54. José Revueltas, *Dialéctica de la conciencia*, ed. Andrea Revueltas and Philippe Cheron (Mexico City: Era, 1982).
55. Quoted in Walter Benjamin, *The Arcades Project*, trans. Howard Eiland and Kevin McLaughlin, ed. Rolf Tiedemann (Cambridge, Mass.: Belknap Press of Harvard University Press, 1999), p. 467.
56. Ibid., pp. 464, 364.
57. José Revueltas, *Las evocaciones requeridas*, ed. Andrea Revueltas and Philippe Cheron (Mexico City: Era, 1987), vol. 1, p. 48.
58. *Conversaciones con José Revueltas*, compiled by Andrea Revueltas and Philippe Cheron (Mexico City: Era, 2001), p. 77.
59. José Revueltas, "*Hegel* y yo . . . ," in *Material de los sueños* (Mexico City: Era, 1979), pp. 20, 13.
60. Ibid., p. 20.
61. Slavoj Žižek, "Lacan—At What Point Is He Hegelian?" trans. Rex Butler and Scott Stephens, in *Interrogating the Real* (London: Continuum, 2007), p. 34. On Freud's notion of *das Ungeschehen-machen* as neurotic compulsion, see also Elizabeth Rottenberg, *Inheriting the Future: Legacies of Kant, Freud, and Flaubert* (Stanford, Calif.: Stanford University Press, 2005), pp. 78–79.
62. Revueltas, "*Hegel* y yo," p. 18.
63. Ibid., p. 16.
64. José Revueltas, *México 68: Juventud y revolución*, ed. Andrea Revueltas and Philippe Cheron (Mexico City: Era, 1978), p. 26.
65. Ibid., p. 21.

5

INFINITE RESTLESSNESS

MARK C. TAYLOR

EITHER/OR ... BOTH/AND

Throughout the latter part of the twentieth century, Hegelianism was repeatedly read as the culmination of the onto-theological tradition in which the will to totality issues in the will to power, which, in turn, unleashes "the fury of destruction" in a holocaust that threatens to become all-consuming. In the wake of the Second World War and the shadow of the Cold War, everywhere people looked they detected what they believed to be totalizing systems that reduce differences—be they religious, racial, sexual, or political—to an identity that is inescapably repressive. As the culmination of the Western tradition, Hegelianism, many argued, is both one of the causes and an effect of hegemonic ideologies on the Left as well as the Right sides of the political spectrum. To counter philosophies of identity, critics developed philosophies of difference, which, contrary to expectation, issued in contrasting versions of an identity politics in which conflict is both inevitable and insurmountable. Many of Hegel's most influential critics drew their inspiration from a misreading of Derridean *différance* as exclusive difference in which opposites can be neither mediated nor reconciled. As the impending threat shifts from totalitarianism to sectarianism, it is becoming increasingly clear that if oppositions can be neither negotiated nor mediated global catastrophe is all but inevitable.

Unlike his many epigones, Derrida always appreciated the complexity of Hegel's philosophy and readily admitted that his own work would have been impossible without it. Concluding the opening chapter in *Of Grammatology*, he writes:

> The horizon of absolute knowledge is the effacement of writing in the logos, the retrieval of the trace in *parousia*, the reappropriation of difference, the accomplishment of what I have elsewhere called the *metaphysics of the proper*. Yet, all that Hegel thought within this horizon, all, that is, except eschatology, may be reread as a meditation on writing. Hegel is *also* the thinker of irreducible difference. He rehabilitated thought as the *memory productive* of signs. And he reintroduced, as I shall try to show elsewhere, the essential necessity of the written trace in a philosophical—that is to say Socratic—discourse that had always believed it possible to do without it; the last philosopher of the book and the first thinker of writing.[1]

In an interview four years later, Derrida clarified and elaborated his position on Hegel's writings. Noting that his own work involves an "infinitesimal and radical displacement" of Hegel's philosophy, Derrida proceeds to explain:

> We will never be finished with the reading or re-reading of Hegel, and, in a certain way, I do nothing other than attempt to explain myself on this point. In effect I believe that Hegel's text is necessarily fissured; that it is something other than the circular closure of its representation. It is not reduced to a content of philosophemes, it also necessarily produces a powerful writing operation, a remainder of writing, whose strange relationship to the philosophical content of Hegel's text must be reexamined, that is, the movement by means of which his text exceeds its meaning, permits itself to be turned away from, to return to, and to repeat itself outside of its self-identity.[2]

The fissure "within" Hegel's text interrupts the circuit of return and thereby exposes an opening that makes possible the "movement by which the text exceeds itself." By reading the Hegelian text against the grain, Derrida makes it possible to detect the activity of an infinite that is neither good nor bad but is something else, something other, which is virtually indistinguishable from nothing. To reread the Hegelian infinite through Derridean *différance* and at the same time to reread Derridean *différance* through the Hegelian *differente Beziehung* (differentiating relation).[3] This double reading creates the possibility of glimpsing an infinite restlessness that is, perhaps, the restlessness of the infinite.

Hegel's entire systematic enterprise turns on a distinction between understanding (*Verstand*) and reason (*Vernunft*). Understanding, which is based upon the principle of noncontradiction, is the analytic activity by which one makes distinctions, establishes antitheses and discerns paradoxes. "Thought, as *understanding*," Hegel argues, "sticks to fixed determinations and to the distinction of one thing from another: every such limited abstraction it treats as having a subsistence of its own."[4] Reason, by contrast, apprehends the dialectical interplay of differences; when rationally comprehended, differences are not exclusive but are codependent and, therefore, coevolve. In an early and important text, *The Difference Between Fichte's and Schelling's System of Philosophy*, Hegel explains that in contrast to understanding,

> the sole interest of reason is to transcend such rigid opposites. But this does not mean that reason is altogether opposed to opposition and limitation. For the necessary bifurcation is *one* factor in life. Life eternally forms itself by setting up oppositions, and totality at the highest vitality of living energy is only possible through its own restoration of the deepest separation. What reason opposes, rather, is just the absolute fixity, which the understanding gives to the dualism; and it does so all the more if the absolute opposites themselves originated in reason.[5]

The contrasting principles of *Verstand* and *Vernunft* lead to different interpretations of the infinite. While understanding conceives the finite and the infinite as mutually exclusive, reason comprehends their reciprocal interrelation. If the finite and the infinite are regarded as antithetical, the infinite is, in fact, limited and bounded by the finite. It is, in other words, a "finite" and therefore "bad" or "spurious infinite [*Schlecht-Unendliche*]." Through a dialectical reversal, the ostensible negativity of the finite and the positivity of the infinite become the positivity of finitude and the negativity of infinitude:

> The infinite determined as such has present in it the finitude that is distinct from it; the former is the *in-itself* in this unity, and the latter is only determinateness, limit in it; but it is a limit, which is the sheer other of the in-itself, is its opposite; the infinite's determination, which is the in-itself as such, is ruined by the addition of such a quality; it is thus a *finitized infinite*. Similarly, since the finite as such is only the negation of the in-itself, but by reason of this unity also has its opposite present in it, it is exalted and, so to say, infinitely exalted above its worth; the finite is posited as the *in-finitized* finite.[6]

The finite, in other words, appears to be independent and self-subsistent and the *in*-finite seems to be dependent on and conditioned by firmly established finitude. According to the dialectical principle of reason, the finitude of *Verstand* negates itself in its very assertion. "*The being of the finite*," Hegel argues, "*is not only its being,* but is also the being of the infinite."[7] Finitude includes within itself its opposite as the indispensable presupposition and essential ground of its own being:

> The finite itself in being elevated into the infinite is no sense acted upon by an alien force; on the contrary, it is its nature to be related to itself as limitation, both limitation as such and as an ought, and to transcend such limitation and to be beyond it. It is not in the sublating of finitude as a whole that infinity in general comes to be; the truth is rather that the finite is only this through its own nature to become infinite.[8]

Infinitude, by contrast, necessarily includes finitude within itself. While the finite realizes itself in and through the infinite, infinitude renders itself infinite in relation to finitude. Then finite is not merely other than or opposed to the infinite but is actually an internal dimension of the infinite. The infinite, therefore, "is on its own account just as much finite as infinite":

> Thus both finite and infinite are this *movement* in which each returns to itself through its negation; they *are* only as *mediation* within themselves, and the affirmative of each contains the negative of each and is the negation of the negation. They are thus a *result*, and hence not what they are in the determination of their *beginning*; the finite is not a d*eterminate being* on *its* side, and the infinite a *determinate* being or *being-in-itself* beyond the determinate being, that is, beyond the being determined as finite.... They occur . . . only as moments of a whole and . . . come on the scene only by means of their opposite, but essentially also by means of the sublation of their opposite.[9]

But is this movement truly circuitous and do the finite and infinite actually form moments of an integral whole? If the Hegelian text is fissured as if from within, there might be an alternative infinite, which could be conceived as the inconceivable mean that is neither either/or nor both/and? Might the very infinity of the infinite imply disruptions, which, though somehow "within," can be neither assimilated nor comprehended by any process designed to contain them? Might this infinite restlessness be Hegel's Absolute, which, contrary to his own intentions can be itself only by not being itself? And might Derridean deconstruction be nothing other than the ceaseless reinscription of the point Hegel made without fully realizing what he was doing? To answer these questions, it is necessary to trace a genealogical trajectory that leads from *différance* back to Heidegger, Schelling, Schlegel, Fichte, and finally Kant. Weaving together what Kant and post-Kantians were saying by not saying, Heidegger exposes the nonoriginal "origin" of deconstruction and thereby shows that the infinitesimal displacement that Derrida claims to effect is already in play in Hegel's system. This play, which "must be conceived of before the alternative of presence and absence," is the infinite restlessness of the infinite.[10]

CRITICAL REFLECTIONS

In 1784, Kant published a brief but influential essay entitled "What Is Enlightenment?" in which he stresses the interrelation of reason and freedom:

> Enlightenment is man's release from his self-incurred tutelage. Tutelage is man's inability to make use of his understanding without direction from another. Self-incurred is this tutelage when its cause lies not in lack of reason but in lack of resolution and courage to use it without direction from another. *Sapere aude*! "Have courage to use your own reason!" That is the motto of enlightenment.[11]

This definition of enlightenment turns on his distinction between heteronomy, which derives from the Greek *hetero* (other) and *nomos* (law), and autonomy, which derives from *auto* (self) and *nomos*. While heteronomy involves determination by another, for example, God, sovereign, parent, or teacher, autonomy is the self-determination or self-legislation through which the subject gives itself the law. Far from arbitrary, free actions are, from this point of view, both rational and normative. Though reason is deployed both theoretically (in thinking) and practically (in acting), Kant insists on the primacy of the practical. Reason and will are inseparable: reason is essentially an *activity*, and if activity is free, it must be reasonable. In the second critique, Kant underscores the primacy of practical reason by arguing that freedom is the pivotal notion for his entire philosophy: "The concept of freedom, in so far as its reality is proved by an apodictic law of practical reason, is the keystone of the whole architecture of the system and even of speculative reason."[12] Freedom, however, proves to be a complex keystone because it harbors an irreducible ambiguity. The more closely one examines Kant's argument, the clearer it becomes that freedom not only involves autonomy but also entails what can best be described as "an-archy." In this context, the term "an-archy" does not mean the absence of form and thus disorder, confusion, or chaos. Rather, an-archy suggests the absence (*an*, without) of any beginning (*arkhe*) and by extension the lack of an originary foundation. That which is anarchic is groundless. While Kant does not always seem to recognize the significant implications of his argument, his critical philosophy demonstrates that autonomy actually presupposes an-archy, which is the nonfoundational foundation or the groundless ground of the law that the self-legislating subject gives to itself. To understand the importance of these two aspects of freedom, it is necessary to consider why autonomy is impossible apart from anarchy.

The notion of autonomy is the structural principle around which all three critiques are organized. The theoretical and practical deployments of reason are isomorphic: a universal principle of reason is brought to bear on particular sense data. While theoretical reason organizes the sensible manifold of intuition through a priori forms of intuition and categories of understanding, practical reason controls idiosyncratic sensible inclinations through universal moral principles. The aim of the *Critique of Judgment* is to reconcile the oppositions and overcome the contradictions within as well as between theoretical and practical reason. The critical faculty in the architectonic of reason in all of its deployments is the imagination.

Kant's three critiques are directed at the triple threat of skepticism, determinism, and atheism. His critical philosophy prepares the way for the defense of religion in terms of moral activity rather than theoretical speculation. Every aspect of his argument is organized around a series of binary oppositions, which he both articulates and attempts to reconcile:

Autonomy/Heteronomy
Freedom/Determinism
Reason/Sensibility
A priori/A posteriori
Universality/Particularity
Objectivity/Subjectivity
Obligation/Inclination
Form/Matter

Kant's immediate successors were divided between those who thought he had not gone far enough and those who thought he had gone too far in formulating a comprehensive philosophical system that could mediate these oppositions. The former argued that his reconciliation of opposites remained incomplete and the latter insisted that his effort to synthesize these opposites was misguided because it obscured the irreducible contradictions and inescapable aporiae inherent in thought and life. The unresolved tensions in Kant's work set the terms of debate in the nineteenth century and continue to influence critical reflection and practice down to the present day.

It has frequently been observed that Kant's "Copernican revolution" is the theoretical equivalent of the political revolution in France. Rarely noted but no less important is the fact that one of Kant's most significant philosophical innovations was his translation of ontology into epistemology. To understand the implications of this development, it is necessary to trace the religio-philosophical genealogy of Kant's epistemology all the way back to Plato and early Christian apologists. In Plato's myth of origin, the world is created by a Demiurge who brings together unchanging forms with the undifferentiated flux of matter. Within this framework the activity of creation is a process of *formation* through which order is brought to chaos. Early Christian apologists, eager to demonstrate that their religion did not involve unsophisticated superstition, which was politically subversive, reinterpreted fundamental theological principles in terms of Platonic philosophy. Instead of an intermediate being situated between eternity and time like the Demiurge, the Christian God, they argued, is the eternal creator of the world. For these apologists, Platonic forms become the mind of God or the Logos, which is understood as the eternal Son of the divine Father. Inasmuch as the Father always creates through the Son, the world is an expression of the divine Logos and is, therefore, logical, reasonable, or, in a more recent idiom, logocentric. Human reason is the reflection of the Logos though which people can comprehend the world God has created. In Kant's account of theoretical reason, Platonic forms and the divine Logos become the forms of intuition and categories of understanding, and the undifferentiated flux of matter becomes the sensible manifold of intuition. Just as Platonic forms and the divine Logos are universal and unchanging, so the forms of intuition and categories of understanding are a priori rather than a posteriori and are therefore universal.

To understand the far-reaching implications of Kant's analysis, it is helpful to translate his epistemology into contemporary information theory. From this point of view, the mind is programmed to process data, which are presented through multiple sensory inputs. Knowledge results from the synthesis of the universal forms of intuition and categories of understanding and the particular data of sense experience. This information processing brings order to chaos by unifying the multiplicity of data to form coherent patterns. The agency through which this synthesis occurs is the imagination—*die Einbildungskraft*. "Now, since every appearance contains a manifold," Kant argues, "and since different perceptions therefore occur in the mind separately and singly, a combination of them, such as they cannot have in sense itself, is demanded. There must therefore exist in us an active faculty for the synthesis of this manifold. To this faculty I give the title, imagination. Its action, when immediately directed to perceptions, I entitled apprehension. Since imagination has to bring the manifold of intuition into the form of an image, it must previously have taken the impressions up into its activity, that is, have apprehended them."[13] Inasmuch as the imagination articulates objects, it is the necessary condition of the possibility of knowledge and as such is *transcendental*. To fulfill this function, the imagination must operate at the edge or on the border *between* understanding and sensation. Kant writes: "Obviously there must be some third thing, which is homogeneous on the one hand with the category, and on the other hand with the appearance, and which thus makes the application of the former to the latter possible. This mediating representation must be pure, that is, void of all empirical content, and yet at the same time, while it must be in one respect *intellectual*, it must in another be *sensible*. Such a representation is the *transcendental schema*."[14] Kant describes the operation of the imagination as the "schematization of the categories." In a manner reminiscent of the transcendent Demiurge who brings form to chaos and the transcendent God who creates through His Logos, the imagination deploys transcendental schemata to organize experience and thereby create the world in which we dwell.[15]

For Kant, all knowledge is synthetic and thus presupposes unification at every level. The data of experience are first processed through the forms of intuition, that is, space and time, and then organized to conform to the categories of understanding through the transcendental imagination. The diverse objects of understanding are, then, unified through what Kant labels the three interrelated Ideas of reason—God, self, and world. Since these Ideas do not arise from and cannot be verified by sense experience, they do not constitute knowledge. Their function is regulative rather than constitutive, that is, they are useful heuristic devices but do not necessarily tell us anything about the world.

Kant was convinced that his analysis of reason provided a response to every version of skepticism and thereby secured the possibility of genuine knowledge. Since the categories of understanding are universal, the knowledge they yield is objective. The data of experience are different but everybody processes them the same way. The principle of causality, for example, is not the result of arbitrary subjective habit but expresses the necessary structure of the human mind. It is clear, however, that such "objectivity" remains subjective because it tells us nothing certain about the way things really are in themselves. Kant's most incisive critics argued that instead of establishing the conditions of the possibility of knowledge, he actually exposed the conditions of the *impossibility* of knowledge. Kant responded by insisting that this limitation is really an advantage. By limiting knowledge of the world, he thought he had made room for the rational affirmation of the freedom of the self and the existence of God.

Kant's argument in *Critique of Practical Reason* is strictly parallel to his argument in *Critique of Pure Reason*. Reason is one though its deployment is triune. In moving from theory to practice, the universal categories of understanding become the universal moral law, and the sensible manifold of intuition becomes multiple sensory intuitions and conflicting sensual desires. The "fundamental law of pure practical reason," Kant argues, is: "To act that the maxim of your will could always hold at the same time as a principle establishing a universal law." He takes this law to be "a fact of reason," which is "plain to all."¹⁶ Just as the first critique is devoted to ascertaining the conditions of the possibility of knowledge, so the second critique seeks to establish the necessary presuppositions of moral activity. In his definitive study, *Between Kant and Hegel*, Dieter Henrich writes: "Kant had already shown that the concept of mind as the subject of knowledge is not possible without the idea of a world that laws govern. Thus a certain concept of the mind implies a conception, an 'image' of the world. We don't have a concept of mind unless we see that the concept of the world is already implied in the self-understanding of the mind. In sum, to develop a conceptual framework for the interpretation of the mind that is based only on mental activity leads directly to the insight that mental activity always implies a world within which such activity occurs."¹⁷ The exercise of practical reason entails a moral *Weltanschauung*, which, Kant maintains, is impossible apart from three postulates: freedom, God, and immortality. Freedom, I have noted, is "the keystone to the whole architecture of the system of pure reason and even of speculative reason." While the limitation of the causality and, by extension, determinism, to a law of the mind preserves the possibility of freedom, the fact of the moral law implies its actuality. In Kant's terms, "freedom is the *ratio essendi* of the moral law" and the moral law is "the *ratio cognoscendi* of freedom."¹⁸ If the subject is not free, moral activity is impossible. In this context, Kant defines freedom as autonomy:

> The autonomy of the will is the sole principle of all moral laws and of duties conforming to them; heteronomy of choice, on the other hand, not only does not establish any obligation but is opposed to the principle of duty and to the morality of the will.
>
> The sole principle of morality consists in independence from all material law (i.e., a desired object) and in the accompanying determination of choice by the mere form of giving universal law, which a maxim must be capable of having. That independence, however, is freedom in the negative sense, while this intrinsic legislation of pure and thus practical reason is freedom in the positive sense. Therefore, the moral law expresses nothing else than the autonomy of the pure practical reason, i.e., freedom.¹⁹

In moral activity, the individual agent regulates personal inclinations and desires through the universal moral law. For an action to be moral, the will cannot be influenced by either desired objects or external pressures but must be determined by nothing other than itself.

While moral action cannot be determined by an object, it is nonetheless unavoidably intentional and, therefore, necessarily entails an object or more precisely an objective. The sole legitimate object of moral action is the *summum bonum*, which Kant defines as happiness proportionate to virtue: "Happiness is the condition of a rational being in the world, in whose whole existence everything goes according to wish and will. It thus rests on the harmony of nature with his entire end and with the essential determining ground of his will." If happiness is the conformity of will and world, it can only be brought about through a being wise enough to discern moral intention and powerful enough to control the natural world. Only God meets these requirements. Moral activity, therefore, presupposes a moral governor who actualizes "the Kingdom of God in which nature and morality come into harmony." It is important to note that while Kant's God is a moral governor, He is not himself a moral being because God's duty and desire are never in conflict. In terms Nietzsche uses in a different though related context, God is "beyond good and evil." Human beings, by contrast, are moral because they never are what they ought to be. When not deceiving himself and others, Kant's moral agent confesses: I am what I am not. The best for which such a divided self can hope is infinite progress in moral development, which is impossible apart from personal immortality. Summarizing the import of the three postulates of practical reason, Kant concludes: "If, therefore, the highest good is impossible according to practical rules, then the moral law, which commands that it be furthered, must be fantastic, directed to empty imaginary ends, and consequently inherently false."[20] Taken together, freedom, God, and immortality provide a schema in which moral action appears to be reasonable, and the world, therefore, makes sense.

Kant realized that his interpretation of reason in both its theoretical and practical deployments deepens the contradictions of subjectivity by inwardizing the conflict between the various binary opposites he articulates. With the movement from heteronomy to autonomy, universality, which had been externally imposed, is inwardly legislated. In the third critique, devoted to aesthetic judgment, Kant attempts to mediate these oppositions through the notion of inner teleology. In contrast to every form of utility and instrumentality in which means and ends are externally related, inner teleology involves what Kant describes as "purposiveness without purpose" in which means and ends are reciprocally related in such a way that each becomes itself in and through the other and neither can be itself apart from the other. Kant illustrates this idea by describing the interplay of whole and part in the work of art:

> The parts of the thing combine of themselves into the unity of a whole by being reciprocally cause and effect of their form. For this is the only way in which it is possible that the idea of the whole may conversely, or reciprocally, determine, in its turn the form and combination of all the parts, not as cause—for that would make it an art product—but as the epistemological basis upon which the systematic unity of the form and combination of all the manifold contained in the given matter become cognizable for the person estimating it.[21]

Though not immediately obvious, this formulation of inner teleology marks a tipping point in cultural and social history whose ramifications are still emerging. In hindsight it is clear that the nineteenth century began with the 1790 publication of the *Critique of Judgment*. The distinction between external and internal teleology is the philosophical articulation of the transition from a mechanical to an organic schema for interpreting the world. What Kant discovered is the *principle of constitutive relationality in which identity is differential rather than oppositional.* While the immediate implications of this insight were worked out by romantic artists and idealistic philosophers during the closing decade of the eighteenth century and early years of the nineteenth century, the structure Kant identifies not only defines modern and postmodern art but also operates in today's information networks and financial markets and anticipates current theories of biological organisms as well as the nature of life itself. For the moment, it is sufficient to note that Kant offers two examples of inner teleology—beautiful works of art and living organisms.

The third critique extends the principle of autonomy from theoretical and practical reason to the work of art understood as both the process of production and the product produced. In contrast to art produced for the market, which is utilitarian and as such has an extrinsic purpose, fine art is not produced for any external end but is created for its own sake. Never referring to anything other than itself, high art is art about art and is, therefore, self-referential and thus self-reflexive. But while seeming to be completely autonomous, the structures of self-referentiality and self-reflexivity are considerably more complicated than they initially appear because they presuppose something they cannot assimilate. The interruption of the self-referential circuit of reflexivity exposes aporiae, which are the condition of creativity. The pivot upon which this analysis turns is the interplay of the imagination and representation in the production of self-consciousness.

AN-ARCHY OF AUTONOMY

For the young writers, artists, and philosophers gathered in Jena in the years immediately following the publication of the third critique, Kant's critical philosophy opened the possibility of completing what began in France by shifting the revolutionary struggle from politics to philosophy and poetry. In a world without adequate social, political, and economic institutions and ravaged by the early stages of industrialization, writers and critics sought to overcome personal alienation and social fragmentation by cultivating new forms of unification and integration. Kant glimpsed the possibility of a unity that nourished rather than repressed differences in his account of the reciprocity of inner teleology but was unable to carry his argument through to its necessary conclusion. Given the limitation of knowledge established in the first critique, he was forced to restrict his notion of beauty to a regulative idea, which might or might not describe the way things really are in the actual world. Since the work of art figures reconciliation as nothing more than an unrealizable idea, it actually deepens the oppositions and fragmentation it is designed to overcome. To accomplish what both the French and the Kantian revolutions leave undone, romantics and idealists argue, it is necessary to realize the Idea by transforming the world into a work of art. As apocalypse by revolution gave way to apocalypse by imagination and cognition, consciousness turned inward and became self-conscious. In pushing itself to its limit, however, autonomous self-consciousness becomes an-archic. That is to say, the subject discovers that it has emerged from a groundless ground that it can never fathom. This fissure creates the opening for the postmodern critique of modernism. Contrary to expectation, the transition from autonomy to an-archy, which is the condition of the possibility of postmodernism, passes through the notion of the infinite elaborated in Hegel's speculative system.

Kant's successors realized that the inner teleological or self-referential structure he identified discloses the self-reflexive structure of self-consciousness. In self-consciousness, the subject (S^S) turns back on itself by becoming an object (S^o) to itself. Self-as-subject and self-as-object are reciprocally related in such a way that each becomes itself through the other and neither can be itself apart from the other. The structure of self-relation constitutive of self-conscious subjectivity presupposes the activity of self-representation (figure 1). Though not immediately obvious, precisely at the point where self-consciousness seems to be complete, it approaches its constitutive limit. Henrich identifies the crucial question in commenting on Fichte's reading of Kant: "We might cast this question another way: Will ontological discourse always make use of the premise that something can be said about the mind that is not of the mind, and that the mind can say something that is of the mind about what is not of the mind, so that the two discourses can never be derived from one another—or even form a third discourse, thereby precluding any fully intelligible linear formulation?"[22] Henrich implies that the impossibility of explaining self-consciousness through linear models does not necessarily mean that the self-reflexivity of self-consciousness is circular. To the contrary, when consciousness turns back on itself, it discovers a lacuna without which it is impossible but with which it is incomplete. The pressing question is: where does that which the self-conscious subject represents to itself come from? If self-as-subject and self-as-object are codependent, neither can be the originary cause of the other. The activity of self-representation, therefore, presupposes a more primordial presentation, which must originate elsewhere. This elsewhere is the limit that is impossible to think but without which thinking is impossible. "Thinking,"

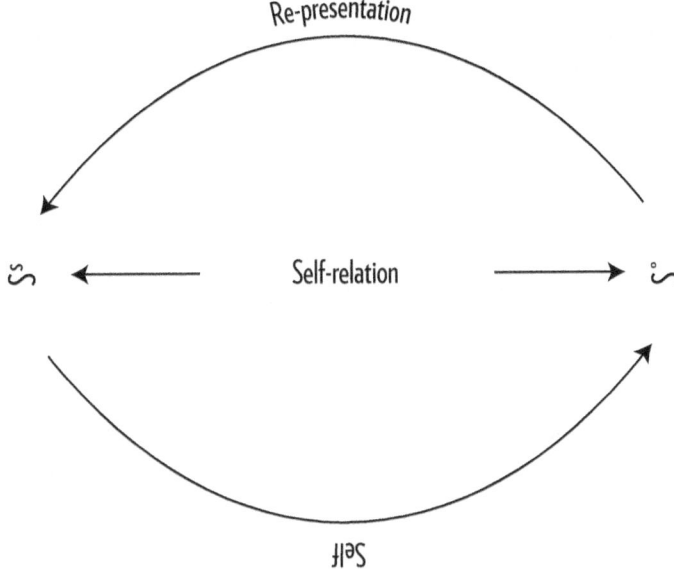

FIGURE 1 Self-consciousness.

as Jean-Luc Nancy explains in another context, "is always thinking on the limit. The limit of comprehending defines thinking. Thus thinking is always thinking about the incomprehensible—about this incomprehensible that 'belongs' to every comprehending, as its own limit."[23] This limit is the edge of chaos where order simultaneously dissolves and emerges. To understand what occurs along this border, it is necessary to consider the dynamics of representation in more detail.

The question of representation—*Vorstellung*—runs through all three critiques. In the first critique, Kant argues: "A concept [*Begriff*] formed from notions [*Notio*] and transcending the possibility of experience is an idea [*Idee*] or concept of reason."[24] In the exercise of practical reason, Ideas that lie beyond experience and hence remain regulative are actualized as they become practically effective in moral activity. But postulates can no more be experienced than ideas and, therefore, yield no knowledge even though they are rational. An Idea or a postulate, Rodolphe Gasché explains, "is a representation by a concept of the concepts that serve to represent representation with consciousness":

> Representation here translates the German *Vorstellung*, a term Kant uses to designate the operation by which the different faculties that constitute the mind bring their respective objects before themselves. Yet when Kant claims that in spite of the impos-

sibility of intuitively representing (and thus knowing) the ideas, they nonetheless play a decisive role for in the realm of cognition, or that in the moral realm they acquire an at least partial concretization, he broaches the question of the becoming present of the highest, but intuitively unpresentable representation that is the idea. This is the problem of the *presentation*, or *Darstellung* of the idea, and it is rigorously distinct from that of representation. The issue is no longer how to depict, articulate, or illustrate something already present yet resisting adequate discursive or figural expression, but of how something acquires presence—reality, actuality, effectiveness—in the first place. The question of *Darstellung* centers on the coming into presence, or occurring, of the ideas.[25]

Coming into presence (*Darstellung*) is the condition of the possibility of representation (*Vorstellung*). But how does such presencing or presentation occur?

In his analysis of Hegel's concept of experience, Heidegger suggests a possible answer to this question when commenting on Hegel's claim that "science, in making its appearance, *is* an appearance itself":

> The appearance is the authentic presence itself: the *parousia* of the Absolute. In keeping with its absoluteness, the Absolute is with us of its own accord. In its will to be with us, the Absolute is being present. In itself, thus bringing itself forward, the Absolute is for itself. For the sake of the will of the *parousia* alone, the presentation of knowledge as phenomenon is necessary. The presentation is bound to remain turned toward the will of the Absolute. The presentation is itself a *willing* [emphasis added], that is, not just a wishing and striving but the action itself, if it pulls itself together within its nature.[26]

This remarkable insight complicates Hegelianism in a way that opens it up *as if* from within. Far from a closed system, which as a stable structure would be the embodiment of the Logos, the Hegelian Absolute here appears to be an *infinitely restless* will that wills itself in willing everything that emerges in nature and history and wills everything that exists in willing itself. Heidegger explains the implications of this reading of Hegel when he interprets the inconceivability of freedom in Kant's philosophy in a way that points toward his own account of the groundless ground of Being: "The only thing that we comprehend is its incomprehensibility. Freedom's incomprehensibility consists in the fact that it resists comprehension since it is freedom that transposes us into the realization of Being, not in the mere representation of it."[27]

The interplay of *Darstellung* (presentation) and *Vorstellung* (representation) occurs through the activity of *Einbildungskraft* (imagination). The etymology of *Einbildungskraft* is important for Kant's argument as well as its elaboration by his followers. *Bild* means picture, image, likeness, or representation, and *Bildung* means formation, forming, generation, and by extension culture as well as education. The verb *bilden* means to form, fashion, shape, mold, or construct. Finally, *Ein* means one. *Einbildungskraft*, then, is the activity of formation or construction by which something is fashioned into a unified image or representation. The multiple nuances of *Einbildungskraft* are captured in the English word "figure." "Figure," which is both a noun and a verb, derives from the Latin *figura* (form, shape, figure). In addition to form or shape, "figure" means the outline or silhouette of a thing as well as a pictorial or sculptural representation. A figure also refers to a diagram, pattern, design, and number. The verb "to figure" means to shape or form something, to make a likeness of, depict, represent, and to adorn with design or figures. In mathematics, to figure is to calculate or compute. Finally, "to figure" can mean both to take into consideration, to solve, decipher, comprehend, and in a more recent twist, to fail to solve, decipher, comprehend, as in "Go figure!" Figuration, by extension, means the act of forming something into a particular shape. What makes the words "figure," "figuring," and "figuration" so interesting and useful is the intersection of the three threads of meaning: form (object), forming (activity), and comprehending or failing to comprehend (thinking or reflecting). Kant's account of the imagination involves all three of these meanings—the imagination figures in all three senses of the word.

While Kant clearly and consistently distinguishes the theoretical and practical uses of reason, I have noted that he insists on the "primacy of practical reason." Cognition presupposes volition but willing does not necessarily presuppose thinking. The imbrication of thinking and willing lies at the heart of the imagination. In his analysis of aesthetic judgment in the third critique, Kant offers a definition of the imagination that proved decisive for many later writers, artists, philosophers, and theologians: "If, now, imagination must in the judgment of taste be regarded in its freedom, then, to begin with, it is not taken as reproductive as in subjection to the laws of association, but as productive in exerting an activity of its own (as originator of arbitrary forms of possible intuitions)."[28] The imagination, then, involves two interrelated activities, which Kant describes as productive and reproductive. In its productive modality, the imagination figures forms that the reproductive imagination combines and recombines to create the schemata that organize the noisy data of experience into comprehensible patterns. Inasmuch as the imagination (*Ein-bildungs-kraft*) is the activity of formation (*bilden/Bildung*), it is, in effect, an in-formation process. Information and noise, as we have already discovered, are not opposites but are codependent: information is noise in-formation and new information disrupts old patterns to create noise (figure 2).

The imagination both fashions schemata that organize experience and disrupts and dislocates stabilizing structures. The figures that the productive imagination

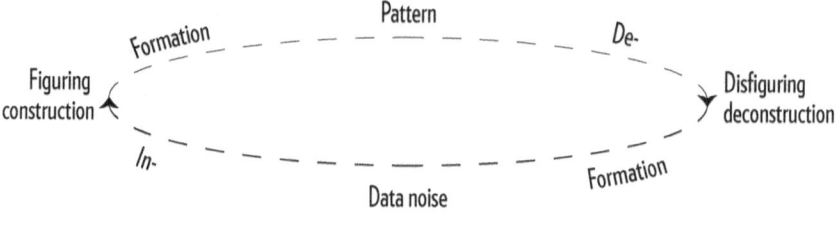

FIGURE 2 Imagination.

forms are *arbitrary* insofar as they are not determined by other figures but are *freely* formed and thus original. Freedom, in other words, is the condition of the possibility of the imagination and, therefore, of knowledge as well. Fichte was the first to recognize implications of this interpretation of the imagination that Kant himself did not fully realize. In *The Science of Knowledge*, he argues:

> Our doctrine here is therefore that all reality—*for us* being understood, as it cannot be otherwise understood in a system of transcendental philosophy—is brought forth solely by the imagination. . . . Yet if it is now proved, as the present system claims to prove it, that this act of imagination forms the basis for the possibility of our consciousness, our life, our existence for ourselves, that is, our existence as selves, then it cannot be eliminated unless we are to abstract from the self; which is a contradiction, since it is impossible that what does the abstracting should abstract from itself.

I will return to the seemingly outrageous claim that the imagination is the basis of all reality in the next section. At this point, it is important to understand why consciousness presupposes the imagination. The argument once again turns on the relation between *Darstellung* and *Vorstellung*. Theoretical and practical reason are impossible apart from representations. Re-presentation, however, is impossible apart from antecedently given data (Latin *datum*, something given; from *do, dare,* to give). The question, then, becomes: What gives? How does *Darstellung* occur? How do representations *emerge*? How are figures figured? According to Fichte, presentation is an act that "occurs with absolute spontaneity" and, therefore, *Darstellung* is "grounded" in freedom. Such freedom is not the freedom *of* subjectivity but the freedom *from* subjectivity through which both subjectivity and objectivity are posited or given.

While autonomy is self-grounded, an-archy is groundless. It "is not the diffraction of a principle, nor the multiple effect of a cause, but is the an-archy—the origin removed from every logic of origin, from every archaeology."[29] Heidegger describes the an-archy of freedom glimpsed in the presentational activity of the imagination as an abyss. In *Kant and the Problem of Metaphysics*, he explains: "In the radicalism of his questions, Kant brought the 'possibility' of metaphysics to the abyss. He saw the unknown. He had to shrink back. It was not just that the transcendental power of the imagination frightened him, but rather that in between [the two editions of the first critique] pure reason as reason drew him increasingly under its spell."[30] This abyss or *Abgrund* from which all determination emerges is the groundless ground that is indistinguishable from nothing. Such an unfathomable ground is the no-thing on which every foundation founders. Hegel explains the relationship between nothingness and freedom: "In its highest form of explication nothingness would be freedom. But this highest form is negativity insofar as it inwardly deepens itself to its highest intensity; and in this way it is itself affirmation—indeed absolute affirmation."[31] Negativity is affirmative insofar as it is the condition of creative emergence of everything that exists. Just as God creates freely ex nihilo, so the productive imagination creates freely out of nothing.

In Kant's doctrine of the imagination, theology becomes anthropology in a way that subverts the simple opposition between word and deed or structure and event. As word issues from will, so structure emerges through event. This process is (the) infinite. Spirit, Hegel argues, "is not an inert being but, on the contrary, is absolutely restless being, pure activity, the negating or ideality of every fixed determination of the understanding; not abstractly simple but, in its simplicity, at the same time distinguishes itself from itself; not an essence that is already finished and complete before its manifestation, hiding itself behind its appearances, but an essence that is truly actual only through the determinate forms of its necessary self-manifestation."[32] This interpretation of the will further deepens the contradictions of subjectivity. Since the will "is actual only through the determinate forms of its necessary self-manifestation," it can be itself only in and through its particular instantiations. While Kant's analysis brings together universality (i.e., categories and the moral law) and particularity (sense data and sensible inclinations), Hegel demonstrates that inasmuch as the will is inescapably active, the universal (will) is *in itself* particular (i.e., determinate) and particulars (determinations) are *in themselves* universal (i.e., instantiations of the will). So understood, the subject can be itself only by *not* being itself. When interpreted in this way, the will is not a unified self-identical ground but is the play of differences that can be itself only by always being other than itself. The noncoincidence of the self with itself issues in its infinite restlessness. Heidegger brings the argument full circle by *not* closing the loop of self-reflexivity: "This original, essential constitution of humankind, 'rooted' in the transcendental power of the imagination, is the 'unknown' into which Kant must have looked if he spoke of the 'root unknown to us,' for the unknown is not that of which we simply know nothing. Rather, it is what pushes against us as something disquieting in what is known."[33] The analysis of the transcendental power of the imagination "reveals" the concealment, which is the origin of the work of art.

INFINITY OF ART

Fichte, we have seen, makes the seemingly implausible claim that the imagination is the basis of objective as well as subjective reality. From this point of view, the world is, in effect, a work of art. Such a comprehensive notion of the imagination only makes sense if we have an expanded notion of art. Art, as Heidegger has learned from Kant and Fichte, is inescapably poetic. The word "poetic" derives from the Greek *poiesis* (*poiein*), which means a making or creation. So understood, *poiesis* is not limited to poetry in the traditional sense but involves all productive and creative activity. Inspired by the third critique but convinced that it did not go far enough, romantic philosophers and poets extended Kant's analysis of the imagination beyond the bounds of the human until it became a creative cosmic principle. Schlegel makes this point concisely in his *Athenaeum Fragments:* "No poetry, no reality. Just as there is, despite all the senses, no external world without the imagination."[34] Jena Romantics identified three distinct but related aspects of poetry:

1. The restricted literary meaning of poetic literature in verse or prose.
2. A faculty of the mind that mediates sensation, understanding, and reason.
3. A cosmic principle informing the entire universe.[35]

As the expression of the productive imagination, *poiesis* is the "putting-into-form of form" or the figuring of figure. In *The Philosophy of Art*, Schelling turns to the notion of genius to explain *poiesis*: "The real side of genius, or that unity that constitutes the informing of the infinite into the finite, can be called *poesy* in the narrower sense; the ideal side, or that unity that constitutes the informing of the finite into the infinite, can be called the art within *art.*" The work of art is not only the created product but is more importantly the *creative process* through which any determinate form emerges. If the imagination is the activity of figuring, which delimits figures, then it is, in effect, an in-formation process that occurs wherever figures are articulated. The so-called natural world is a work of art de-signed by an anonymous artist. Wherever forms are figured, the imagination is active. In other words, the imagination is not merely a subjective process but is also the creative origin of the so-called natural world.

Insofar as objectivity and subjectivity emerge in and through the same information process, they are isomorphic. The formal identity-within-difference and difference-within-identity of subject and object make knowledge possible. If knowledge is to be something other than a projection or construction of human schemata, the structure and operation of the mind and the world must be the same. In knowing the world, the subject knows itself, and in the subject's self-consciousness, the world becomes aware of itself. Through the self-reflexivity of the subject, the figurative process of the world bends back on itself and manifests itself to itself. This is implied in Kant's account of genius: "*Genius* is the talent (natural endowment), which gives the rule to art. Since talent, as the innate productive activity of the artists, belongs to nature, we may put it this way: *Genius* is the innate mental aptitude (*ingenium*) *through which* nature gives rule to art."[36] Insofar as the activity of the genius is "natural," nature manifests itself to itself in the work of art. The most important point to stress in this context is that such self-manifestation is always incomplete and, thus, self-reflexivity is inevitably short-circuited. Since the groundless ground of the imagination can never be fathomed, knowledge and self-consciousness are necessarily incomplete and must constantly be revised and reformulated. Far from an insufficiency, the lacuna, which is constitutive of all knowledge and every figure, is infinitely generative. As Blanchot observes when commenting on Schlegel's *Athenaeum Fragments:* "The poet becomes the future of humankind at the moment when, no longer being anything—anything but one who knows himself to be a poet—he designates in this knowledge for which he is intimately responsible the site wherein poetry will no longer be content to produce the beautiful, determinate works, but rather will produce itself in a movement without term and without determination."[37] When the movement of the imagination is without term, the conversation becomes infinite.

The in-finity of the work of art is the unending process of its own production. The work (verb) of art is the creative activity through which determinate works (noun) of art emerge. As the formation of form or figuring of figure, art is the infinite process of creative emergence. Here production is autoproduction and as such is autotelic; the work of art, in other words, is purposeless or has no purpose other than itself. This infinite process is both complete/closed and incomplete/open—it is complete/closed insofar as it always becomes *itself* in and through itself and it is incomplete/open insofar as it can become itself only by becoming *other* than itself and, thus, never secures its own identity. In his book *Hegel: The Restlessness of the Infinite*, Jean-Luc Nancy explains:

> Now, there is no thing—neither being nor thought—that is not determined. But becoming is not a process that leads to another thing, because it is the condition of everything. Its absolute restlessness is itself the determination of the absolute. Becoming

is quite exactly absolution: the detachment of each thing from its determination, as well as the detachment of the Whole in its determination. And it is thus that the absolute is what it is: equal to itself and, consequently, in absolute repose—but it is so only thus, quite exactly as non-repose. And the process or progress of the absolute is an infinite process or progress.[38]

The structure of this infinite process is isomorphic with the structure of the creative imagination. Since creativity is "grounded" in the groundless abyss of nothing, its expression is always new. As Schlegel insists, "creative art is still in the process of becoming, and it is even its essence proper never to obtain perfection, to be always and eternally new; no theory of art can exhaust it, it alone is infinite just as it alone is free."[39] Since the imagination is what it is by becoming other than itself, it constantly "strives," "hovers," "oscillates" between opposites it simultaneously brings together and holds apart. "Being free," according to Novalis, "means to waver between extremes that have to be united and also to be separated necessarily. From the light point of the wavering radiates all reality; object and subject exist through it, not it through them."[40] Another name for this oscillation is "altarity." The neologism "altarity" harbors three implications that are important in this context. First, altarity specifies the endless alternation through which binary and dialectical differences are articulated in such a way that their oppositions are overcome. Second, altarity names the unnameable outside that is inside every system, structure, and schema as its necessary condition. As such, it is the irreducible trace that marks and remarks the openness and incompletion of seemingly closed systems. And third, altarity suggests a dimension of sacrality, which is neither simply transcendent nor immanent but is an immanent transcendence that disrupts and dislocates systems, structures, and schemata that seem to be secure.

The immanent transcendence of altarity transforms human agents into vehicles of an infinite creative process that is more encompassing than any individual activity. The artist, as Nietzsche observes in *The Birth of Tragedy*, is the *medium* through which "the True Subject celebrates His redemption in illusion."[41] This True Subject is the incarnation of the transcendent Creator who dies and is reborn in the creative imagination of the artist. Another name for this creative activity is the infinite. While Nietzsche restricts the genuine work of art to the activity of the genius, Schlegel's vision is more inclusive: "Everyone is an artist whose central purpose in life is to educate his intellect." Education (*Bildung*) is cultivation (*Bildung*). To educate oneself is, therefore, to cultivate oneself and to cultivate oneself is, in effect, to become God. Schlegel continues: "Every good human being is always progressively becoming God. To become God, to become human, to cultivate oneself are all expressions that mean the same thing."[42] Cultivation occurs through the imagination. Coleridge, who heard Fichte's lectures in Jena and transmitted German philosophical idealism and romanticism to British romantics and American transcendentalists, reformulates Kant's doctrine of the imagination in a way that translates theology into anthropology and vice versa: "The *imagination*, then, I consider either as primary, or secondary. The primary *imagination* I hold to be the living Power and prime Agent of all human Perception, and as repetition in the finite mind of the eternal act of creation in the infinite I AM. The secondary Imagination I consider as an echo of the former, coexisting with the conscious will, yet still as identical with the primary in the *kind* of its agency, and differing only in *degree* and the *mode* of its operation."[43] Whereas the primary imagination is emergent, the secondary imagination is recombinant. In different terms, the imagination involves both the activity of figuring through which schemata emerge and the activity of recombining and reconfiguring schemata to adapt to changing circumstances. Though figuring cannot be represented, there is nonetheless a mimetic dimension to creative emergence. In a gloss on Kant's notion of art, Derrida describes a mimesis that is not simply a repetition of preformed figures:

> *Mimesis* here is not the representation of one thing by another, the relation of resemblance or identification between two beings, the reproduction of one product of nature by a product of art. It is not the relation of two products but of two productions. And of two freedoms. The artist does not imitate things in nature, or if you will, *natura naturata*, but the acts of *natura naturans*, the art of an author-subject, and, one could even say, of an artist-god, mimesis displays the identification of human action with divine action—of one freedom with another.[44]

With this notion of nonrepresentational mimesis, we return to the issue of freedom, which we have been exploring from the outset. Far from restricting freedom, the restlessness of the infinite is its necessary condition, which is not to say its original ground.

Freedom, I have argued, is neither simple nor monolithic but is inwardly divided and, thus, irreducibly complex. Though the modern subject is self-legislating, autonomy presupposes an originary givenness, which is groundless and hence an-archic. In relating itself to itself through the activity of self-representation, the creative subject relates itself to an altarity, which, as a condition of its own possibility, is not simply heteronomous. The "inward" disruption of altarity issues in the infinite restlessness of desire. Appearances to the contrary notwithstanding, desire that is vital never strives for fulfillment; to the contrary, when it is creative, desire desires desire. Originary lack does not involve loss but is the supplementary excess that keeps everything and everyone in play. The purpose of this play is nothing other than the creative process itself. Far from satisfying desire, the infinite engenders an endless restlessness that is the eternal pulse of life.

NOTES

1. Jacques Derrida, *Of Grammatology*, trans. Gayatri Chakravorty Spivak (Baltimore: Johns Hopkins University Press, 1976), p. 26.
2. Jacques Derrida, *Positions*, trans. Alan Bass (Chicago: University of Chicago Press, 1972), pp. 77–78.
3. Jacques Derrida, "Différance," in *Margins of Philosophy*, trans. Alan Bass (Chicago: University of Chicago Press, 1982), p. 14.
4. G. W. F. Hegel, *Lesser Logic*, trans. W. Wallace (New York: Oxford University Press, 1968), para. 80.
5. G. W. F. Hegel, *The Difference Between Fichte's and Schelling's System of Philosophy*, trans. and ed. H. S. Harris and Walter Cerf (Albany: State University of New York Press, 1977), pp. 90–91.
6. G. W. F. Hegel, *Science of Logic*, trans. A. V. Miller (New York: Oxford University Press, 1969), p. 145.
7. G. W. F. Hegel, *Lectures on the Philosophy of Religion*, trans. E. B. Speirs and J. B. Sanderson (New York: Humanities Press, 1968), vol. 3, p. 254.
8. Hegel, *Science of Logic*, p. 138.
9. Ibid., pp. 153, 147.
10. Jacques Derrida, "Structure, Sign, and Play," in *Writing and Difference*, trans. Alan Bass (Chicago: University of Chicago Press, 1978), p. 292.
11. Immanuel Kant, "What Is Enlightenment?" in *On History*, trans. Louis White Beck (New York: Bobbs-Merrill, 1963), p. 3.
12. Immanuel Kant, *Critique of Practical Reason*, trans. Lewis White Beck (New York: Bobbs-Merrill, 1956), p. 3.
13. Immanuel Kant, *Critique of Pure Reason*, trans. Norman Kemp Smith (New York: St. Martin's Press, 1965), p. 144.
14. Ibid., p. 181.
15. I will consider further implications of Kant's account of the imagination later.
16. Kant, *Critique of Practical Reason*, pp. 30, 31, 39.
17. Dieter Henrich, *Between Kant and Hegel: Lectures on German Idealism*, ed. David Pacini (Cambridge, Mass.: Harvard University Press, 2003). Henrich proceeds to explain the significance of Kant's argument: "This insight into the interconnection between concepts of the mind and images of the world is the origin of the modern methods of historical interpretation. Fichte was the first to bring the word *Weltanschauung* (image of the world) to philosophical prominence; it captured the theoretical correlation he was developing in his own work. Similarly, employed methodologically, this correlation between mind and world image is the foundation of Hegel's *Phenomenology*: because all stages of the development of the mind are simultaneously stages of the development of the conception of the world, we cannot talk about either one apart from the other" (20). I was fortunate enough to hear Henrich's lectures when he first delivered them at Harvard in 1972. I also took a seminar with Henrich on Hegel's *Science of Logic*. The lectures and the seminars decisively shaped my interpretation of Hegel and have influenced my thinking for more than three decades.

18. Kant, *Critique of Practical Reason*, p. 4.
19. Ibid., pp. 33–34.
20. Ibid., pp. 114, 133, 118.
21. Immanuel Kant, *Critique of Judgment*, trans. James Meredith (New York: Oxford University Press, 1973), part 2, p. 21.
22. Henrich, *Between Kant and Hegel*, p. 287.
23. Jean-Luc Nancy, *The Experience of Freedom*, trans. Bridget McDonald (Stanford, Calif.: Stanford University Press, 1993), p. 54.
24. Kant, *Critique of Pure Reason*, p. 314.
25. Rodolphe Gasché, "Ideality in Fragmentation," foreword to Friedrich Schlegel, *Philosophical Fragments*, trans. Peter Firchow (Minneapolis: University of Minneapolis Press, 1991), pp. xix–xx.
26. Martin Heidegger, *Hegel's Concept of Experience*, trans. Kenley Dove (New York: Harper & Row, 1970), pp. 48–49.
27. Martin Heidegger, *Schelling's Treatise on the Essence of Human Freedom*, trans. Joan Stambaugh (Athens: Ohio University Press, 1985), p. 162.
28. Kant, *Critique of Judgment*, p. 86.
29. Nancy, *Experience of Freedom*, p. 13.
30. Martin Heidegger, *Kant and the Problem of Metaphysics*, trans. Richard Taft (Bloomington: Indiana University Press, 1997), p. 118.
31. *The Logic of Hegel*, trans. William Wallace (New York: Oxford University Press, 1968), p. 162.
32. *Hegel's Philosophy of Mind*, trans. William Wallace (New York: Oxford University Press, 1971), p. 3.
33. Heidegger, *Kant and the Problem of Metaphysics*, p. 112.
34. Schlegel, *Philosophical Fragments*, p. 70.
35. This is a revised version of Ernst Behler and Roman Struc's formulation in their introduction to Friedrich Schlegel, *Dialogue on Poetry and Literary Aphorisms* (University Park: Pennsylvania State University Press, 1969), p. 15.
36. Kant, *Critique of Judgment*, vol. 1, p. 168.
37. Maurice Blanchot, *The Infinite Conversation*, trans. Susan Hanson (Minneapolis: University of Minnesota Press, 1993), p. 354.
38. Jean-Luc Nancy, *Hegel: The Restlessness of the Infinite*, trans. Jason Smith and Steven Miller (Minneapolis: University of Minnesota Press, 2002), p. 12.
39. Quoted in Blanchot, *Infinite Conversation*, p. 356.
40. Quoted in Henrich, *Between Kant and Hegel*, p. 227.
41. Friedrich Nietzsche, *The Birth of Tragedy and The Case of Wagner*, trans. Walter Kaufmann (New York: Vintage Books, 1967), p. 5.
42. Schlegel, *Philosophical Fragments*, pp. 96, 55.
43. Samuel Taylor Coleridge, *Biographia Literaria*, ed. J. Shawcross (New York: Oxford University Press, 1967), vol. 1, p. 202.
44. Jacques Derrida, "Economimesis," *Diacritics*, June 1981, p. 9.

6

BETWEEN FINITUDE AND INFINITY

On Hegel's Sublationary Infinitism

WILLIAM DESMOND

EQUIVOCAL DIALECTIC

I approach the interpretation of Hegel's philosophy of religion with diffidence for the obvious reason that it generates opposite interpretations. At one extreme, we encounter the pious Hegelians who find great consolation in what they take to be Hegel's magnificent defense of religion, not least his efforts to make philosophy and Christianity at one with each other. At the other extreme, we find the atheistic Hegelians who finally do not take Hegel's engagement with religion seriously, deeming it as perhaps nothing but a concession to the pious hoi polloi, a concession freeing up space for the inner secret of a postreligious humanism. I am not just referring to the split into the Right- and Left-Hegelians that occurred shortly after Hegel's death. In some more contemporary commentary, we find the practice of *ventriloquizing* through Hegel—the Hegelian corpus becomes a means for the commentator to voice what he considers most dear to his own heart. I do not object to making use of Hegelian ideas, but the ventriloquizing approach often practices the incomparable art of Cinderella's ugly sisters—the glass slipper must fit the foot, never mind the blood on the carpet. There are pious ugly sisters—they downplay the difficulties for religion entailed by Hegel's philosophy, while playing up the putative advantages. There are impious ugly sisters—their faces turn stony at the suggestion of anything "metaphysical" in Hegel as they render an account not alarming to the comfort levels of the contemporary secular *Zeitgeist* wherein mention of the word "God" has an effect analogous to the effect in a respectable Victorian parlor of the word "sex."

The pious Hegelians read Hegel too innocently. They are beguiled by the surface rhetoric of religious language that easily—too easily—invokes the sacred commonplaces of a Christian culture. Hegel can then be quoted almost as an edifying preacher, complete with pet citations from the good Book itself. The impious Hegelians read Hegel too suspiciously, or at least in a manner withholding of a certain credit, a credit that would acknowledge that there is more to the rhetoric than a concession to the religious *Zeitgeist* of his own time. The pious Hegelians give us a simplistic Hegel, the impious Hegelians give us a simplified Hegel. Neither seems entirely true to Hegel. Speaking for myself, I would prefer to speak for the community of the religious and the philosophical, and in that respect I have some sympathy for the intentions of the pious Hegelians. Nevertheless, the final effect of Hegel's thought is to point to a postreligious humanism, and hence I understand something of what the impious Hegelians recommend. What they recommend I cannot endorse, namely, the loss of seriousness about the religious as such, not least its great challenge to living philosophical thought. We must inhabit the space between religion and philosophy and think in that space differently—neither as a pious nor impious Hegelian, nor indeed as any kind of Hegelian.

This split into Left- and Right-Hegelians is very revealing, symptomatic of an inherent equivocity in Hegel's claim to provide a *coincidentia oppositorum* all along the line, whether of religion and philosophy, the finite and infinite, or the human and divine. Hegel's speculative dialectic claims to surpass equivocities, but in my view it suspends equivocity in its own claim to a more inclusive unity. With a different pressure now from this side, now from that side, the equivocity reappears, and Hegel's descendents will plump for one side of the "unity" rather than the other, for one side over against the other. You might say this proves the point in Hegel's favor vis-à-vis his desire to be true to the many-sidedness of an issue. Yes, but this desire may play false with the equivocal situation, just in its claim to include opposites in its embrace. It may recess serious difficulties just in claim to meet these serious difficulties.

Note that, despite their difference, these interpretations are held together by this point of convergence: the *immanence* of Hegel's God. This immanent God might be given a pantheist interpretation or a postheist, atheist interpretation—if you like, a pious or impious reading. This immanent God may even make use of the Christian claim that God entered into time and became human, hence offering even a very highly qualified theist interpretation. But, one must ask if this interpretation counterfeits the biblical God in so reconfiguring divine transcendence, so that in the end there is no divine transcendence as irreducibly other. God becoming human in time is the human in time becoming God. Some commentators applaud Hegel's immanence but I find serous difficulties with it. The Christian story is put to a use that risks emptying the story of its properly religious meaning.

Claims about the end of divine transcendence are exploited to buttress pious platitudes sacred to the secular *Zeitgeist* of a putatively postreligious humanism. I suspect this is special pleading on the basis of a counterfeit double of God that evades the seriousness of the religious while seeming to make friends with it. Hegel's own philosophical practice does not properly address the potential for equivocation in the relation of the human and divine but raises the potential to a "higher" equivocity in claiming to effect a dialectic-speculative reconciliation that overcomes equivocation. That the equivocation is only held in suspense by Hegel seems to be confirmed by the split into the pious and the impious, the religious and the atheist interpretation that followed him, that followed from him.

In regard to this I want to look at significant responses to the space between finitude and infinity, with special reference to what I will call Hegel's sublationary infinitism. There are different ways of understanding our being between finitude and infinity, and Hegel's way is not the only one and is by no means immune from serious question. I will look at an easy-too-easy dialectic, Kant's postulatory moral deism, then more closely at Hegel's own sublationary infinitism, as well as at what I call the postulatory infinitism and postulatory finitism of some of his successors. At the end, I will offer some remarks on the space between finitude and infinity, looked at in terms of a metaxological agapeics. This tries to stay true to the overdeterminacy of infinitude as communicated in the hyperboles of being in immanent finitude. In due course, what these terms mean will become evident, at least in some measure.

BETWEEN FINITUDE AND INFINITY: EASY-TOO-EASY DIALECTIC

A first approach to the space between finite and infinite might be described as the easy-too-easy dialectic against dualism. In this approach, we univocalize the finite and the infinite as two terms set over against each other. A certain operation of negation is at work here. The infinite is *not* what the finite is; the finite is *not* what the infinite is. The finite is defined in more or less determinate terms. The infinite, as what the finite is not, is not so determinable. The infinite is the indeterminate and indeed has nothing but a privative character. We find a more privative definition of the infinite in ancient thought, for instance, in Aristotle (*Physics* 3.4–8). While this is not Hegel's infinite, there is something of crucial relevance, namely, Hegel's own attitude to the indeterminate. This is quite negative: without some determination there is for him no articulated intelligibility. For him, we might grant the indeterminate as a beginning but must move beyond it, not only in the direction of determination, but also self-determination. I will come to this later.

Here the stress on the determinate, wedded to the operation of negation, sets the finite and infinite over against each other, and the purported univocalization of each produces a dualism between them. By way of response, the easy-too-easy dialectic is found in many standard descriptions of Hegel's thought. Starting with dualism, we find we cannot stay with dualism. If we think the finite, we also have to think what the finite is not. The fixed determination of finitude over against the infinite cannot be the last word. To think the first is necessarily to think the second and to pass over from finitude to the infinite. This easy dialectic works the other way also. If we think of infinitude over against the finite as determinable, we think a mere indetermination, and to think an indetermination is not to think. To think the infinite then must entail more than indeterminacy, and we find ourselves in a passage beyond indeterminacy to the finite. The coimplication of finite and infinite seems to result, and we begin on one side or the other.

Hegel is committed to some such view but, of course, the delicate question is the nature of this coimplication. I speak of an easy-too-easy dialectic since it seems to work all but *analytically* as simply trying to think what either finitude or infinity means. We find in thinking one, we cannot but think about the other, and this works both ways from finite to infinite, from infinite to finite. It all seems so easy. Why then do we not bow before the wisdom of this logic in a more docile way?

DUALISM BETWEEN FINITUDE AND INFINITY: KANT'S POSTULATORY MORAL DEISM

One response might be offered in the terms of Kant, a thinker whom Hegel normally judges guilty of fixating on a dualism of finitude and infinite. There is something of the latter in Kant. He does think of the infinite as a regulative ideal, and something about his philosophy as a whole marks it as a philosophy of finitude. Any defense of Kant has to meet the Hegelian objection: any plotting of a limit shows itself to be on both sides of the limit, and hence the limit plotted turns out not to be unsurpassable, as initially claimed. Hegel is right to press that argument, especially if our presupposition is that there is no fundamental heterogeneity between the finite and infinite. But it might well be that the Hegelian objection begs the question concerning *homogeneity* between what happens to be on the two sides of the limit. If we question this homogeneity, we must also look at limit differently, and this is so even if we grant that there is a surpassing of limit. The surpassing does not preclude the possibility of a fundamental heterogeneity relative to what lies on the different sides of a limit. One must consider this especially with respect to God: if there is an absolute singularity to God, then that cannot be homogenized into what is determinable in finite intelligibilities.

Otherwise put, there may be a passing between finite and infinite, but the passage one way may not be the same as the passage the other way. Heraclitus posits, to the contrary, that the way up and the way down may not be the same. There may be an irreducible asymmetry in the passages. The passage from infinite to finite may exhibit an otherness to the passage from finite to infinite. Whether or not such an asymmetry constitutes an element of Kant's discourse, it raises an issue that complicates the situation against the standard Hegelian objection to plotting a limit without presupposing what lies beyond the limit plotted. Relevant to the God of biblical monotheism, I would say there is a difference of our erotic self-transcending from the side of finitude and the agapeic communication from the side of the God beyond finitude. These two passages cannot be reduced to the one same form of self-mediating speculative dialectic. Their heterogeneity requires a different inhabitation of the middle space between finite and infinite. Pascal offers us one instance where something of this difference to Hegel is evident.[1]

To return to Kant, his response to the implied dualism of finite and infinite is postulatory. On one side, and on the basis of our moral being, we are driven to postulate a God. This is a response that need not simply collapse before the Hegelian objection, if there is an asymmetry between one side of the limit and the other, if there is something about the beyond that does not yield to the speculative homogenization. I am not attributing such an explicit idea to Kant,[2] but if there is this asymmetry, then the Hegelian objection loses some of its force, which comes just from the presupposition of homogeneity. Of course, Kant does speak of reason as the faculty of the unconditioned, and the unconditional is defined by the notion of totality. Thus, there are significant continuities between his philosophy and Hegel's, continuities Hegel can exploit while claiming to correct and complete their inner intention. Nevertheless, whatever Kant's explicit statements, there may be something about his deeper intentions, perhaps despite himself, which might be concerned with, so to say, keeping gaps open. Think of his strong demurral, by contrast with Hegel, with respect to anything smacking of Spinozism.

Kant is not free of equivocity in all of this, as in so much else. One might see him as bordering on a great tension: committed to respect what he saw as the limit, yet impelled to think at the boundary of the limit and indeed beyond, pulled on one side back within the limit, driven out from finitude on the other side, but driven out without the relatively secure univocities of the former. He is between finitude and infinity, though he often masks that intermediacy in a manner more intent on securing coherent univocity on this immanent side of the limit and letting the equivocal darkness beyond take care of itself. In truth, however, these two sides cannot be kept from each other in an uncontaminated purity. One might see the antinomic character of Kantian thinking as a kind of *hovering* on the limit in its equivocal character. But as Kant perhaps came to know, one cannot really hover for very long, and Kant often seems more vacillating than hovering: either tempted to reassert the secured univocities on this finite side of the limit or still equivocally longing for the epistemically unsecured unconditional beyond the limit.

With respect to the latter, Kant's approach to God might be called a postulatory moral deism. It is postulatory because it projects from finitude into the beyond. It is moral because the postulation or projection is carried out on the basis of Kant's understanding of our moral being. It is deism because the beyondness of his moral God seems to have little of the intimate involvement in immanence of the theistic God of biblical monotheism. A certain gap always remains, turn whichever way one will within finitude. The dualistic transcendence of this postulated deity remains a beyond. I think one can read the stress on transcendence more appreciatively and approach the beyond in a less dualistic frame of mind. Some of Kant's successors do not evidence this appreciation, and they enact projects of a more radical, autonomous immanence. They postulate, they project something other to the moral God and feel licensed to do so in just that gap. Why a moral God of good will, they ask; why not, say, an amoral "god" of will to power, either in a Schopenhauerian or Nietzschean modality? The question calls out for a fuller exploration of our finite condition as communicating what exceeds finite immanence.

BETWEEN THE INFINITE AND ITS OWN FINITIZATION: HEGEL'S SUBLATIONARY INFINITISM

I turn more fully to Hegel's sense of the infinite. First, one notes his rejection of the dualistic way of thinking. This is epitomized by the *Verstand* under whose dominance, Hegel claims, Kant philosophizes. The *Verstand* fixed on determinacies, fixes rightly, but it becomes fixated and hence cannot do justice to the passage between determinations or beyond them. Dialectic unfixes these fixations and allows us to see that opposites are defined by their own opposites. There is an internal relation between one thing and its opposites. As we saw, this holds for the finite and infinite as well: they are mutually implicated.

Something of this is portended in Kant's discovery of the antinomic structure of reason itself. Fix as reason might on this determination, it will do so only to discover that an opposite determination equally has a claim on rational validation. Kant did not see the affirmative significance of the antinomies. This has much to do with the internal contradiction of merely finite thinking: finite thinking contradicts itself and points beyond finitude. Hence for Hegel one cannot define the infinite over against the finite. This would be a finite infinite. Equally, an infinite of succession is a merely indefinite becoming and not the true infinite. Here indeterminacy replaces determinacy, but its openness is empty. Beyond the determinate and the indeterminate, we need the self-determining.

Think of it this way: we move along the infinite of succession, which is one finite item after another. We move, and in moving from a determinacy to its beyond, then to the beyond of this beyond, it always seems we are attaining a different determinacy. But this is not quite so. There is something the *same* in the passing beyond, more than this determinacy following that. This is not just a mathematical rule that determines the move from one to the next and so on. It is the mindfulness of passage that comes to itself in passing from one to the next and so on. Mindfulness not only grasps the rule of passage but comes to itself in the passage. This coming to itself in passage is not one determinacy over against an other, is not the endless unfulfilled line that stretches out to empty indeterminacy. It is more a self-relating process that comes to itself, recovers itself again in passing beyond itself. In passing beyond itself it comes to be at home with itself in what seems other. The circle seems closed in this self-mediating process. Rather than definition by determination, or indefinition by indeterminacy, this is self-definition by self-determination.

Consult now Hegel's description: "The infinite is . . . the self-sublation of [the one-sided] infinite and finite, as a *single* process—this is the *true or genuine infinite*."[3] The self-sublating infinite cannot be rendered by the dualistically defined finite and infinite. Hegel stresses the singleness of the process. No fixated determinations can do justice to process as such. Does a single process qua process suppress the differences of determinacy and give us no more than formless flux? I take Hegel's response to stress a forming, indeed a self-forming. This is entailed by the self-sublating character Hegel mentions. To sublate is to negate, to surpass, and to preserve—to self-sublate is to self-negate, to self-surpass, and to self-preserve. The infinite of succession is not enough. If the negation of the earlier term by the later is not a replacement of the earlier but a self-negation of it, the process is a self-surpassing of itself. It is also a recurrence to itself, for in surpassing itself, it is still itself in the process of passage: in this consists the self-preservation of the self-sublation. This recurrence to self betokens a *logic of self-mediation through its own otherness* in the process of self-surpassing. If there is otherness to this Hegelian infinite, it is also an immanent otherness. The finite, if negated, is taken up into the self-mediating infinite process. On its own, as the one-sided finite, finitude has no standing but gives way to its other. In giving way the finite reveals itself as what it is—a moment of this more inclusive, self-including infinite.

Compare this with what he says of the "bad infinite" (*die schlecte Unendlichkeit*) as a mere "ought-to-be."[4] This is a rejoinder to the postulatory character of Kant's infinite as a regulative ideal which may heuristically guide a process of becoming but is not constitutive of process as such. Hegel does have a point here, though one that has to be qualified differently than he does. A regulative ideal must be constitutive in some sense, if it is to function as a regulative ideal—otherwise its postulation merges uneasily into wishful thinking. That said, its modality of constitution must allow some openness to the further unfolding of process. If this is so, its constitutive nature might not be quite the same as the total immanence suggested by Hegel's option. There can be an immanence of the infinite that yet reserves something of the fullness of itself, such that no immanence can exhaust what it communicates. The immanent can betoken the beyond of immanence. I will return to this with the hyperboles of being.

Hegel again: "But this infinite progression is not the genuine infinite, which consists rather in remaining at home with itself in its other, or (when it is expressed as a process) in coming to itself in its other."[5] The "bad infinite" does not come to itself, does not remain at home with itself in its own otherness. Of course, this begs the question in favor of an immanent otherness and hides the possibility of being at home in an otherness that is not one's own, or for that matter being in a middle space between one's own and what is not one's own. It recesses the possibility that such a between is more truly communicative of the excess of the infinite to finite determinacy. Hegel is intent on closing the circle rather than of opening up the porosity of the between to what is beyond it, even in the network of immanent relations that define it.

I underscore Hegel's stress on "coming to self." Hegel once again (*Encyclopaedia* §95): "In its passing into another, something only comes together with itself; and this relation to itself in the passing, and in the other, is the genuine infinity."[6] Some commentators, admirers of Hegel who want to make him palatable in the postmodern discourse of difference, underplay this logic of coming to self which can be found pervasively in Hegel's texts. Without this coming to self, there is no true infinite for Hegel, more accurately, no true whole. For coming to self is what closes the circle of a passage of becoming into a single process, now not inarticulate, formless flux, but forming that is self-forming and containing its own immanent differentiations within itself. Coming to self in one's other is at the center of Hegel's philosophy as a whole and his philosophy of religion. For instance, his critique of the Hindu Trimurti is precisely with respect to the lack of a proper third to close the circle, unlike the truer Trinitarianism of the Christian tradition. Of course, Hegel also owes much to Kant's turn to the transcendental subject, even if that subject is rewritten by him as transcendental (inter)subjectivity, or self-relating negativity, or self-mediating *Geist*. Hegel famously speaks of "*das reine Selbsterkennen im absoluten Anderssein*, pure self-recognition in absolute otherness, or being-other."[7] This phrase is sometimes cited by Hegel's admirers who want to make him a philosopher of radical otherness. I take the "absolute otherness," *Anderssein*, being-other, precisely to be an "absolved" otherness that is a *medial* otherness through which the self passes to "*pure self*-recognition." Hegel himself emphasizes the *pure* nature of the self-recognition: the absolute being-other is its own otherness, that is, of the self itself.

The equivocal nature of Hegel's relation to otherness also holds for his true infinite. It may be questionable to think of a dualistic opposition of finite and infinite, as the easy-too-easy dialectic suggests. But there are questions equally to be asked about conceiving infinity entirely as holistic immanence. The self-sublating character of Hegel's true infinite is intended to address just that absolute immanence. There is no irreducible otherness because the otherness is owned by the process of immanent formation itself. Is there a thinking of infinity and a certain transcendence to it that is not defined either by dualistic opposition or speculative dialectic? To see or grant this point we have to orient ourselves differently to the middle space between finite and infinite than does Hegel's speculative dialectic and its self-sublating infinite.

Who or what is the "self" of the self-sublating infinite? You might object that "self" here is merely a placeholder for an operation for which there need be no "self." I think this will not do, since Hegel clearly wants to ascribe some agency to *Geist*. It is not a mere selfless operation. Perhaps one might better call it a "selving." To deny any kind of agency seems all but impossible if we insist on the language of self-sublating. Clearly, Hegel wants to think substance as subject, and hence the language of selving seems necessary. The selving is self-othering as process and in process is also self-returning, hence coming back to itself, beyond the strung out infinity of endless succession.

We might connect this with how Hegel resorts to the language of the Trinity: God as selving, God as self-othering, God as self-recognizing in self-othering: Father, Son, Spirit. This triadic movement also corresponds to Hegel's logic of the concept (*Begriff*): universality, particularity, and individuality (or concrete universality). The first is indeterminate, the second determinate, the third self-determining. One might say: God-selving, God-othering, God-self-recognizing. But if these three correspond to indeterminacy, determinacy, and self-determination, once again there is no overdeterminacy. This is one reason I speak of Hegel's God as an erotic absolute.[8] God-selving takes the form of an erotic process of coming to self. The indeterminacy of the beginning is not properly absolute but must become itself to be fully itself. It must determine itself in otherness, and since this is its own self-othering, the determination is really self-determination. Only in the consummated self-determination is the lack of the indeterminate beginning overcome, and only God is truly absolute.

Taking the overdeterminacy into account, against Hegel, I would speak of an agapeic God. An agapeic God need not create itself to become itself; and when it creates, there is a giving that is not the self-othering of the divine, nor yet a necessitated return in which the second moment of otherness must be recuperated in the third and last, wherein the original first can truly be said to be itself. An absolute that has to become itself to be itself is not an agapeic absolute. There is surplus to the agapeic origin that is not spent either in the middle or the end and that yet frees the finite middle of creation to be for itself—and not just as the agapeic origin in self-externality. Here and there, Hegel might speak of a release of the absolute, but this release cannot be described as agapeic. There is no surplus plenitude in the Hegelian origin, no overdeterminacy that would give beyond itself from its surplus. The Hegelian origin is an indeterminate, abstract, and impoverished beginning, which is nothing without its determination and self-determination.

There is no outside self-sublating infinitude in the God of Hegel. As Hegel puts it: "What God creates God himself is."[9] The circular metaphorics so loved by Hegelians is a spatialized way of thinking that is very representational—even when they accuse others of thinking representationally. "What God creates, God himself is": divine creation would be God cloning himself. In an agapeic understanding of origination, the other to God that is given to be in creation is not God self-othered. The qualification "ex nihilo" in *creatio ex nihilo* is extremely important in so far as it tries to mark the infinitely qualitative difference of God and creature (to speak with Kierkegaard). With Aquinas, I find the notion of God as self-creating to border on the incoherent. A God that creates itself would have to be itself to create itself; but if it were itself, why would it have to create itself? An absolute that is only absolute by becoming absolute does not seem absolute in the first instance, much less capable of making itself absolute.

In sum, the Hegelian God is not truly agapeic, because the *unsurpassable whole* always comes in the return to self that completes the circle. This is self-determining freedom as absolute. "Freedom is only present where there is no other for me that is not myself."[10] Release of or for the other is penultimate to return to self. I find this at every level in Hegel—from the immanent life of Hegel's God to the intermediations of social self-determination in the ultimate community of God on earth, the modern state. I have often asked the pluralistic Hegelians what they make of Hegel's citation of Aristotle's *noēsis noēsis neoseōs* at the end and apex of the *Encyclopaedia* (§577). I have never received a satisfactory answer and often have been greeted by uneasy silence. Whatever else one might say, Aristotle's God is not agapeic.

If this is correct, Hegel is talking more about his sense of the whole than of the infinite as in excess of every whole. Hegel may grant the excess of the infinite to determinate finite wholes, but the self-sublating character of his infinite shows the holistic nature of his thinking. Given its active nature, one might even speak of the wholing of the whole. Nevertheless, any excess to the whole is reconfigured as immanent to the wholing as such. In religious terms, there is no longer any transcendence to the divine. There is no irreducible space between finite and infinite. The process of the wholing is *between the infinite and itself in the forms of its own finitization*. God, so to say, is making faces of himself in immanence and seeing himself again in those faces. The only between is between the whole and itself, articulated in an entirely immanent process of wholing. I have to ask then, if Hegel's true infinite is a counterfeit double of the true infinite, then is the true infinite in excess not only of finite determinate wholes but of every self-determining whole?

BETWEEN HEGEL AND HIS INHERITORS: REVERSING SUBLATION

Returning to the divide between those who take Hegel to preserve religion and those who take him to surpass and negate it, can we *reverse* the movement of sublation? Sublation moves from negating to surpassing to preserving; reverse sublation would move from preserving to surpassing to negating. Does Hegel's sublationary infinitism preserve religion in a way that allows a reverse sublation in which preservation itself becomes a surpassing, and surpassing gives way to negation—itself claiming to be the true completion of the process?

I ask this because of the manner in which Hegel mingles the religious and the postreligious, giving encouragement to both the pious and the not so pious Hegelians. The admirers who affirm religion's preservation might sympathetically cite consoling texts such as Hegel's claim that his *Science of Logic* represents the "exposition of God [*die Darstellung Gottes*] as he is in his eternal essence before the creation of nature and finite spirit."[11] Hegel also says that the logical determination of his *Encyclopaedia Logic* "may be looked upon as definitions of the Absolute, as the *metaphysical definitions of God*" (*Encyclopaedia* §85, Hegel's emphasis). The nonmetaphysical Hegelian will be stony to all of this. They are not entirely wrong if there is something like a reverse sublation of the religious. We can take these citations seriously without becoming too pious, for they are still not the whole, and not the whole of Hegel's concept of God. Speaking theologically, the immanent self-mediating life of Hegel's God overreaches itself to nature and history. This overreaching is God's own self-externalization: nature and history are the two temples in which God manifests himself.[12] In the *Lectures on the Philosophy of Religion* the "inclusive Trinity" comes into play, but this clearly communicates that neither in the abstraction of God without the creation of the world, nor in God's concretely consummated actuality, which includes nature and history in its own immanent intermediation, is there any otherness genuinely outside of this God. God is consummately self-actualized in entirely immanent form as absolute spirit in the religious community first, but then in the worldly community of the modern state, indeed the Protestant state as the worldly consummation of the otherwise merely spiritual Protestant church. "It is nothing but a modern folly to try to alter a corrupt moral organization by altering its political constitution and code of laws without changing the religion,—to make a revolution without having made a reformation."[13] "Changing the religion": there are changes and changes, and some changes finally offer us political changelings in place of the religious original changed. Reversing sublation? No revolution without a reformation, he says; but the revolution completes the immanent worldly self-determination won spiritually by the reformation. Nietzsche dreamed of "a Roman Caesar with the Soul of Christ," but it is of a "higher" Caesar he dreams, not of Christ.[14] We might conceive of Hegel saying: "A post-Napoleonic sovereign with the soul of Luther," but it would be to the sovereign that would fall the last judgment in immanence: the State "actualizes and reveals itself . . . in world history as the universal world spirit [*Weltgeist*] whose *right* is *supreme*."[15]

This is where we wonder about the reverse sublation: religion preserved as community of spirit is surpassed by the modern state as the immanent objective community of worldly freedom. Preserving religion by thus relativizing its ultimacy has consequences for the not so pious reading of Hegel, for the relativizing can now claim to complete itself only by radicalizing the *negation* of the religious. And this is precisely what we starkly see with some of Hegel's most immediate inheritors.

Consider again how in Hegel's version of the "inclusive Trinity" the difference of time and eternity is speculatively sublated. This is not an Augustinian view in which the difference in time of the cities of God and Man, in their equivocal minglings, must always be kept in mind, asking of us a religious discernment and historical finesse not amenable to a speculative system. Hegel's overcoming of the difference of humanity and divinity ultimately points in the direction of a postreligious humanism. He is not to be absolved from all responsibility for cruder employments of dialectic by his inheritors. In his philosophy of history, it is unmistakable that the modern secular state is the more ultimate ethical community than the religious community of spirit. In the language I use,[16] Hegel has not enough finesse for the religious community of agapeic service, which is nothing without reference to God as exceeding the measure of every immanent totality. He thinks too dominantly of the immanent political community of erotic sovereignty. One can legitimately argue that the Left-Hegelians were simply more honest in pushing through the consequences of Hegel on this score. To say this is not at all to endorse the Left-Hegelian's project. But that these might be closer to the true inheritance of Hegel must give us pause about the full consequences of his postreligious humanism.

They enacted a kind of reversed form of sublationary infinitism in humanistic form. Their reversed sublation becomes a postulatory infinitism, as we shall see.

On this issue, I grant that there is no uncontroversial way of reading Hegel. Recall the equivocities I noted at the outset in connection with Hegel's immanent God. That his immanent God could engender atheistic successors who insisted that they were true to Hegel's essential spirit is one of the most glaring facts that must be confronted by any reading of the religious Hegel. What was there in Hegel that could engender such an outcome? I do not find myself philosophically or religiously in sympathy with that line of inheritance, and Hegel is not marked by the crude atheism we find with figures like Marx, but there is a true sense in which he and others like him are genuinely Hegel's sons. They were attuned to something in Hegel that in Hegel himself was much more wrapped in dialectical qualifications, qualifications I believe are dialectical equivocations. What more pious Hegelians take to be speculative solutions are dialectical equivocations that hide essential differences, even while claiming to sublate them into a reconciling unity. The way the Left-Hegelians broke apart that unity and found atheism at its kernel is not entirely untrue to Hegel, even if it is a coarse version of what Hegel was trying to effect. They thought Hegel mystified reason by appealing to religion. They might not be entirely wrong about that, but Hegel and the Left-Hegelian are closer to each other than someone who would affirm the transcendence and personalism of the biblical God.

By contrast with these early iconoclastic inheritors, the nonmetaphysical and humanistic readers of Hegel common today are blandly bourgeois. The humanists of the revolutionary Left have been overtaken by the humanists of postreligious persuasion for whom the critique of religion is not the basis of all critique: it is just an embarrassment. At most, religion is an expression of human "values." By contrast with the last men of postreligious humanism, there is something to be said for the impatience of the young Hegelians in calling a spade a spade, in relation to Hegel's speculative reconciliation of the human and divine. *Humanus heisst der Heilige* (Humanity is the holy of holies), they could say with their father Hegel, but they said it out louder. Hegel held an equivocation in suspense and called it a speculative reconciliation, but the young Hegelians were impatient with the suspense and the equivocation and turned the speculative reconciliation more radically in the humanistic direction, toward which Hegel himself pointed. One has to chuckle at the chutzpah of that "Trumpet of the Last Judgment Against Hegel the Atheist and Anti-Christ: An Ultimatum"[17]—a marvellous outburst by that onetime devoted Right-Hegelian, later apostate and young Hegelian, Bruno Bauer. The impatient sons shouted it out loud. The shuffling caressing whispers of the father Hegel kept it hidden. That being said, I prefer the shout and the whispering to the silence of the postreligious humanists. I would also prefer to speak otherwise than this shout, this whisper, or this silence.

BETWEEN FINITUDE AND ITS OWN INFINITIZATION: POSTULATORY INFINITISM

I will now speak of two major developments that react to Hegel's sublationary infinitism, what I call "postulatory infinitism" and "postulatory finitism." Though they can pass into each other, for now I concentrate on postulatory infinitism. This view claims that the agency of Hegelian *Geist* is human. We are asked to return to the horizon of human finitude without speculative mystifications. Hegel's inflated claims for his speculative system are taken to bring into discredit all metaphysical theology. Rather, the humanism hidden in Hegel must be further developed in directions outside of the reassuring embrace of the Hegelian system. Metaphysical theology comes to seem like a philosophical bubble blown up to remarkable proportions by thinking intoxicated with the thinking of itself. At a certain limit of idealistic inflations the bubble bursts, but a new bubble begins—a humanistic, antitheological bubble.

Reacting against the self-sublating infinitude, when *Geist* as the selving of the sublation is identified with God, the Left-Hegelians transcribe the process of the infinite from the divine Sprit to the human being. Humanity becomes the self-sublating infinity in history itself. One thinks of the humanistic Marx's account of labor. Human labor is self-sublating in contributing to human self-creation in time. True labor sublates: we work on the otherness of nature but this otherness need be no alienated other if we recognize our own power in and through that otherness. Alienated labor, by contrast, short circuits the process of "self-recognition in being-other."

This account is not only continuous with Hegel's dialectic but also with what Kant speaks of as *subreption* (*Critique of Judgment* §27). Subreption, Kant says, is to attribute to an other what is truly of ourselves. For instance, in the experience of the sublime, we attribute to an object what is of the subject. The sublime is a subreption when we think that there is a sublime object. There is no sublime object; rather we, as supersensible moral beings, are the truly sublime. Hegel supplies the logic of subreption by calling systematic attention to our self-recovery in the being-other. Hegel's logic is the process of subreption becoming self-knowing and systematic. When the process is unknowing, there are a whole series of subreption where we attribute to otherness what is properly our own. Waking up to ourselves, we realize we have been in thrall to our own subreptions, our self-otherings, all along. Being free is coming to recognize ourselves in that otherness. As coming back to ourselves out of the otherness, it is sublating oneself as an other. For the Left-Hegelians, if and when Hegel's sublationary infinitism attributes the process of selving to *Geist* as a divine other, then he merely reinstates the speculative subreption and has not truly freed us into our immanent humanity. This freeing must be completed—self-completed.

Note that these critics are themselves marked by something like the Hegelian logic of self-mediation through the other and are in agreement with Hegel's critique of divine transcendence, though they often attribute to Hegel unexpurgated allegiances to a transhuman transcendence. Divine transcendence is now reinterpreted, in line with the desired autonomy of human praxis in modernity, as a form of infinity not appropriate to enlightened and emancipated humanity. It must be surpassed by autonomous humanity, now claiming to be more completely self-sublating. The critics of Hegel, in my view, also participate in a similar culture in which a logic of self-determination has a kind of privilege. Even the post-Hegelian *anti-Hegelians* are often in agreement with Hegel in relativizing the claims of divine transcendence as other in favor of immanent self-determination.

Relevant again is the reconfiguration of the Christian story of God becoming human in time. Hegel reads that as the death of divine transcendence as irreducibly other, a transcendence he finds in the Father of the Old Testament, in Judaism as a kind of religion of dualism, in religions shaped by the opposition of divine master and human slave, in the unhappy consciousness divided without redress between immanence and transcendence as other. The postulatory infinitism of post-Hegelian atheism is the human project of that immanent redress. This is not a Kantian postulation of a beyond; it is the human being projecting itself into its own becoming divine. Here, Feuerbach is crucial in moving the discussion, after Hegel's death, in the direction of a more humanistic interpretation of dialectic. A student of Hegel, he wrote to him that the inner essence of speculative philosophy was humanism. The younger son saw the older master as wearing a religious mask. All divine spirits are merely mystifications of the human spirit, as Marx will claim. Feuerbach's claim is worth pondering: whatever Hegel's avowals, the logic of the position must lead to the reduction of theology to anthropology. Hegel equivocates on the speculative subreption and fails to come clean on what is entailed if the other is the self-projected, the self-sublated. All of the attributes of God are secretly the attributes of humanity as the infinite genus and must be repatriated to the human home, recuperated fully for immanence itself.

Marx was delighted with this so far as it goes, but it does not go far enough. Beyond the contemplative recognition that there is no absolute beyond the human being, we need revolutionary praxis in which the implications of sublationary infinitism become no postulation of a beyond but a project for the transformation of history into the very process by which social humanity more and more fully mediates with itself. Postulatory infinitism becomes projective infinitism: the self-sublation of the communist totality as a single process—communist freedom is One. Mimicking the logical Hegel, the single infinite mediates with itself through the one-sided finite and one-sided infinite. A process of social self-sublation will allow humanity to overcome alienation and become absolutely self-determining. What is truly our own is not to be attributed to an other, for such an other then has stolen from us our own. It is somewhat the reverse of the mythical Prometheus. Prometheus, the thieving Titan, steals fire from Zeus, just as self-sublating humanity must do. What happens in alienated labor is that the fire of Prometheus is stolen by the owners, each an immanent Zeus of corporate capitalism: "All property is theft." We need a reverse subreption. In postulatory infinitism thieving gets an immanent self-sublating humanistic interpretation, which becomes the basis of expropriation, reappropriation.

Postulatory infinitism here differentiates itself from the speculative overinflation of the Hegelian self-sublating infinite, sharing its return to immanence but reacting differently to the announcement: "There is no beyond." "There is no beyond" issues in a different postulatory project than Kant's postulatory moral deism. If one holds to Kant's moral deism, there is still a kind of beyond. Hegel dialectically deconstructed that beyond, but the Marxist return to immanence is not a humble project of human finitude. It is the fullest possible appropriation of nature as other and human productive power, hitherto alienated from itself: dialectical mastery of human history in classless society. The project is between finitude and its own self-infinitization. Marx's conviction that there was an immanent logic to this is very Hegelian. The atheology of the human *Geist* in history is determined to the end of the absolutely self-determining One: absolute social freedom, determined by the logic of productive humanity's immanent self-determination. In time we have seen how this can produce a counterfeit of community in the name of "social justice." The communist will to bring into being the socially redeemed totality reveals a mutation of erotic self-surpassing marked by unexpurgated will to power. The implications of the counterfeiting of community were initially perhaps more recessed. Later, when they came into power, the unpurged will to be the one totality was overtly expressed in the form of world-historical determinations, wherein social self-determining concretized itself in unsurpassed systems of tyranny.

BETWEEN FINITUDE AND ITSELF: POSTULATORY FINITISM

Another major reaction to Hegel's sublationary infinitism is postulatory finitism. This can also mutate into a variety of postulatory infinitisms, or it can be diversely deconstructed, into, say, autonomy disillusioned with itself, or self-lacerating, rather than full of confidence in its own powers of self-determining. We tend to find the confidence earlier, the self-laceration later. The self-laceration can also conceal deficiency in how we understand the relation of finite and infinite.

Elsewhere I have discussed postulatory finitism in Nietzsche and post-Nietzschean philosophy (in Heidegger, for instance).[18] What is rightly addressed here is the need of a philosophy of finitude as such. In reaction to "metaphysics," caricatured somewhat as a two-world Platonic theory of ideas, or as escape into the outer space of an empty beyond, or as Hegel's onto-theology of absolute *Geist*, finitude as such is postulated as the ultimate context of all human significance. In truth, it is impossible to think finitude without invoking infinity in some manner. The question is how to invoke and what infinity to invoke. Postulatory finitism refuses any invocation, at least on the surface: there is nothing beyond finitude. Finitude is the horizon greater than which none can be conceived.

Postulated finitude here replaces Kant's moral God and Hegel's self-sublating *Geist*. That "greater than which none can be conceived" is how Anselm spoke of God in the ontological proof. Here, finitude as such functions as the absolute horizon. Such a position is finally incoherent as so stated, and Hegel's arguments against it are not negligible. But while this is so, we need not commit ourselves to his self-sublating infinitism. There is a thinking between finitude and infinity that is neither sublationary infinitism nor postulatory finitism nor either postulatory infinitism. Nevertheless, I see some continuity between these last three: postulatory finitism develops in reaction against Hegel, with some resonances of Kant's postulated deism but without the moral God. What is important is the resort to the "as if" structure. Kant: If the human person as a moral being must be thought of in such and such terms, then we must think "as if" there is a moral God. Postulatory finitism and its "as if" structure: If we must think of the finite qua finite and nothing but the finite, then certain things will follow, such as *no* resort to a transcendent God.

Consider Nietzsche, for whom a kind of postulatory atheism emerges rather than a postulatory moral deism. Very revealing is the declamation of his Zarathustra ("On the Blissful Islands"):

> God is a supposition; but I want your supposing to reach no further than your creating will. Could you *create* a god?—so be silent about all gods! But you could surely create the superman. . . . God is a supposition: but I want your supposing to be bounded by conceivability. Could you conceive a god?—but may the will to truth mean this to you: that everything shall be transformed into the humanly conceivable, the humanly evident, the humanly palpable! You should follow your senses to the end. And you yourself should create what you have hitherto called the World: the World should be formed in your image, by your reason, your will, and your love![19]

Here we see the explicit connection of the "as if" with the postulatory structure: "But let me reveal my heart to you entirely, my friends: *if* there were gods, how could I endure not to be a god! *Therefore* there are no gods. Though I drew this conclusion, now it draws me."[20] (Sartre gives a similar "argument" in the twentieth century: If God, no freedom. I am free, therefore no God.) The entire declamation urges a putatively new project: the turning away from God and gods and the turning to the human. This is not quite so new: it is rhapsodic homiletics, a lyrical version of Feuerbach's reduction of theology to anthropology.

This is not an argument; it is preaching. Zarathustra is delivering an exhortation on the basis of a different supposition. It is preaching that urges an orientation to life, said to follow from the rejection of a supposition now deemed impossible or unacceptable—namely, the suppositions of gods or God beyond humanity. "Rejection" is maybe too light-headed a word, since Nietzsche himself uses a bloodier word: murder. And after the murder of God? "Must we ourselves not become gods ourselves simply to appear worthy of it?"[21] The faith of the new project for the liberated higher humanity: "being true to the earth." This is the repeated refrain of this philosophy of finitude, but again it is postulatory: it proposes a project on the basis of a certain understanding of the human being from which God and gods have been excluded.

Notice how *the supposition can now go underground*. Once granted, it becomes taken for granted and falls asleep to its own suppositional character. "Though I drew this conclusion, now it draws me." What first I proposed, now proposes for me. The supposing, as it were, disposes me, or disposes of me, in becoming a later hidden presupposing. Suppose the postulatory finitism goes underground in a more widespread sense, namely, with respect to *an era* in general, not just one or two particular thinkers. The supposition then turns into something like a kind of absolute presupposition, and the "as if" is entirely lost from sight in a wider sense. Affirming finitude and nothing but finitude, we fall into the sleep of finitude.[22]

A token of this, for instance, is the continuity between Kant and Nietzsche, despite the surface impression of great discontinuity. Nietzsche was more a (grand) son of Kant than he knew or acknowledged, but he did know the *als ob* of a postulatory moral deism mutates into the *als ob* of a postulatory amoral a-theism. Was Nietzsche blowing Kant's cover: taking off the mask on the equivocation of the *als ob* of God as beyond: there is to be no transcendence as other, only human self-transcendence? No God above us, and no man either! Not unlike the impatient Left-Hegelian sons of Hegel, Nietzsche is perhaps an impatient grandson, the black sheep even, in the family of German will, where good will now mutates into will as good in the form of will to power. I do not wish to homogenize Kant and Nietzsche. For Kant draws attention to a very important consideration in his own postulatory endeavor, namely, the *unconditional* dimension manifest with our moral being, and this must surely be of immense importance in thinking about God, restraining us from projecting just anything we wish. To his credit, Kant stood firm on something ethically fundamental, but religiously, theologically, he equivocates on the brink of disaster. Religion is not morality, though it is not immoral or antimoral and cannot be seamlessly folded back into practical reason consumed with satisfying itself, all the while asleep to its own defect of spiritual finesse and perhaps also lack of love.

Be that as it may, and turning to the sons of Nietzsche, we must ask if the philosophers of finitude are also being drawn by an "as if" similar to Nietzsche's. If this is so, are they really being true to finitude? Is their project not also motivated by its own "suppose," its own *Muthmaassung*: the supposition of finitude and nothing but finitude? For if this supposition has become a presupposition about the whole of being, almost inevitably its suppositional character falls in a space within which our transcending energies circulate, and since they circulate we have the feeling there is the utmost freedom, which is even more so the case since these energies also seem most intimately to circulate around themselves. What if this circling around ourselves were a *counterfeit* form of infinitude? Have we created the "false infinity" as this self-encirclement? I do not mean Hegel's "bad infinite." It is because of opposition to Hegel's "sublationary infinitism" as not true enough to finitude, that "postulatory finitism" derives not a little of its contemporary persuasiveness. Nevertheless, once again they have in common a stress on unremitting *immanence*. Do we need a philosophy of finitude that is not postulatory, a philosophy of infinitude that is not sublationary or postulatory, a philosophy in which we are not closed off from rethinking transcendence in another sense?

Nietzsche seems entirely other to Marx and, as we know, he despised socialism as much as Christianity. In postmodern times we find strange mutations, one of which is the Left-Nietzschean. For there comes to be a postulatory infinitism in Nietzsche too, and it is the project(ion) of the *Übermensch*. Both Marx and Nietzsche are philosophers of immanent will to power. The ruling ideas of an epoch are the ideas of the ruling powers. Marx said this, but Nietzsche is in basic agreement. That their philosophies are both projects indicates their origin in the same gene pool. The genes of immanence in the different mutations do not themselves mutate into an opening to transcendence as other. To pretend otherwise is to perpetuate the dissimulation. Again, we suffer from the sleep of finitude, though we claim at last to now be awake.

In time we can come to understand, in the light of finitude, that immanent self-determination is not sufficient, even for itself. But we can also be paralyzed from raising the question of an other transcendence if our agreement with Hegel, despite the disagreement, continues. Early successors of Hegel were less diffident about the attempt to absolutize immanent autonomy. Even though we are finite, in seeking to circle around ourselves, we also enact our own configuration of infinite movement. The issue of infinity reappears, as we saw, newly postulatory and projecting the immanent self-infinitization of the human as such. But circling around ourselves, the circling is going nowhere, certainly not anywhere genuinely beyond itself, for in this self-encirclement the beyond of itself is again its own immanent beyond. The more lucid of postmodern thought has the suspicion that this is like padding around a cell of self-reflecting mirrors. We feel we are glutted with ourselves and might even want to smash the mirrors. That is no true way out. One must wonder if there is something askew in all of this. Have we been true to the full happening of human finitude, both its self-surpassing and its porosity that allows in what communicates to it from beyond itself? We need a further exploration of the space between finitude and infinity.

METAXOLOGY BETWEEN FINITUDE AND INFINITUDE: ON THE HYPERBOLES OF BEING

In a final approach, I propose a metaxological position that is neither sublationary infinitism nor postulatory finitism nor postulatory infinitism. Postulatory finitism leads to certain *aporiai* of finitude that it cannot address on its own terms. We may be the measure of things other than ourselves in finitude, but we are not the measure of our own finitude. We infinitely surpass ourselves—and not again toward ourselves only. Sublationary infinitism falls asleep, not just to finitude, but to the infinite as exceeding all wholes, even self-determining wholes. The metaxological approach affirms the difference between finite and infinite, yet allows that this difference grants a space of porosity across which communication can happen, though never such as to be captured by an immanent totality. The God of the between is not the between but is beyond the whole, a beyond at issue in the question of God being infinite.

In *God and the Between* I discuss God's being infinite more fully with four conceptions of infinity: the numerical (or quantitative) infinite, the infinite of succession, the intentional infinitude, and actual infinitude.[23] These correlate with the indeterminate, the determinate, the self-determining, and the overdeterminate. The first two infinitudes correlate with determinacy and indeterminacy (in the sense of the indefinite) and their interplay; the third correlates with self-determination; the fourth with the overdeterminate. There is also a correlation with respective dominances in each of the univocal, equivocal, dialectical, and metaxological senses of being. The first form of infinity is based on the unit of numbering and the possibility of infinitely redoubling this unit. The second form of infinity explicitly implicates the mindfulness of process as dynamic; as marking successiveness it is temporal and temporizing infinity rather than mathematical or quantitative. A third form of infinity I call intentional infinitude.[24] I do not mean a process that is just master of itself; I mean more a mindful transcending that is as much an undergoing as a self-directing, as much a suffering as an acting. This is the kind of infinitude we might ascribe to human beings. The fourth sense of the actual infinite is defined by way of excess, not primarily relative to erotic infinity, but relative to communications of the surpluses of agapeic being in finitude itself. Agapeic, being in the between, is the hyperbolic image of this actual infinite. Given present limitations, I cannot say anything more about this fourfold conception, but must confine myself to connecting the infinite with the overdeterminate beyond the indeterminate, the determinate, and the self-determining. We will also see how this resituates Hegel's concept of the self-sublating infinite.

In the metaxological space between finitude and infinity, we have to attend to what I call the hyperboles of being, which point to something of the overdeterminate excess of the divine infinity. The hyperbolic stresses something different to the postulatory and the self-sublating. The original Greek meaning of *hyperballein* suggest a "throwing above" or a "being thrown above."[25] Being thrown above takes us beyond postulatory finitism, for we do not postulate but are carried above ourselves in a surpassing of self-exceeding. Nor is it self-sublating infinitism, for the infinite restlessness of our being caught up in self-exceeding is not the determining measure of its own movement above itself. Neither is the *hyperballein* a postulatory infinitism, for it is not our project or projection, as if it were we who threw ourselves above. (This entails a reversal of the directionality of the self-transcending of our intentional infinitude.) Between finitude and infinity there is a movement of being carried beyond every whole. This comes home to us when we attend to the signs of the overdeterminate in immanence. The hyperboles are happenings in immanence that are not determined by immanence alone: neither merely determinate, nor merely indeterminate, and not yet self-determining, something about them communicates of the overdeterminate. We need to attend to four especially significant hyperboles.

First, there is what I call the idiocy of being (in the Greek sense of idiot): the sheer "that it is" of given finite being. This can stun us into astonishment and rouse thought that is hyperbolic to finite determinacy or to our own self-determination. In the stunning of mindfulness, our thinking can become porous to what exceeds finite determination rather than insisting that immanent finitude is the horizon greater than which none is to be thought. The overdeterminacy of the "that it is" plays no role in Hegel's thinking of the infinite. The "that it is" is a contingency that while acknowledged in its immediacy is merely indeterminate until mediated, and hence given proper intelligible determination. Hegel is deficient in ontological wonder and the agapeic astonishment that is the more original source of fertile metaphysical mindfulness.[26]

Second, there is the aesthetics of happening: the incarnate glory of aesthetic happening as given also rouses astonishment and appreciation before finite being, yet it seems to exceed finitization. The aesthetic glory of finitude is impossible to characterize exhaustively in finite terms. We are inclined to liken it to a great work of art: richly determinate, yet exceeding fixation in any one determination or set of finite determinations. Something more is incarnated in the beauty and sublimity of finitude that communicates an otherness exceeding all finitization. Hegel again here strikes me as lacking in finesse: at most the sublime is an aesthetic *Jenseits* that he especially associated with the transcendence of the Jewish God.[27] Hegel does not understand the meaning of this asymmetrical transcendence. Its very beyondness is for him a defect. His defect is that he cannot see that a different sense of the overdeterminate infinite is to be acknowledged. (He would not appreciate Levinas's privileging infinity over totality.) There is also a lack of appreciation of the sensuous as such—this is also a beyond resistant to Hegel's will to sublate it in the philosophical form of thought thinking itself. The defect of the aesthetic for him is its tie to the sensuous as such. We might understand and appreciate this differently in a truly incarnational sense: the infinite as bodied forth in the sensuous finitude.

Third, there is the erotics of selving: finite though we are, we are also infinitely self-surpassing. We surpass ourselves beyond every finitely determined limit. But beyond the measure of ourselves as measure, we point and are pointed to a measure exceeding finite measure. The measure of human self-transcending that measures and makes the finite determinable is beyond the determination of finite measure. Marked as both finite and infinitely restlessness, we are the incarnate conjunction and tension of these two. The erotics of selving is more than a self-overcoming driven to its own most complete self-determination in immanence. It incarnates a primal porosity to what exceeds its own determination and self-transcending. In the fecund poverty of its given porosity, it is an opening to transcendence as other beyond immanent self-transcendence.

I see Hegel deriving the energy of his thinking from this source (in some ways corresponding to the intentional infinitude trying to self-sublate into actual infinity). For him the self-surpassing becomes self-sublating, for the surpassing of self to the other is again surpassing to self in the form of otherness. The circle is closed even on this level into a whole mediating with itself, and infinity is refigured in the whole or totality. I do not think this is true to the erotics of selving as hyperbolic, nor is it true to what is beyond the erotics of selving. Hegel does not metaxologically dwell on the boundary of the erotic selving and know its porosity to the overdeterminacy of the divine that is beyond its own self-mediation and self-sublation. (There is something about the erotics of selving that is also beyond the Dionysian self-transcendence of Nietzschean self-infinitizing—though at a certain limit, Nietzsche lays himself open to what is mysteriously beyond him.) We need to pay special attention to this fourth hyperbole to grant this.

Fourth, there is the agapeics of community: in our relation to others, our being is in receiving and in giving; we are receptive to the gift of the other, and we are free to give beyond ourselves to others, simply for the good of the other as other in some instances. In the finiteness of our lives, there is the promise of a generosity beyond finite reckoning. We are given to be before we can give ourselves to be. Finitude as such is given, but not given from itself alone. Nothing is alone; hence, the idea of finitude as for itself alone and nothing other cannot be taken as the last word or the first. Thus our being freed into ethical responsibility is difficult to render on purely finite terms, since the call of something *unconditional* emerges (Kant is to be heard here). In our ethical relation to the other, this unconditional is given before one's freedom to determine oneself (Kant does not get this quite right). There is an agapeics of generosity beyond even moral reckoning. We are invited to consider a religious agape, more unconditional than the moral unconditional, a hyper-unconditional generosity toward finitude exceeding finitization. The agapeics of community intimates a surplus source of good that makes itself available in an absolute porosity, an absolved porosity of the *passio essendi* that ethically lives itself as a *compassio essendi*. This is a sign of something more than the ethical, since it incarnates the holy. The infinity of divine goodness is communicated in the holy.

The agapeics of community does not figure in a significant systematic way in Hegel's account. Some commentators have claimed Hegel's God is agapeic, but this is ventriloquizing through one or two sentences about love, which has an ambiguous suggestion of the agapeic. The agapeics of community are in no way thought through or assimilated to the systematic substance of Hegel's philosophy as a whole.[28] Hegel's God, as previously indicated, shows itself to be an erotic not an agapeic absolute.

I conclude that there are signs of the infinite in the idiotic overdeterminate givenness of being. There are signs in aesthetic happening, especially as shown in the sublime as the overdeterminate appearing in sensuous determinacy. There are signs in erotic selving as carried in its self-surpassing by an energy of being overdeterminate to all our self-determinings. There are signs in agapeic communications, where the overdeterminacy of divine goodness passes between finitude and infinity in a released metaxological community of surplus generosity.

NOTES

1. On this, see William Desmond, *Is There a Sabbath for Thought? Between Religion and Philosophy* (New York: Fordham University Press, 2005), chap. 2.
2. Kant's differentiation between a "boundary" (*Grenze*) and a "limit" (*Schranke*) has some relevance here: "Bounds (in extended beings) always presuppose a certain definite space and inclosing it; limits do not require this, but are mere negations which affect a quantity so far as it is not absolutely complete. But our reason, as it were, sees in its surroundings a space for the cognition of things in themselves, though we can never have determinate concepts of them and are limited to appearances" (*Prolegomena to Any Future Metaphysics*, trans. James W. Ellington [revised from Paul Carus] [Indianapolis: Hackett, 1977], § 57, p. 93). The contrast of the determinate and the indeterminate is at work here, and Kant clearly sees the heterogeneity between what is mathematically and scientifically determinable and what is metaphysically thinkable. Whether he handles that heterogeneity satisfactorily is another question.
3. G. W. F. Hegel, *Wissenschaft der Logik* I, in *Werke in zwanzig Bänder (Theorie-Werkausgabe)*, ed. Eva Moldenhauer and Karl Markus Michel (Frankfurt: Suhrkamp Verlag, 1970), vol. 5, p. 149; *Science of Logic*, trans. A. V. Miller (New York: Humanities Press, 1969), p. 137 ("Das Unendliche ist . . . das Sichaufheben dieses Unendlichen wie des Endlichen als *ein* Prozeß—ist das *warhhafte Unendliche*").
4. G. W. F. Hegel, *Encyclopaedia*, §94, *Zusätze*.
5. G. W. F. Hegel, *Enzyclopädie der philosophischen Wissenschaften* I, in *Werke (Theorie-Werkausgabe)*, ed. Eva Moldenhauer and Karl Markus Michel (Frankfurt: Suhrkamp Verlag, 1970), vol. 8, p. 199; *The Encylopaedia Logic*, trans. with intro. and notes by T. F. Geraets, W. A. Suchting, and H. S. Harris (Indianapolis: Hackett, 1991), p. 149.
6. Hegel, *Enzyclopädie* I, p. 201; *Encylopaedia Logic*, p. 151 ("so geht hiermit Etwas in sienem Übergehen in Anderes nur *mit sich selbst* zusammen").
7. G. W. F. Hegel, *Phänomenologie des Geistes* (Hamburg: Felix Meiner, 1952), p. 24; *Phenomenology of Spirit*, trans. A. V. Miller (Oxford: Clarendon Press, 1977), p. 14.
8. On this more fully, see William Desmond, *Hegel's God: A Counterfeit Double?* (Aldershot: Ashgate, 2003), esp. chap. 4.
9. G. W. F. Hegel, *Lectures on the Philosophy of Religion: The Lectures of 1827*, ed. Peter C. Hodgson, trans. R. F. Brown, P. C. Hodgson, and J. M. Stewart (Berkeley: University of California Press, 1988), p. 129.
10. "Freiheit ist nur da, wo kein Anderes für mich ist, das ich nicht selbst bin" (Hegel, §24A2; *Enzyclopädie* I, p. 84; *Encyclopaedia Logic*, p. 58).
11. Hegel, *Wissenschaft der Logik* I, p. 44; *Science of Logic*, p. 50.

12. Hegel, §140A; *Enzyclopädie* I, pp. 274ff.; *Encyclopaedia Logic*, pp. 210ff.
13. *Hegel's Philosophy of Mind: Part Three of the Encyclopedia of the Philosophical Sciences (1830), Translated by William Wallace, Together with the Zusätze in Boumann's Text (1845)*, trans. A. V. Miller (Oxford: Clarendon Press, 1971), §552, p. 287.
14. On this more fully, see Desmond, *Is There a Sabbath for Thought?* chap. 6.
15. G. W. F. Hegel, *Elements of the Philosophy of Right*, ed. Allan W. Wood (Cambridge: Cambridge University Press, 1991), §33, pp. 62–63; see also §30.
16. G. W. F. Hegel, *Ethics and the Between* (Albany: State University of New York Press, 2001), chaps. 15 and 16.
17. Bruno Bauer, *The Trumpet of the Last Judgment Against Hegel the Atheist and Anti-Christ: An Ultimatum*, trans. Lawrence Stepelevich (Lewiston, N.Y.: Mellen Press, 1989).
18. Desmond, *Is There a Sabbath for Thought?* esp. chap. 1.
19. Friedrich Nietzsche, *Also sprach Zarathustra*, in *Werke*, ed. G. Colli and M. Montinari (Berlin: De Gruyter, 1968), vol. 6, pt. 1, pp. 105–106. The German word that Nietzsche uses is *Muthmaassung*, which Walter Kaufmann translates as "conjecture" (*The Portable Nietzsche* [New York: Viking Penguin, 1982], p. 197), and R. J. Hollingdale, as "supposition" (*Thus Spoke Zarathustra* [Harmondsworth: Penguin, 1961], p. 110); it might also be rendered as something like "guess" or "surmise." (The quotation is from the Hollingdale translation.) Kant's "Conjectural Beginning of Human History" (*Mutmaßlicher Anfang der Menschengeschichte*, 1786) uses the same word as *Zarathustra*. Kant's conjecture wants to substitute a secular "likely story" or *muthos* for the religious *muthos*. In *Die Religion innerhalb der Grenzen der blossen Vernunft* [*Religion Within the Bounds of Reason Alone*], he makes up a moralized version of the Kingdom of God. I suspect this "ecclesiology" of being a rationalized (counterfeit) double of the intimate universal of the religious community.
20. Nietzsche, *Also sprach Zarathustra*, pp. 105–106.
21. Friedrich Nietzsche, *The Gay Science*, trans. Walter Kaufmann (New York: Vintage Books, 1974), §125
22. Desmond, *Is There a Sabbath for Thought?* chap. 1.
23. William Desmond, *God and the Between* (Oxford: Blackwell, 2007), part 6, Seventh Metaphysical Canto: God Being Infinite.
24. A term I use in *Desire, Dialectic and Otherness: An Essays on Origins* (New Haven, Conn.: Yale University Press, 1986), a work that, taken as a whole, plots the convergence of intentional and successive infinitudes in the between, convergence that metaxologically intermediates a sense of the hyperbolic infinity. I would now stress more strongly the qualification of our infinite self-surpassing by its being first a *passio essendi* in a received sense before being a *conatus essendi* in an endeavouring sense.
25. Contrast this with symbol as a *sumballein*, a "throwing together" or a "being thrown together." The sense of "conjecture" I noted in Nietzsche and Kant (note 19) is more projective than genuinely con-jectural (in the meaning of "being thrown together or with" [*jacere-con*]). The sense of conjecture in Cusa as symbolic (*sumballein*) of the infinite stresses more this sense of *con*—opening it more to the *huper*, the "above" of *huperbal-*

lein. The religious significance of imagination as not just projective is here at stake; on this, see Desmond, *Is There a Sabbath for Thought?* chap. 4.

26. William Desmond, "Surplus Immediacy and the Defect(ion) of Hegel's Concept," in *Philosophy and Culture: Essays in Honor of Donald Phillip Verene*, ed. Glenn Alexander Magee (Charlottesville, Va.: Philosophy Documentation Center, 2002).
27. William Desmond, *Art, Origins, Otherness: Between Art and Philosophy* (Albany: State University of New York Press, 2003), chaps. 3 and 4.
28. See Peter C. Hodgson, *Hegel and Christian Theology: A Reading of the Lectures on the Philosophy of Religion* (Oxford: Oxford University Press, 2006), and the exchange between Hodgson and me concerning *Hegel's God* in *Owl of Minerva* 36, no. 2 (2005): 153–163, 189–200.

7

THE WAY OF DESPAIR

KATRIN PAHL

The twentieth century has read the *Phenomenology of Spirit* as a coherent narrative of progress. It has commonly accepted that "the *Phenomenology* raises empirical consciousness to absolute knowledge," understanding this "raising" as an improvement and "absolute knowledge" as the final mastery of truth.[1] Eugen Fink, for example, describes the itinerary of the *Phenomenology* as a straightforward movement with "a definite point of departure and a definite end. The point of departure is the ordinary conception of being, in which we lodge, as it were, in a blind and ignorant fashion.... The end of the path is for Hegel the attained insight in what being is, that is, the truth of being or absolute knowledge."[2] Robert Solomon spells out the common assumption that this passage is a progression from darkness to light when he suggests that "the 'root-metaphor' of the entire *Phenomenology* [is development understood as] growth and education. Hegel several times uses the image of a growing tree or a growing child to illustrate his model of philosophy, but perhaps the dominant philosophical image is Plato's metaphor of education, in which the philosopher leads the uneducated out of the shadows and into the light of truth."[3]

The introduction to the *Phenomenology*, however, describes consciousness's path toward Absolute Knowledge as a "way of despair" (*Weg der Verzweiflung*; 49/61).[4] Quite contrary to the optimistic interpretations of many of its readers, "this path has a negative significance" for consciousness, which is the protagonist of this narrative of *Bildung* (49/61).[5] The *Phenomenology* emphasizes repeatedly that the formation, or *Bildung*, of the subject means "the loss of its own self" (49/61). The way to Absolute Knowledge is blazed by the loss of self and the loss of truth, "for it does lose its truth on this path" (49/61). Consciousness starts its journey of formation righteously with a clear idea of the world. Then, not once, but many times, again and again, consciousness loses itself and is forced to abandon the certainty of its knowledge until it "achieve[s], through the complete experience [*vollständige Erfahrung*] of itself, the awareness of what it really is in itself": a crushed and consumed subject (49/60, translation corrected).

The *Phenomenology* presents the way of despair as a spiritual and physical ruin (*Zerrissenheit*). The subject in despair loses its head, its every bone is broken, it self-digests, its heart breaks, its spirit is crushed but restless. One of the later figures of the protagonist, the self-alienated spirit of culture (*Bildung*), rather poignantly registers the despair of this way: it has the "feeling that it has been rolled upon the wheel through all the stages of its existence [*durch alle Momente ihres Daseins hindurch gerädert*] and that its every bone has been shattered [*an allen Knochen zerschlagen zu sein*]" (328/356, translation corrected). With all its bones broken, the protagonist feels like rubber. In that moment, the reader realizes together with the phenomenologist and the protagonist that *Bildung* is torture.

Yet the despair of the *Phenomenology* remains strangely impalpable. After the brief but powerful mention of it in the introduction, despair barely ever becomes a topic again. The feeling of despair is largely covered over by the teleological narrative that the phenomenologist tends to construct. It is for the most part lost on the protagonist as well. Consciousness does not have the face of despair. In fact, every time it is crushed, it cheerfully starts anew. The introduction to the *Phenomenology* announces that this is a text of despair. But once the text begins, it seems to forget this proclamation.

Nevertheless, despair affects the entire organization of the *Phenomenology*. It plays a structural and performative rather than a thematic role. In this article, I will attend to the significance of despair for the structure of the *Phenomenology*. I will follow a twofold approach. First, I will examine two of Hegel's rather curious and, in the traditional sense, nonphilosophical mentions of despair: despair (*Verzweiflung*) as an etymological relative of doubt (*Zweifel*) and despair as an emotion of animals. Then, I will explore two structural operations of despair that Hegel does not name as such: the (dis)organization of rational thought and the (dis)organization of the *Phenomenology*'s narrative.

Throughout my discussion of Hegel, I will draw upon *The Passion According to G. H.*, a novel by the Brazilian writer Clarice Lispector that describes an unexpected crisis in the life of an upper-middle-class Brazilian woman: the encounter with a cockroach. An insignificant incident that is usually aborted by the quick killing of the cockroach takes greater, spiritually transformative dimensions for this woman who, for no particular reason, opens herself to the experience of the encounter. In my view, *The Passion According to G. H.* resonates across a productive distance with the *Phenomenology of Spirit*. It offers a poetic phenomenology of the (self-)crushing and (self-)consuming qualities of despair.

A PLAY WITH WORDS

In the introduction to the *Phenomenology*, Hegel links the two rather conceptually disparate terms *Verzweiflung* (despair) and *Zweifel* (doubt, skepticism). As is often the case with Hegel, his attention to the linguistic material determines the thrust of his conceptual operation here. Bringing to bear the prefix *ver-* (which can express the thorough accomplishment, but also the negation of the action expressed in the verb it modifies) and the suffix *-ung* (English: "-ing"; regularly used to turn verbs into nouns, it emphasizes the continuous aspect of the action expressed) on the root *zweifel*, he describes despair as a thoroughgoing self-doubt or a "self-accomplishing skepticism" (*sich vollbringende Skeptizismus*; 50/61; translation corrected).[6] With this phrase, Hegel draws attention to three characteristics that make him validate despair over skepticism. First, with the use of the reflexive pronoun "self" in the phrase "self-accomplishing" (*sich vollbringend*), he affirms the self-reflexivity of despair. In contrast, he critiques the skeptical "I" for directing its negativity solely toward the outside, that is, for being skeptical about everything except its own power to negate.[7] Second, he considers despair as more genuine than skepticism. While skepticism pretends to negate accepted opinions and prejudices, it ends up reenforcing them.[8] Despair actually accomplishes what skepticism claims to do. Finally, Hegel underscores the extent to which despair is a process: the gerund "self-accomplish*ing*" (*vollbring*end) presents despair as an ongoing movement that does not come to completion.

The subject in despair negates itself and disarticulates the certainty of its own (positive or negative) opinions. Yet, despair ruins the self without ever completely annihilating it. Mere negations are too simple for a hyperactive consciousness in despair. That is why despair doesn't open onto an abyss of nothingness:

> Nothingness is specifically [*bestimmt*] the nothingness of that *from which it results*. . . . In that case it is itself a *determinate* [*bestimmtes*] nothingness, one which has a *content*. When . . . the result is conceived as it is in truth, namely, as a *determinate* [*bestimmte*] negation, a new form has thereby immediately arisen. (51/62)

The subject in despair keeps changing its form and it does so to no end (no purpose, no limit). Despair is unending (the self). On (or rather, under) the wheel of determinate negations, the despairing subject rolls through its various shapes, on and on. It is crushed by the wheel, but it never falls apart completely, because the self-reflexive energy of despair's determinate negations holds together the different shapes or shreds of the subject. While despair ruins the original unity, it also prevents the shreds from settling into a shape completely of their own. For the protagonist of the *Phenomenology* is "an 'I' that in its simplicity is genuinely self-differentiating [*sich wahrhaft unterscheidendes*], or that in this absolute differentiation remains identical with itself [*sich gleichbleibendes*]" (119/136). "Qua self . . . [the 'I'] is absolute elasticity" (*die absolute Elastizität*; 314/341): a rubber subject.

The elasticity of its rubber nature governs consciousness. Despairing, it always ruins its current existence, but this self-loss never keeps it down for long. Consciousness always bounces back. It neither stands nor falls: it does both at the same time, and so it wobbles or hovers. Like a rubber tumbler, consciousness is easily tipped, but it cannot lie down. Even though it feels heavy with despair, it always flips up again. This is not its own freely exercised decision. Consciousness simply does not have the choice to find peace on the ground. While it keeps its head up high, it is ruled by its butt. And even though its butt is heavy, it touches the ground only ever so slightly, and this makes its head always flip up again, without a purpose.[9]

Consciousness keeps staggering and flipping up until, almost by accident, it realizes that it cannot stop. That does not mean that it has reached its goal. Despair is unending in the active sense; it undoes the final teleology of the *Phenomenology*. When the protagonist realizes that it cannot stand still, all it has understood is that going beyond itself and being beside itself are parts of itself. On the path of despair, the protagonist "achieve[s] . . . the awareness of what it really is in itself"—a self in despair (49/60).

Despairing, consciousness loses the legs that provide stability. It begins to float. Despair lets consciousness lo(o)se: it unleashes consciousness's (self-)destructive forces. It is a liberating way of despair that has its own pleasure: "a very difficult pleasure; but it *is* called pleasure."[10] When the path of despair opens onto the pleasure of despair, this pleasure consists in the difficult bliss of living the elastic tension between two irreconcilable yet unending pulls: to unify (without ever reaching complete unification) and to fragment (without ever reaching complete dissolution).

The word "despair" might carry too much pathos for the lighthearted despair that the *Phenomenology* produces. The term tends to leave us with our false imaginations of the worst. As an elastic transport, despair keeps its subject bouncing back and forth between its torturous and its pleasurable poles. The German word is perhaps more felicitous in that it draws us playfully into the double twist of *Ver-*

zwei (two)-*fl-ung*.¹¹ In the *Phenomenology*, despair doesn't take itself seriously. From the start, it is *aufgehoben*, or ironic, in the sense that the early German Romantics developed of irony as the double gesture of simultaneously affirming and negating. Consciousness remains quite unpossessed by despair; it experiences not the absolute depth of nothingness, but different degrees of despair that it is ruined from the onset.

ANIMAL DESPAIR

Now that we have touched on the pleasurable aspect of despair, it might not be surprising anymore that Hegel describes as despair what we usually consider to be an enjoyment, namely, eating. His first explicit example of a despairing act is the literal consumption, the eating up, of that which has no stable being. Sense Certainty, the first and most immediate figure of consciousness, must, according to its own notion of truth, conclude the unreality of sensuous objects. For Sense Certainty, true reality means unchangeable, everlasting being. Therefore, this figure of consciousness that has staked all its certainty on the reality of sensuous things will have to despair:

> We can tell those who assert the truth and certainty of the reality of sense-objects that they should go back to the most elementary school of wisdom, viz. the ancient Eleusinian Mysteries of Ceres and Bacchus, and that they still have to learn the secret meaning of the eating of bread and the drinking of wine. For he who is initiated into these Mysteries not only comes to doubt the being of sensuous things, but to despair of it. (65/77)

Hegel in no way says here that sensuous things are in and for themselves unreal. Rather, he says a consciousness that views reality as everlasting being must come to the conclusion that sensuous things are not real.¹² This does not preclude the protagonist of the *Phenomenology* from changing its understanding of what counts as truth. In fact, after a long process of self-education, consciousness will begin to appreciate the notion of a dynamic and transient truth. At that point, the status of sensuous things will be reevaluated. This said, we can turn our attention to the puzzling fact that Hegel describes the consumption of sensuous objects—"the eating of bread and the drinking of wine," for example—as a way of despair. In the introduction, Hegel contends that despair actually annihilates what skepticism merely "resolves" to negate. In the first chapter of the *Phenomenology*, this actual annihilation takes the form of a physical or sensuous negation: the gobbling-up of the object. Often, this kind of negation disagrees with the voice of human conscience. Therefore, those who are presumed to have no conscience, such as animals, are better at it:

> The animals are not shut out from this wisdom [of the Eleusinian Mysteries] but, on the contrary, show themselves to be most profoundly initiated into it; for they do not just stand idly in front of sensuous things as if these possessed intrinsic being, but, despairing of their reality, and completely assured of their nothingness, they fall to without ceremony [*ohne weiteres*] and eat them up. And all Nature, like the animals, celebrates these open Mysteries which teach the truth about sensuous things. (65/77)

Hegel considers animals to be able to despair but unable to doubt. In speculative circularity, a step forward is a step backward. Animals don't doubt because doubt requires a distancing from the object of doubt, a separation that creates the other as an object, as a *Gegenstand*, as something that *stands* stationary opposite (*gegen*) the subject. But animals don't freeze the frame and "do not just stand idly in front of sensuous things." Instead, by eating the other, they acknowledge their own and the other's changeability and their interrelatedness with the other. To eat the other means to abolish the separation between subject and object; it means to become or to exist as the other: *Man ist, was man isst*. Eating the other alive draws both parties into a mutual, death-and-life-giving relation. Animals can openly engage in a behavior that humans must keep a secret. They grasp the truth that remains a mystery to humans. Lispector suggests that the moral categories of victim and executioner do not exist in the animal realm precisely because they are based on the distance between subject and object.

> The most profound of murders: one that is a mode of relating, a way of one being existing the other being, a way of our seeing each other and being each other and having each other, a murder where there is neither victim nor executioner but instead a link of mutual ferocity.[13]

Partaking in the cycle of eating and being eaten, animals consume in despair. "Without ceremony," they expose themselves to the whirl of consumption and thus show that they not only grasp the truth about sensuous things, namely, that sensuous beings (including animals) are transient, but that they also accept the higher, speculative notion of truth, namely, that truth itself is dynamic. For these animals, changeability does not mean unreality, and negation does not end in nothingness.

The element of self-reflexivity that distinguishes despair from doubt might not be immediately obvious in the context of the *Phenomenology*'s first chapter, on sense-certainty, but it becomes clearer against the background of Hegel's discussion of life at the beginning of the *Phenomenology*'s second part, on self-consciousness (107–110/122–127). Here, Hegel describes the "cycle" (*Kreislauf*) of life as a "circulation" of (self-)consumption, where eating the other means eating oneself, and devouring means giving birth (108/125).

Hegel at first distinguishes between life in general and individual life. Organisms, animal and otherwise, are individual forms of life, while life in general exists physically as inorganic matter. Living organisms eat life matter. Here, consumption functions as separation: the animal "preserves itself by separating itself from this its inorganic nature, and by consuming it" (107/124). The organism defines and sustains itself as individual living being over against life in general. When the living being eats life, "what is consumed is the essence" (*was aufgezehrt wird, ist das Wesen*; 108/124). The animal *isst, was es ist*. It negates its own essence. It incorporates that against which it means to stand out and thereby undoes the separation. *Es ist, was es isst.* In other words, the essence negates the individual; life consumes the living. The negation is mutual, not only in the sense that every animal that lives on others is in turn eaten by another, but also because in the very act of eating the other, the animal is unable to maintain its own individuality. Thus, consumption means both the destruction of the other and the ruin of the self.

But consumption also restores the self and gives life to the other:

> Conversely, the suppression of individual existence is equally the production of it.... [W]hen this substance places the *other* within itself [*das Andre in sich setzt*] it supersedes ... its *simplicity* ... i.e. it divides it, and this dividedness of the differenceless fluid medium is just what establishes individuality. (108/124)

Life eats the living. Life in general—that is, inorganic and undivided matter—literally swallows the individual and thereby introduces a difference into the general fluidity, which in turn individuates life. The mutual (self-)negation is a mutual (self-re-)production. Each part of the cycle of life has its essence in the other. In the end, it becomes clear that the distinction between life in general and individual life doesn't hold: "The fluid element . . . is *actual* only as shape; and its very articulation of itself is . . . a dissolution of what is articulated into form" (*Das flüssige Element ist . . . nur als Gestalt wirklich; und dass es sich gliedert, ist wieder ein Auflösen* [*des Gegliederten*]; 108/125, translation corrected). To say that the living eats life and that, in the same act, life eats the living, is therefore just another way of saying that the living eats itself. Animals (and not only animals) eat each other alive. This "alive" is to be taken in both the attributive and the predicative sense. Animals eat living animals and they make what they eat come alive.

Lispector articulates the same thought in different terms. The first person narrator of *The Passion According to G. H.* has caught a cockroach between the two doors of a wardrobe. For G. H., the cockroach exemplifies eternal life, impersonal, unindividuated life matter that has survived millions of years on earth unchanged.

> A cockroach is an ugly, shiny being. The cockroach is inside out. No, no, I don't mean that it has an inside and an outside; I mean that [it] is what it is. What it has on the outside is what I hide inside myself.[14]

The cockroach is what it is: undivided, divine being. Its absolute nakedness reveals without revealing since it knows not even the trace of a secret. G. H. keeps many secrets. She is capable of lying.[15] In other words, G. H. has a heart. She is the proud proprietor of an interiority, in which she can hide "behind the appearance" (52/63).[16] And yet she begins to see herself, if inverted, in the cockroach: "What it has on the outside is what I hide inside myself." Then, G. H. watches how white pus slowly oozes out of the cockroach's cracked body: "The cockroach's pulp, which was its insides, raw matter that was whitish and thick and slow, was piling up on it."[17]

> Mother, I only pretend to want to kill, but just see what I have cracked: I have cracked a shell! Killing is also forbidden because you crack the hard husk and you are left with viscous life. From the inside of the husk, a heart that is thick and white and living, like pus, comes out, Mother, blessed be you among cockroaches, now and in the hour of this, *my death of yours*, cockroach and jewel.[18]

The whitish pulp—life in general—slowly dissolves the boundaries of the individual, that is, of G. H. G. H. sees herself in the cockroach. She has projected her heart onto the cockroach, which has no heart but wears its insides out. "A heart that is thick and white and living, like pus, comes out" of the first person narrator G. H.—Georg Hegel, perhaps—who abandons the attachment to interiority: "As if saying the word "Mother" had released a thick, white part in me . . . like after a violent attack of vomiting, my forehead was relieved."[19] Cockroach and G. H. are each other. They eat each other and birth each other. G. H. not only lets herself be touched by the neutral, nonindividual eyes of the cockroach; she also tastes the white pus, the thick matter of life. In doing so, she abandons the defining traits of her persona, the adornments of her ego, the initials that mark her property.[20] To kill the other means to kill the self. She gives the cockroach her death: "my death of yours."

Both—the narrator and the cockroach—are but different pieces of "hard husk" or dried surface from the same continuous fluidity of life. G. H.: two pieces from the alphabet, that's all, nothing behind it. The same goes for the "I." I is an exchangeable letter. "I, neutral cockroach body, I with a life that at last is not eluding me because I finally see it outside myself—I am the cockroach," says G. H.[21] To eat is to give life, says Georg Hegel.

So much attention has been paid to the supposedly life-devouring character of knowledge in Hegel that the inverse operation has been overlooked: eating is a form of self-reflection, a way of sharing in some truth and sharing it. By eating each other and themselves alive, animals grasp some truth about sensuous beings. For Hegel, eating is a way of thinking.

DESPERATE ANALYSIS

"All of nature, like the animals, celebrates these open Mysteries," this "link of mutual ferocity." But man likes to separate from the feast. While animals "show themselves to be most profoundly initiated" into the mysteries of despair, man emerges from the revel of mutual reflection (*gegenseitiges Erkennen*) by way of a peculiar kind of stupidity (65/77). He fixes his gaze, wherever he looks, on the dull but stable opacity of self-identity.

This mode of reflection relies on the rational work of the understanding: "The activity of separating [*Tätigkeit des Scheidens*] is the power and work of the *Understanding*, the most astonishing and mightiest of powers, or rather the absolute power" (18/25, translation corrected). Men—including Hegel—take great pride in this rational faculty, which nevertheless stops short of the speculative movement of reflection that animals are capable of. By cultivating the power of differentiation and analysis (*Scheiden*), man protects himself against the destabilizing effect of despair's self-reflection-by-another. He refuses to join the cycle, run around in circles, and lose his head in despair.

This rational dissection of and withdrawal from fluid life has a deadly ring to it (*Scheiden* also means "to depart this life," "to die"):

> This is the tremendous power of the negative; it is the energy . . . of the pure "I." Death, if that is what we want to call this non-actuality [*Unwirklichkeit*], is of all things the most dreadful, and to hold fast what is dead requires the greatest strength. (19/26)

The source of man's power is his ability to analyze, that is, to detach elements from the fluid whirl of life and to assign object status to these elements, which as such really don't exist. "That . . . what is bound and is actual only in its context with others, should attain an existence of its own and a separate freedom—this is the tremendous power of the negative; it is the energy . . . of the pure 'I'" (19/26). By sheer hypnotic force—by facing death and staring the nonactual in the face, as it were—man gives this nonactuality a face.[22] By fixing the gaze on abstractions he confers upon them an objective identity: "This tarrying . . . is the magical power that converts it into being" (19/26). The same prosopopoietic operation will also be applied to its source: the "pure 'I'" is itself an abstraction with no actuality; it comes into being by way of a concentrated self-contemplation, a form of autosuggestion. "To hold fast what is dead requires the greatest strength": man flaunts his self-importance by giving himself his own death.

He keeps a cool head and abhors nothing more than to "roam about as a crowd of frenzied females [*als ein Haufen schwärmender Weiber*], the untamed revelry [*der ungebändigte Taumel*] of Nature in self-conscious form" (437–438/472). Hegel here combines women, animals (via the adjective "untamed"), and gods (Dionysos, Demeter) in one dizzying semantic field of ecstasies and rebellions against the authority of the rational "I." Lispector reclaims this potentially misogynous trope for a feminine phenomenology of the intensity of neutral life: "Living life instead of living one's own life is forbidden. It is a sin to go into divine matter. And that sin has an inexorable punishment: the person who dares go into that secret, in losing her individual life, disorganizes the human world."[23] Neutral life, life in general, which is indifferent to the individual's life and death, cannot be owned; its ecstasy is improper and unpossessed. Lispector calls this impropriety of living neutral life "immund" (*immundo* in Brazilian Portuguese).[24] With this word she retrieves connotations not only of "unclean" (for example, animals that are unclean in the sense that the adherents of a given religion are not allowed to consume them), but also of "unadorned" (the Latin adjective *mundus* can refer to a woman's dress and ornaments, in that case meaning "elegant") and of "chaotic" (the Latin noun *mundus* means "world"; it translates the Greek *cosmos*, which represents the world as an orderly arrangement; the antithesis of *cosmos* is *chaos*). Since this unclean nakedness of chaotic life cannot be attributed to the individual, the punishment for this sin strikes not a single individual, but human society as a whole: it "disorganizes the human world." Living neutral life instead of living one's own life ruins the intelligibility of the anthropocentric world. The cosmos becomes unpredictable. We fall into despair. We stagger.

To prevent this staggering and to remain in control as best as possible, man analyzes his world. But rational analysis produces fragmentation. Tarrying with the negative, the Understanding gives object status and separate existence to what in itself exists only as a passing moment in a fluid movement. The analysis was meant as an intellectual exercise and a rational self-disciple, but it has literal and physical effects. Against its intention, the Understanding creates despair by scattering the dynamic whole. Rational analysis brings about precisely the ruin or disruption (*Zerrissenheit*) that characterizes speculative, despairing self-reflection. The locus of agency in man's "activity of parting" (*Tätigkeit des Scheidens*), thus, turns out to be rather uncertain. As doer, man is done. Avoiding despair, he falls into despair. Pentheus, who separates from Dionysian revelry, will have his head torn off by his mother, and, like him, every king will lose his head on Hegel's path of despair. Hegel is ready to tear to pieces anyone who "should . . . ask for a royal road [*königlichen Wege*] to Science" (43/51).

NARRATIVE (DIS)ORGANIZATION

The protagonist of the *Phenomenology*, however, is not ready to be transported by a lighthearted despair. It resists despair's unending movement. Instead, it develops a "tremendous power" (*ungeheure Macht*; 19/26) to hold fast to the purely intellectual and therefore unreal elements that it abstracts from a concrete context. It employs the same power to hold fast to itself even though, or precisely because, each of the *Phenomenology*'s figures (*Gestalt*) of consciousness is only an abstraction of the whole way. Not one of the figures of consciousness wants to change. In their desire for stability, they fear the truth: "Its fear of the truth may lead consciousness to hide . . . from itself and others behind the appearance" (52/63). Or, as the narrator of *The Passion According to G. H.* puts it:

> I'm terrified of that profound disorganization. . . . I know that I can walk only when I have two legs. But I sense the irrelevant loss of the third one, and it horrifies me, it was that leg that made me able to find myself, and without even having to look.[25]

When it absolutely has to change, consciousness goes blank. It slips into oblivion. Then, it looks rather comical on its path of despair. Consciousness repeatedly gets knocked down, but it always gets up again. As soon as it is back on its feet (however many) or (for those who grew up in the United States of the 1950s and 1960s) as soon as it is back on its wheels, the protagonist is happier than ever:

> For Hegel, tragic events are never decisive. . . . What seems like tragic blindness turns out to be more like the comic myopia of Mr. Magoo whose automobile careening through the neighbor's chicken coop always seems to land on all four wheels. Like such miraculously resilient characters of the Saturday morning cartoon, Hegel's pro-

tagonists always reassemble themselves, prepare a new scene, enter the stage armed with a new set of ontological insights—and fail again.[26]

After each crisis, consciousness is more than happy to start anew. Each time it is convinced that it has found the truth now and that this time it will last forever. This enthusiasm is a version of despair and differs from the difficult pleasure of despair only in that it stakes all its bets exclusively on oblivion, rather than affirming the dismembering effect of remembering. Because none of the figures of consciousness remembers its previous life or recollects the many torturous self-negations that have led it to where it is, the protagonist of the *Phenomenology* falls apart into many protagonists. Analytic thinking is a way of eating the self.

The fragmenting force of despair at work in the narrative of the *Phenomenology of Spirit* is supported by the hermeneutic activity of most of its readers, who, as mentioned at the beginning of this article, assume that Spirit's self-formation (*Bildung*) ends in stability. Like the protagonist(s), most readers prefer a happy ending to the path of despair. They lose the sense of despair by integrating it quickly into an economy of sacrifice or into the machinery of teleology.

And yet, the pathbreaking sentence of the *Phenomenology*'s preface—"Spirit... wins its truth only when, in utter dismemberment [*in der absoluten Zerrissenheit*], it finds itself"—does not mean that finding itself undoes the dismemberment (19/26). Spirit finds itself *in* dismemberment, that is, it finds itself as dismembered. Its self-remembrance is self-dismembering. Therefore, the way of despair that concerns us here is not an avoidable breakdown along the lines of "don't despair now, we are almost there." Without despairing, we would never be there. Despair transports Spirit, and each section of the road springs from the despair of the readers, the protagonists, and the phenomenologists.

The despair of the *Phenomenology* is structural. And so, the attempt to produce a coherent story of progress has the ironic effect of tearing the exposition into pieces. The *Phenomenology* in its entirety is a path of despair because despair shreds the dynamic "whole" that is the True into separate chapters, figures of consciousness, or "stations" (*Stationen*):

> This exposition ... can be regarded as the path of the natural consciousness which penetrates to true knowledge; or as the way of the Soul which journeys through the series of its own configurations as though they were the stations [*Stationen*] appointed for it by its own nature, so that it may purify itself into the Spirit [*daß sie sich zum Geiste läutere*]. (49/60, translation corrected)

The word "stations" (*Stationen*) echoes the Stations of the Cross. The passage, then, figures the *Phenomenology* as the passion of the Christ, the passion of the phenomenal aspect of God in the process of purifying physical existence into the Holy Spirit. This is the Passion according to G. W. F. Hegel—according to most of his readers. But the word "stations" also evokes the stations through which the *Mystai* were required to pass on their initiatory travels to Eleusis.[27] The cult of Demeter and Dionysos taught its followers the secrets of death, resurrection, and life. It effectively absolves the initiated from the terror or panic that death induces (Pan is a companion of and at times another name for Dionysos):

> This cultus . . . is based on serenity. The path of purification is one that is traveled (physically) [*durchwandert*]. . . . The physical traveling [*Durchwanderung*] of the road (is regarded) as an actually accomplished purification of the soul, an absolution.[28]

The description of the *Phenomenology*'s path as purifying the soul into the life of the Spirit resonates with the rites of the Eleusinian mysteries. The myths of Dionysos's double birth and repeated dismemberment and of Persephone's rape-rapture-capture by the underworld and her periodic reemergence from it remind Hegel of Spirit's mediation with itself.[29]

> The chief basis of the representations of Ceres and Proserpine, Bacchus and his train, was the universal principle of Nature; representations mainly bearing on the vital force and its metamorphoses. An analogous process to that of Nature, Spirit has also to undergo; for it must be twice-born, *i.e.* abnegate itself [*sich in sich selbst negieren*]; and thus the representations given in the mysteries called attention . . . to the nature of Spirit.[30]

In the *Phenomenology*, Spirit is not just born twice, but with each transition to a new chapter and a new figure of consciousness, Spirit is born anew. This parceling out of Spirit's truth, as Hegel states in one of his early works, "can easily cause the wanderer to lose sight of the path over its bends and distracting or scattering stations [*zerstreuende Stationen*]."[31] None of the *Phenomenology*'s chapters, stations, or figures of consciousness speaks the absolute truth (not even the chapter on "Absolute Knowledge"). Their truth and reality are relative. Each chapter presents an incarnation of the absolute subject and, as such, reaches a certain independence or station; but not one, in the end, can stand on its own. Butler puts her finger on the comical aspect of this textual despair; she even finds it sexy:

> We begin the *Phenomenology* with a sense that the main character has not yet arrived. . . . Our immediate impulse is to look more closely to discern this absent subject in the wings; we are poised for his arrival. As the narrative progresses beyond . . . the various deceptions of immediate truth, we realize slowly that this

subject will not arrive all at once, but will offer choice morsels of himself, gestures, shadows, garments strewn along the way, and that this "waiting for the subject," much like attending Godot, is the comic, even burlesque, dimension of Hegel's *Phenomenology*.[32]

The subject is segmented; truth is offered up in morsels. This has its sex appeal. We can linger on each part of the textual body. While reading, we disjoint the body of this truth that is figured as an "organic unity" (2/4). The sex act has a dismembering effect.[33] Some might be disappointed in the end. Those who were not distracted enough by the activity of taking the narrative apart and tasting its bits might actually realize that Godot never came, that the grand subject never arrived, that their love for Absolute Knowledge was never consummated. Or was it? The sexiness of this text, if it exists, lies not in deferred gratification, but in the orgiastic pull at any bend of the way: "The True is . . . the Bacchanalian revel [*Taumel*] in which no member [*kein Glied*] is not drunk" (27/35).

Hegel superimposes the path of the *Phenomenology of Spirit* on the passion of Christ and the initiation rites of the Eleusinian mysteries. I take the liberty to add *The Passion According to G. H.* In all four cases, some body will have been torn apart and consumed. Christ breaks the bread that is his body and gives it to his disciples to eat. Dionysos is torn to shreds by the Titans and incorporated by the human race.[34] G. H. cracks and tastes the cockroach. The readers of the *Phenomenology* are supposed to digest and recollect the stations of this book. It's always us, the mortals who are to swallow the pieces. But can we make them whole?

According to one topos of our cultural imaginary, true love can heal fragmentation: "To reconstruct 'this shipwreck of fragments, these echoes, these shards . . .' needs a special love. . . . 'Break a vase,' says Walcott, 'and the love that reassembles the fragments is stronger than the love that took its symmetry for granted when it was whole.'"[35] This statement symptomatically expresses the idea that desire is fed by lack and that we therefore love the imperfect more than the perfect. It also presupposes the idea of a proper shape (genuine and symmetrical) and bespeaks a strong investment in its restoration. The commitments to lack and integrity, to the whole and the cracks are equally strong. This topos presents love as the (neverending) desire to heal (in both the transitive and the intransitive sense). But it puts the burden again on us, asking us to unify emotional energies and to focus them exclusively on the one god, the one work, or the one life.

Hegel does not opt for this notion of love. Instead, he invites us to disperse emotional energy in the crushing, consuming, and negativity-sharing movement of a lighthearted despair. There is no reason that we should indulge the desire to heal when we read Hegel. Rather than labor to restore a presumed (w)holiness, my aim is to read the *Phenomenology* in a way that remains faithful to the emotionality of the text, to its lighthearted despair.[36]

The logic of lighthearted despair makes the processes of remembering and dismembering overlap. To remember (to incorporate—to consume—to join and hold together—to learn by heart—to keep secret) and to dismember (to shatter—to scatter and become scattered—to distract and get distracted—to forget—to open—to reveal) play each other and echo one another. "Dismembering" literalizes "remembering," and "remembering" spiritualizes "dismembering." Despair is fragmentation *and* stickiness. For the rubber subject of the *Phenomenology*, falling and getting up are one and the same movement. The elastic self stretches until it tears; and when it tears, its pieces still stick together, without pathos or ambition. The cracks of the cockroach heal without leaving scars. This healing is just as little triumphant as the cracking is dramatic. And yet, a humble and unexcited emotionality pervades and propels all of these movements.

NOTES

1. Jean Hyppolite, *Genesis and Structure of Hegel's Phenomenology of Spirit*, trans. Samuel Cherniak and John Heckman (Evanston, Ill.: Northwestern University Press, 1974), p. 39.
2. "hat einen bestimmten Ausgang und ein bestimmtes Ende. Der Ausgang ist das alltägliche Verstehen von Sein, in dem wir gleichsam blind und unverständig hausen.... Das Ende des Weges ist für Hegel die erreichte Einsicht in das, was Sein ist, eben die Wahrheit des Seins oder das absolute Wissen." (Eugen Fink, *Hegel: Phänomenologische Interpretationen der Phänomenologie des Geistes* [Frankfurt: Vittorio Klostermann, 1977], p. 42).
3. Robert E. Solomon, *In the Spirit of Hegel: A Study of G. W. F. Hegel's Phenomenology of Spirit* (Oxford: Oxford University Press, 1983), p. 277.
4. G. W. F. Hegel, *Phänomenologie des Geistes* (Hamburg: Felix Meiner, 1988); *Phenomenology of Spirit*, trans. A. V. Miller (Oxford: Clarendon Press, 1977). For this and subsequent references, page numbers are included in parentheses—English followed by German.
5. Cynthia Chase foregrounds the "disarticulation of the figure of progression" in her rapprochement of Hegel with Baudelaire in "Getting Versed: Reading Hegel with Baudelaire," in *Decomposing Figures: Rhetorical Readings in the Romantic Tradition* (Baltimore: Johns Hopkins University Press, 1986).
6. See *Grimm's Deutsches Wörterbuch*, s.v. "ver."
7. "The skeptical [sic] self-consciousness thus experiences in the flux of all that would stand secure before it its own freedom ... the unchanging certainty of itself" (124/142).

8. "Skepticism engages only in a shaking of this or that presumed truth, followed by a return to that truth again, after the doubt has been thoroughly dispelled" (49/61, translation corrected).
9. The German word for "stagger" (*taumeln*) evokes the Bacchanalian revel (*Bacchantischer Taumel*) in the notorious phrase of the preface: "The True is thus the Bacchanalian revel in which no member is not drunk" (27/35).
10. Clarice Lispector, *The Passion According to G. H.*, trans. Ronald W. Sousa (Minneapolis: University of Minnesota Press, 1994), p. i.
11. The prefix *ver-* (which can mean both thorough accomplishment and negation) adds an additional and ambiguous twist to the word *Zweifel*, which is etymologically related to *Zwiefalt* (twofold).
12. For the importance of deriving the concept of truth from the consciousness, one observes instead of judging that consciousness is based on an external standard of truth, see 52–55/63–66.
13. Lispector, *Passion According to G. H.*, p. 74.
14. Ibid., p. 69.
15. For Lacan, nonhuman animals are incapable of lying. See Jacques Lacan, *Seminar II: The Ego in Freud's Theory and in the Technique of Psychoanalysis, 1954–1955*, trans. Sylvana Tomaselli (New York: Norton, 1988), pp. 244–245.
16. See the beginning of the section on "Narrative (Dis)organization" later in this essay.
17. Lispector, *Passion According to G. H.*, p. 54.
18. Ibid., p. 86 (emphasis mine).
19. Ibid.
20. "Eating of living matter would expel me from a paradise of adornments"; and "learn from this one who has had to be laid completely bare and lose all her suitcases with the engraved initials" (ibid, pp. 64, 107).
21. Ibid., p. 57.
22. "Spirit is this power only by looking the negative in the face" (19/26).
23. Lispector, *Passion According to G. H.*, p. 136.
24. "I had committed the forbidden act of touching something impure [*immundo*]" (ibid., p. 64).
25. Ibid., pp. 3–4.
26. Judith Butler, *Subjects of Desire: Hegelian Reflections in Twentieth-Century France* (New York: Columbia University Press, 1999), p. 21.
27. Hegel is well aware of the historical link of Christianity to the Greek cults of Demeter and Dionysos.
28. G. W. F. Hegel, *Vorlesungen über die Philosophie der Religion*, vol. 2, *Halbband* 1, ed. Georg Lasson (Hamburg: Felix Meiner, 1974), p. 179; *Lectures on the Philosophy of Religion*, vol. 2, *Determinate Religion*, trans. R. F. Brown, P. C. Hodgson, and J. M. Stewart (Berkeley: University of California Press, 1987), p. 180.
29. In Greek myth, Dionysos/Bacchus was taken out of the burned body of his mother, Semele (first birth), and inserted into his father Zeus's thigh, out of which he was born again once fully developed, according to the authoritative source on Greek mythology

during Hegel's time (Benjamin Hederich, "Bacchus," in *Gründliches Mythologisches Lexikon*, a photographic reprint of the first edition from 1770 [Darmstadt: Wissenschaftliche Buchgesellschaft, 1996]). According to another version of Greek myth, he was the child of Zeus and Persephone/Proserpina. Zeus's jealous wife, Hera/Juno, incited the Titans to lacerate the child and devour the pieces. Athena saved his pulsating heart and brought it to Zeus, who gave it Semele to eat, which caused her to become pregnant with Dionysos (second birth). Under the entry "Dithyrambus," Hederich explains that one epitaph of Dionysos was Dithyrambus ("double door" or "twice-born") because he was torn apart by the Titans and then put back together by Ceres/Demeter. Dionysos's dismemberment as a child is repeated in the stories of raving female followers (Maenads) who dismember those who refuse to worship Dionysos. Like all her siblings, Ceres/Demeter was eaten by her father, Saturn/Kronos, but he vomited her out again after Metis had given him an emetic (Hederich, "Ceres"). During the time of her grief for Persephone/Proserpina/Kore, Ceres hides in a cave. According to Hederich, this was meant to symbolize the seed in the earth, before it comes to light or sprouts (when Pan discloses Ceres's dwelling place to Jupiter). Persephone/Proserpina spends part of the year in the underworld and part of the year with her mother, Ceres, above ground. Her name has been taken to mean "concealed fruit," which can refer to the seed in the ground or to the harvest stored in the barn during winter (Hederich, "Proserpina").

30. G. W. F. Hegel, *Vorlesungen zur Philosophie der Geschichte*, vol. 12, *Werke in zwanzig Bänden* (Frankfurt: Suhrkamp, 1986), p. 303; *Philosophy of History*, trans. J. Sibree (New York: Dover, 1956), p. 248.
31. G. W. F. Hegel, "Die Positivität der christlichen Religion," in *Frühe Schriften*, vol. 1, *Werke in zwanzig Bänden* (Frankfurt: Suhrkamp, 1986), p. 116; "The Positivity of the Chrisitian Religion," in *Early Theological Writings*, trans. T. M. Knox (Philadelphia: University of Pennsylvania Press, 1988), p. 79.
32. Butler, *Subjects of Desire*, p. 20.
33. Elizabeth Grosz, "Animal Sex: Libido as Desire and Death," in *Space, Time, and Perversion: Essays on the Politics of Bodies* (New York: Routledge, 1995).
34. According to the Orphic variant of the myth, the first humans emerged from the ashes of the Titans, who were burned by Zeus's lightning after they had devoured Dionysos. Thus humans are made of pieces of Titans and pieces of Dionysos. See *Encyclopædia Britannica*, 2008, s.v. "Dionysus"; Encyclopædia Britannica Online, March 18, 2008, www.britannica.com/eb/article-9030551.
35. Derek Walcott, quoted in Geoffrey Hartman, "Public Memory and Its Discontents," in *The Longest Shadow* (Bloomington: Indiana University Press, 1996), pp. 111–112.
36. See also my forthcoming book, *Tropes of Transport: Hegel and Emotion*.

8

THE WEAKNESS OF NATURE

Hegel, Freud, Lacan, and Negativity Materialized

ADRIAN JOHNSTON

FREUD AND THE NEGATIVE: A DYSFUNCTIONAL PRINCIPLE ALONE

Freud's 1920 book *Beyond the Pleasure Principle*, despite being one of the most closely scrutinized portions of his picked-over corpus, contains a relatively neglected theoretical shift that has major philosophical repercussions. Of course, everyone familiar with Freud knows that this is a transitional text; it's common knowledge that he here ushers in a fundamentally revised version of libidinal dualism, replacing prior oppositions such as sexual and self-preservative tendencies with the novel foundational distinction between *Eros* and the *Todestrieb*. This shift to a new dual-drive model involving the infamous death drive tends to be identified as the primary metapsychological significance of this particular piece of the Freudian oeuvre.

Jonathan Lear enjoys the merit of being one of the few thinkers engaging with Freud to have pointed in the direction of another 1920 change of enormous, sweeping import, obfuscated by an excessive focus on the different versions of the *Todestrieb* (or, at least, the widely accepted exegetical renditions of this fuzzy, multivalent concept-term designating a far-from-coherent cluster of various notions). Lear criticizes Freud's *Beyond the Pleasure Principle* for its hypostatization of the failures of the pleasure principle to assert itself as the dominant rule-like tendency of mental life. More specifically, he argues that certain Freudian formulations apropos the death drive illegitimately posit a second, deeper principle distinct from the pleasure principle to speciously explain how and why the pursuit of satisfaction and well-being goes awry.[1] As Lear summarizes his critique, "what lies 'beyond the pleasure principle' isn't another principle, but a lack of principle."[2] What the pre-1920 Freud treats as an unbreakable law governing the psyche proves to be susceptible to disruption, even self-subversion. There is just the dysfunctional pleasure principle and nothing more.

Lear's criticism is justified: Freud indeed repeatedly succumbs to the temptation to elide the nonteleological negativity of the pleasure principle's malfunctioning by transforming these glitches and short-circuits into evidence of another principled teleology, that is, the positive content of a shadowy, hidden undercurrent following its own distinct aims and purposes in ways that pull away from the directions normally pursued for the sake of gratifying contentment. But, as Lear might be willing to grant, despite engaging in this sort of hypostatization, Freud acknowledges and describes, in *Beyond the Pleasure Principle*, the phenomenon of the pleasure principle's own dynamics and mechanisms leading to its autointerruption. With regard to the repetition compulsions tormenting his traumatized patients, he hypothesizes that these sufferers' recurrent mnemic revisitations of their traumas result from psychical functions working in the service of the pleasure principle. Through repetition, this principle struggles to tame and domesticate experiences of overwhelming pain, to inscribe the unsettling traces of these experiences within the economy of calm, homeostatic equilibrium characterizing tolerable psychical existence. But, the whole pathological problem is that this tactic doesn't work. Reliving the nightmares of traumas again and again doesn't end up gradually dissipating (or, as Freud himself would put it, "abreacting" or "working-through") the horrible, terrifying maelstrom of negative affects they arouse. Instead, the preparatory labors of repetition dictated by the pleasure principle have the effect of repeatedly retraumatizing the psyche caught in looping movements supposedly preparing for the reestablishment of this same principle's disrupted dominance. Obviously, this strategy for coping with trauma is a failing one. And yet, the psyche gets stuck stubbornly pursuing it nonetheless, not managing to sensibly and adaptively abandon this vain Sisyphean activity in favor of other more promising maneuvers.[3]

In line with Lear's perspective, one reasonably could conclude that the pleasure principle is not sufficiently clever or strong enough to do better. As a mental legislator, it possesses relatively limited powers. And it has no more powerful Other standing behind it as a secret, profound metalaw steering things when its feeble regime is in default and disarray. These implications of the 1920 dethroning of the pleasure principle as the invariantly operative fundamental inclination of mental life are often overlooked by those seduced by Freud's musings about a mysterious, enigmatic drive-toward-death.

Apart from this overlooked feature, *Beyond the Pleasure Principle* also manifests a certain pervasive Freudian penchant widely lamented by his readers, especially those approaching him through the interpretive lenses of Continental European psychoanalytic and philosophical orientations. Specifically, Freud therein and elsewhere indulges in a biologistic naturalism (in keeping with his long-standing ambitions for and anticipations of a scientific grounding of analytic theory) as part of his speculations concerning the *Todestrieb*; with reference to, among others, the pre-Socratic Greek thinker Empedocles, he wonders aloud about a cosmic clash between the forces of life and death saturating all layers and levels of material being.[4] For those whose views of psychoanalysis are shaped by their understandings of French styles of metapsychological theorizing, the purported primacy of language and all of the social, cultural, and historical mediation it entails ostensibly require dismissing Freud's appeals to the natural sciences as a self-misunderstanding on his part—an erroneous conception of his own endeavors, perhaps indicative of the insecurities of a groundbreaking explorer of uncharted territory occasionally succumbing to the anxiety-prompted urge to cling to old cognitive maps (in this case, nineteenth-century positivist scientism) for the sake of some kind of reassurance.

For such antinaturalist readers, the "good Freud" of the signifier must be saved from the "bad Freud" of biology. The basis for this splitting into two Freuds already can be seen in Freud's work as early as 1893. That year, in his paper "Some Points for a Comparative Study of Organic and Hysterical Motor Paralyses," Freud distinguishes between the body examined by somatic medicine (i.e., the organic matter of living flesh) and an ethereal double of the body cobbled together out of impressions and ideas (i.e., the body as it exists within psychical reality in the form of ideational representations [*Vorstellungen*]). This latter body, constituted out of a mix of images, concepts, and symbols, shows itself (exemplarily through psychosomatic conversion symptoms) to be capable of perturbing the former body. However, the signifier-shaped body image isn't in the least constrained to being a faithful reflection of physiological reality.[5] In the eyes of many, one of the accomplishments of Lacan's "return to Freud" is, as it were, the killing off of the first of these two bodies (i.e., the body of natural materiality), effectuated through both stressing the autonomy possessed by the body of *Vorstellungen* as well as correlatively erasing, within the theory and practice of analysis, the presence of the corporeal substance of interest to the life sciences.

And yet, not only, as will be seen here, is this construal of Lacan's relation to the topic of embodiment wrong in several important respects—one ought to take note of an all-too-often unnoticed baby thrown out with the proverbial bathwater in any and every antinaturalist disavowal (be it Lacanian in inspiration or otherwise) of Freud's naturalizing gestures and frequent references to biology and related fields. To cut a long story short, the Freudian naturalization of the psyche's conflict-ridden libidinal economy entails, so to speak, a corresponding transformative denaturalization of nature itself—in other words, a defamiliarizing alteration of the protoconceptual pictures and metaphors informing what nature is taken to be in both quotidian and scientific senses.[6] That is to say, psychoanalytic naturalism, instead of being summarily written off as an anachronistic aberration, a compromised ideological concession, or an outright category mistake, can and should be employed as a Trojan horse introducing into the core of the sciences considerations forcing a serious reconsideration of the very materiality of human corporeality.

To be quite specific, combining the neglected aspect of *Beyond the Pleasure Principle* (i.e., the shift from a strong to a weak pleasure principle, as arguably distinct from the shift to another dual-drive model involving the death drive) with its rejected aspect (i.e., Freud's anchoring of his hypotheses and speculations in biomaterial nature itself) has the startling consequence of pointing to a somewhat counterintuitive notion: Nature itself is weak, vulnerable to breakdowns and failures in its functions.[7] This challenges the intuitive notion of it as being an almighty monistic nexus of seamlessly connected elements controlled by inviolable laws of efficient causality. In such a vision of the material universe, human nature can be imagined only as an overdetermined subcomponent of a macrocosmic web of entities exhaustively integrated through causal relations. By contrast, a nature permitting and giving rise to, for example, beings guided by dysfunctional operating programs not up to the task of providing constant, steady guidance doesn't correspond to the fantasy of a quasidivine cosmic substance as a puppet master from whose determinative grasp nothing whatsoever, including forms of psychical subjectivity reduced to the status of residual epiphenomena, escapes. Apart from psychoanalysis, a veritable avalanche of current research in genetics and the neurosciences reveals the brains and bodies of humans to be open qua massively underdetermined by preestablished codes.[8]

Francisco Varela and some of his collaborators (Humberto Maturana, Evan Thomson, and Eleanor Rosch), apropos the utterly aleatory status of evolutionary systems, maintain that, with respect to evolution, a change in thinking is needed "from the idea that what is not allowed is forbidden to the idea that what is not forbidden is allowed."[9] Put differently, biomaterial nature establishes a relatively small number of limiting parameters for living beings, but it hardly functions as an iron-fisted dictator issuing micromanaging commandments bearing down upon each and every of the smallest details of life. In this vein, Varela and company describe the ontogenetic and phylogenetic unfolding of organic existences as *bricolage*-like processes of "satisficing," namely, as meandering trajectories of "drifting" in which the bare-minimum requirement of "good enough to survive, long enough to reproduce" permits a great deal of things, other than what is evolutionarily advantageous (i.e., for things "suboptimal" vis-à-vis evolution), to emerge and flourish.[10] Evolution neither produces nor forces the production of what would be evolutionarily optimal; it may even permit the persistence of highly dysfunctional loopholes in the circuitry of organisms (such as Freud's malfunctioning pleasure principle), so long as these organisms aggregately function in a manner sufficient to propagate their genetic material. Consequently, these authors claim, on the basis of the preceding observations, that "much of what an organism looks like and is 'about' is completely *underdetermined* by the constraints of survival and reproduction."[11] This underdetermination, unacknowledged by those who unjustifiably fear that the inevitable price to be paid for forays into the life sciences is selling one's psychoanalytic-philosophical soul to a reductionist devil, is precisely what is at stake in the long-overdue transition from the image of nature as strong (qua overdetermining) to one in which it figures as weak.

Moreover, positing the corporeality of this weak nature, this fragile matter of error-prone contingency and complexity, as the minimal, ground-zero foundation for a materialist metapsychology, involves a renewed fidelity to the ontological implications of German idealist philosophies of nature (as elaborated primarily by Schelling and Hegel). In particular, Hegel insists, in his 1807 *Phenomenology of Spirit*, on comprehending "*Substance . . . as Subject.*"[12] He clarifies, on the heels of this insistence, that such axiomatic substance-as-subject is "pure, *simple negativity*,"[13] that is, the immanent self-sundering of incarnate being, its autointerrupting movements. An anti-antinaturalist renaturalization of select components of Freudian-Lacanian metapsychology accomplishes nothing less than putting real flesh on the bones of this Hegelian axiom. Against the tired trend of a now-misinformed and utterly outdated antinaturalism, the true materialist path to be pursued today, insofar as this path runs through the territories of psychoanalysis and several sectors of recent European philosophy, must involve resurrecting an unfamiliar incarnation of the biomaterial body to be found not only in Freud's writings, but also within select moments in the teachings of Lacan.

LACAN'S TWO BODIES: NATURE BETWEEN THE NATURAL AND THE UNNATURAL

What sorts of bodies, if any, are acknowledged by Lacanian theory? And—this additional question is even more pressing for a contemporary materialism both informed by the natural sciences as well as interested in engaging with Lacan's ideas—does Lacan have a brain? A certain strain of popular interpretive *doxa* frequently leads people to conclude that the sole type of corporeality posited by Lacanian psychoanalysis is that of a "cadaverized" or "corpsified" flesh overwritten by the lifeless, mortifying signifiers of the big Other of the symbolic order (i.e., a body analogous to that of the mind of empiricism à la Locke and Hume, namely, a passive, receptive *tabula rasa* merely waiting to receive exogenously imposed inscriptions). Such a conclusion is not entirely without support in particular portions of Lacan's corpus; admittedly, especially during the height of his flirtations with structuralism in the mid-1950s, he sometimes speaks as though this body of signifiers is the only body at stake in his conceptions of analysis. But, from his early texts of the 1930s through his later pronouncements of the 1970s, Lacan never completely loses sight of other dimensions of the corporeal underlying and irreducible to Imaginary-Symbolic *Vorstellungen* (dimensions serving as material conditions of possibility for the body of signifiers).[14] Furthermore, for several reasons that will become apparent in what follows, his frequent denunciations of biologistic naturalism shouldn't be construed as entailing a wholesale banishment of "natural" materiality from the intertwined practical and theoretical domains of analysis. One should keep in mind that these are responses mainly to mid-twentieth-century analytic appropriations of biology, not to biology per se (and, obviously, especially not to twenty-first-century biology).

In the ensemble of concepts deployed by Lacan at various stages of his thinking, there are several obvious indications of theoretical roles being played by bits of bodily being different from the images and inscriptions constitutive of the psychical representations of the body: the "body in pieces" (*corps morcelé*) of the mirror stage, "need" as per the need-demand-desire triad, and specific definitions of *jouissance*, to list a few. Like Freud's *Beyond the Pleasure Principle*, Lacan's 1949 *écrit* on the mirror stage has been read and reread countless times. But, surprisingly, peculiar details therein and their potential ramifications have been passed over in silence by the vast majority of commentators on this short-yet-incredibly-influential essay. Not only does Lacan invoke a number of zoological examples from the life sciences in elucidating the mirror stage (locusts, pigeons, and various primates)—like Freud, the early Lacan exhibits few qualms about borrowing liberally from these sciences[15]—he also directly refers to the human brain, speaking of "the central nervous system" with its "cerebral cortex" as that "which psychosurgical operations will lead us to regard as the intra-organic mirror."[16]

In the mid-1990s, the neurophysiologist Giacomo Rizzolatti and his colleagues discover what they dub, in a quite serendipitous coincidence, "mirror neurons" (i.e., premotor neurons that fire both when an organism with such neurons observes another similar living being performing a given action as well as when this organism itself performs the same given action). And, despite the neuroscientists' likely ignorance of Lacanian theory, this isn't just an accidental linguistic link: mirror neurons can be legitimately viewed as the physiological evidence the Lacan of 1949 announces that he awaits of such phenomena as transitivism, identification, mimesis, and the pervasive dynamic through which "a gestalt may have formative effects on an organism"[17] (again like Freud, Lacan voices hopes for future empirical confirmations of key psychoanalytic conjectures). Three years later, in a 1951 lecture presented to the British Psycho-Analytical Society explaining the mirror stage (entitled "Some Reflections on the Ego"), Lacan refers once more to the brain, voicing his suspicion that "the cerebral cortex functions like a mirror";[18] he then proceeds to speculate that this neural locale is "the site where the images are integrated in the libidinal relationship which is hinted at in the theory of narcissism."[19]

In recent years, pioneering work by, first and foremost, philosopher Catherine Malabou and psychoanalyst François Ansermet (the latter partly in collaboration with neuroscientist Pierre Magistretti) has fleshed out the neurological configurations and operations Lacan explicitly points to as *à venir* scientific substantiations of some of his models and assertions. Both Malabou and Ansermet spell out the plethora of philosophical and psychoanalytic ramifications of the now-verified fact of "neuroplasticity," a fact stating that the human brain is organized and reorganized by an open dialectical economy continually undergoing multiple oscillations between malleable flexibility and resistant fixity[20] (Slavoj Žižek too, in his 2006 tome *The Parallax View*, likewise calls attention to the theoretical indispensability of this plasticity for a revivified dialectical materialism).[21] The plastic nature of the brain makes it function as (à la Lacan) an "intra-organic mirror" simultaneously constituting and being constituted by its phenomenal and structural milieus (i.e., images, signifiers, and so on). Additionally, this connects neuroplasticity with, and adds a further twist to, the earlier discussion of underdetermination in evolution (as per Varela et al.). The brain's plastic synapses, in a paradoxical manner Hegel certainly would appreciate, are the product of contingent evolutionary factors that necessarily determine the indeterminacy of the brain. Malabou convincingly argues that a Hegel-inspired dialectical framework is essential for, in Hegelian parlance, raising the neurosciences to the dignity of their Notions.[22] This determined lack of determination results from genes preprogramming the central nervous system to be reprogrammed by epigenetic variables (i.e., by the mediating matrices of more-than-biological dimensions operative in the individual's always-unique ontogenetic life history).[23] The biomaterial substances of evolution appear to be self-sundering, reflexively negating their own causal controls and influences by giving rise to beings whose complex plasticity, epitomized by human body-brain systems, comes to escape governance by evolutionary-genetic nature alone—"the individual can be considered to be biologically determined to be free, that is, to constitute an exception to the universal that carries him."[24]

Malabou and Ansermet also each draw parallels between evidence from the neurosciences and specific notions in Lacan's metapsychology.[25] (As an aside, one should note here that the Anglo-American trend known as "neuro-psychoanalysis" interfaces the neurosciences exclusively with non-Lacanian metapsychological frameworks.) Returning to Lacan in light of this work in contemporary neuroscience, other facets of his elaborations regarding the mirror stage (in both the famous 1949 *écrit* and the less-referenced 1951 English-language presentation) become more glaringly prominent and deserving of closer scrutiny. In 1949, Lacan, after talking about the "social dialectic" distinctive of humanity, declares that "these reflections lead me to recognize in the spatial capture manifested by the mirror stage, the effect in man, even prior to this social dialectic, of an organic inadequacy of his natural reality—assuming we can give some meaning to the word 'nature' "[26] (Lacan's reasons for placing "nature" in quotation marks will be elucidated subsequently). In the second paragraph following this declaration, he proceeds to preface his discussion of the biological reality of human beings' premature birth and ensuing prolonged state of helplessness once outside of the womb (this being the biology of a nature in need of nurturing). Thus, "in man ... this relationship to nature is altered by a certain dehiscence at the very heart of the organism, a primordial Discord betrayed by the signs of malaise and motor uncoordination of the neonatal months."[27] For both Freud and Lacan, this physical "fetalization" has enormous psychical consequences,[28] with the latter, in his 1948 *écrit* "Aggression in Psychoanalysis," speaking of "neurological and humoral signs of a physiological pre-maturity at birth."[29]

Lacan proposes that a flawed and conflicted biomateriality constitutive of the human organism (as a first body) both ontogenetically precedes as well as catalyzes the embracing of what come to be the Imaginary-Symbolic avatars of ego-level subjectifying identifications (as a second body) erected on the groundless ground of this natural foundation. Bodily and affective negativities (for instance, physiological prematuration and the distressing anxiety it generates) must be recognized as contingent-yet-a-priori variables inclining the human organism in the direction of subjectification in and by its enveloping intersubjective and transsubjective environs.[30] Moreover, thanks to neuroplasticity—as observed, Lacan appears to anticipate its scientific discovery—the brain of this strange organism is marked and re-marked by these surrounding matrices of mediation, becoming a locus wherein the volatile material of nature and the nurture of more-than-material culture collide, creating complexities and antagonisms literally embedding themselves in and through the tangible flesh of the physical body.

In "Some Reflections on the Ego," Lacan revisits Freud's 1893 distinction between the two bodies involved with hysterical conversion symptoms (i.e., the organic body versus the psychical body) equipped with his account of the mirror stage. In so doing, he flatly repudiates the notion that the transbiological body of images and signifiers can be conceived of as a sociocultural construct entirely separate from and independent of biological factors; against the antinaturalist picture of embodiment in Lacanian theory as a matter of being overwritten by the non-natural traces of the big Other, he refuses to affirm the absolute autonomy of the representational dimensions of embodiment relative to an underlying organic substratum.[31] As in this 1951 lecture, Lacan, in several other places, alludes to prefigurations of Imaginary-Symbolic structures within the brute material Real.[32] The body image and the signifiers shaping it don't magically emerge ex nihilo as purely external impositions pressed upon the raw inertness of a pliable corporeal surface as a blank slate. Lacan is enough of a sober-minded materialist not to believe that the unnatural subjectivities dealt with by psychoanalysis miraculously spring into existence entirely without the consent and participation of what is usually designated, in a loose, imprecise fashion, as "nature."

In a recently published book-length overview of Lacan's teachings from start to finish, Lorenzo Chiesa addresses the Lacanian treatment of nature from the viewpoint of the life sciences, claiming that the fact of humans' premature birth is the sole element of biology appropriated by Lacan over the course of his entire intellectual itinerary[33] (even if true, the phenomena of fetalization, as illustrated previously, harbors multiple implications entwined with speculations pertaining to the brain's plasticity). On Chiesa's reading, Lacan opts for an anti-Darwinian depiction of humanity as maladapted with respect to the exigencies and pressures of evolution; Chiesa underscores how prematurely born human beings, leaning on and into the denaturalizing support networks of Imaginary-Symbolic structures available to them as compensations for their hardwired deficiencies, exhibit a "disadaptation to nature."[34] However, what about (without disagreeing with Chiesa) subtly shifting the weight of emphasis here? What if it isn't that humans are distinctively disordered and out of joint with regard to nature, but that nature itself is disordered and out of joint? What if subjects operating in excess of the algorithms of evolution and genes are outgrowths of an inconsistent, fragmented materiality from which these same algorithms (and the brains and bodies they congeal) also arise? How must a materialist theory of denaturalized subjectivity reconceive of material nature so that the possibility of subjectivity surfacing out of substance(s) is a thinkable possibility?

Lacan's references to organic matter are far from strictly confined to his early theories of the 1930s and 1940s. From the 1950s through the late 1970s he repeatedly speculates about "nature" along the preceding lines, namely, as a disharmonious, self-sundering Real[35] (i.e., as a barred Real).[36] This is the properly Hegelian-Lacanian move to make apropos the distinction between the natural and the nonnatural: what initially presents itself as an opposition between two terms external to each other turns out, upon further consideration, to be an opposition internal to one of the two terms—more precisely, the opposition between nature and antinature (as Lacan's "*antiphusis*" or "*contre-nature*") is internal to nature itself. Paraphrasing the Lacanian one-liner according to which "there is no Other of the Other," there is no Nature of nature. That is to say, the barred Real of weak nature, split between itself and its internally generated countercurrents of denaturalization, is all there is, with no encompassing cosmic balance to (re-)absorb this fissuring stratification into the synthesis of a greater whole.

These rather abstract pronouncements can perhaps be concretized through a much too brief recourse to cognitive scientist Keith E. Stanovich's interesting 2004 study *The Robot's Rebellion: Finding Meaning in the Age of Darwin*. Therein, Stanovich, on the basis of a combination of meme theory (à la Richard Dawkins) with a view of evolution and genetics similar to that sketched earlier, argues that a multitude of evolutionary processes have created out of themselves certain beings (i.e., humans) of such a degree of complexity (especially neural complexity) that two interlinked results occur. First, intracerebral conflicts become both possibilities and actualities in a brain shaped by a highly elaborate anatomical differentiation into a plurality of interacting constituents, constituents that aren't entirely synchronized with each other and often push in incompatible mental or behavioral directions. Second, these intracerebral conflicts, which are the materialized products of the sedimentation in the folded matter of the human central-nervous system of various distinct periods and pressures from the history of evolution, make possible human beings' naturally unique "rebellion" against nature qua evolutionary and genetic determinants (this amounts to an evolutionarily immanent break with evolution itself). According to Stanovich's account, genes, in obedience to the patterns of evolution, have come to code for humans as vehicles (i.e., carriers capable of transmitting genetic material) with incredibly elaborate and flexible intelligences. From the genes' perspective (if one can talk in this fashion for a moment), such elaborateness and flexibility—which also involves a plastic brain sensitive and responsive to a vast range of contexts and temporalities—is a form of "long-leash control," namely, a genetic strategy of outsourcing the planning and implementation of what is required for propagating genes to the guidance of a "robot" (i.e., the human vehicle built by these genes for the sake of their own replication).

However, through a twisted turn quite familiar to aficionados of the genres of science fiction and horror, the evolutionary-genetic creators, in the case of created human beings, end up manufacturing unnatural monstrosities, creatures that escape from their control, disregard their planned purposes, and run amok in unpredictable ways.[37] The hypercomplexity of human body-brain systems, attuned to and altered by rapidly changing environments of numerous types, is, from the perspective of genes as blind replicators, a double-edged sword: while enabling the execution of tactics for replication of far greater cunning and sophistication than those deployed by other living beings, humanity's exceptional biomaterial complexity precipitates a plethora of antagonistic inconsistencies interfering with, or even disrupting, the natural dictates of evolution as conveyed via the genes.[38]

(What's more, the powerful cognitive-analytic faculties of the human neurological apparatus enable it to become self-reflectively aware of its status as a robotlike vehicle for genetic replication and thereby call into question, at least in some instances, whether it desires to serve its genes' desires.)[39] These complexity-generated axes of conflict arise between a series of related variables: natural-evolutionary time and cultural-historical time, archaic pasts and unprecedented presents, as well as, on top of everything else, anticipations of multiple modes of futurity.[40] (Additionally, for Stanovich, human beings' special cognizance of various forms of temporality, apart from the immediate here and now to which other animals are riveted by naturally programmed stimulus-response repertoires, is an evolutionary adaptation helping to enable a defiance of evolutionary nature itself.)[41] Humans' plastic, multilayered brains, retaining residues of the primordial while taking on traces of newness (with the primordial sometimes being partially, although not completely, altered by this newness),[42] are the embodied instantiations of these clashing temporal-material discrepancies. Stanovich partially encapsulates the upshot of all this when he says that "sometimes a person may have a brain that is, in an important sense, at war with itself."[43] Although these assertions are more involved and intricate than the early Lacan's invocations of physiologically premature birth and neurological fetalization, how could one not construe this as a rigorous scientific specification of what is at stake in Lacanian ruminations regarding nature as self-shattering material Real?

Stanovich comments that "ironically, what from an evolutionary design point of view could be considered design defects actually make possible the robot's rebellion."[44] Human beings and the structures of subjectivity to which they accede are byproducts of a weak nature, rebellious offspring of creators incapable of crushing this rebellion and reestablishing their undisputed authority. Or, as Malabou puts it apropos the role of plasticity in Hegel's philosophical anthropology, "what is exemplary about man is less human-ness than his status as an *insistent accident*."[45] As she goes on to note, "The investigation of 'plastic individuality' brings out one of the fundamental aspects of the Hegelian theory of substance: the recognition of the essential status of the *a posteriori*"[46] (more specifically, the acknowledgment of "an *essence a posteriori*").[47] In the spirit of Malabou's reading of Hegel, one can claim, with respect to the lines of argumentation advanced earlier, that natural substance produces more-than-natural subjects when the material ground of being contingently gives birth to things accidental that can and do autonomize themselves apart from heteronomous determination by this same ground (being able to do so in part because of the underdetermining weakness of natural substance as a necessary-but-not-sufficient material-a-posteriori condition of possibility for the genesis of subjects immanently transcending their natural conditions). Human subjectivities are glitches and loopholes internal to an autodenaturalizing nature,

Frankenstein-like creatures of material discrepancies and temporal torsions whose negativities pervade the very "stuff" of substance itself.

HOLEY SPIRIT: HEGELIAN-LACANIAN STIGMATA IN THE REAL

It ought to be admitted at this juncture that Lacan's direct references to neurological matters are few and far between. Long after his pronouncements heralding the discovery to come of neuroplasticity articulated during the preliminary delineations of the mirror stage, Lacan, in 1967, briefly mentions the brain again. Implicitly addressing the rapport between, as it were, the word and the flesh, he depicts language as relating to the brain like a spider,[48] straddling the lump of meat it catches as its prey and spinning structuring cobwebs draped over its bumpy surfaces. Lacan here seemingly repeats, with regard to the central nervous system, what many take to be the fundamental gist of his overall account of embodiment: The brain, like the rest of the body, is nothing more than the malleable recipient of inscriptions impressed upon it from the Elsewhere of the big Other, from enveloping sociosymbolic external surroundings. Of course, one could labor to reconcile this mid-1960s remark with Lacan's characterizations of nature from both the early (1930s and 1940s) and late (1970s) phases of his theorizing, so as to mitigate against its appearing to endorse antinaturalist, even social constructivist, readings of the body in Lacanian theory. These characterizations, outlined earlier, point to his awareness of the need to envision nature differently than usual in order to explain how and why denaturalizing subjectification ever occurs to begin with.[49] But, from a perspective informed by both the style and content of Hegelian philosophy, it promises to be much more interesting and productive to confront head-on and put to work such tensions and contradictions (rather than to hastily smooth over these rough patches encountered in interpreting Lacan's elaborations of his doctrines).

As Žižek observes, Lacan is at his most Hegelian not when explicitly referring to Hegel (more often than not relying on Alexandre Kojève's interpretations of the *Phenomenology of Spirit*), but, instead, in places where Hegel's name isn't invoked. In other words, Lacan's Hegelianism is of an unconscious kind (with Žižek alleging that his conscious assessments of Hegel suffer from a host of inherited blind spots).[50] And one of the times in Lacan's ongoing articulations of his ideas when this is quite evident also functions as a point of condensation for conflicting, yet-to-be-resolved renditions of the interlinked problematics of the body, nature, and the Real. The time in question occurs on December 5, 1956, in the third meeting of Lacan's fourth seminar of 1956–1957 on *The Object Relation*. Jacques-Alain Miller entitled this session "The Signifier and the Holy Spirit" (Le signifiant et le Saint-

Esprit). What's more, both Žižek and Chiesa refer in passing to this curiously (insofar as Lacan is an avowed atheist) entitled session in recent texts.[51] It merits reexamination specifically in conjunction with the preceding considerations concerning Lacanian theory vis-à-vis the life sciences (primarily for the sake of manageable succinctness, references to Lacan's work in what follows will be restricted exclusively to this one seminar meeting).

This session of Lacan's fourth seminar, like so many moments in his teaching, involves a critique of other psychoanalytic schools. In particular, Lacan lambastes those analysts—he likely has in mind both ego psychologists and object-relations theorists (if not certain portions of Freud's oeuvre too)—who appeal to a naturalistic substratum, conceived of in the vein of the biology of the time, as an ultimate underlying foundation for the psychical and libidinal phenomena handled in analyses. Echoing the quintessentially Hegelian quip that the notion of concreteness apart from abstraction is itself the height of abstraction—concrete quotidian reality is saturated with the materially efficacious effects of supposedly abstract categories and concepts—Lacan berates the "material reality" of analytic biologism as a "mythical notion."[52] There are epistemological and ontological levels to this critique. At the epistemological level, Lacanian theory generally highlights, in a somewhat Kantian manner, the limits of possible experience in psychoanalysis. The practicing clinician as well as the metapsychological theoretician is able to know the Real—at this time in Lacan's thinking, this register frequently includes the idea of naked matter *an sich* in its asubjective objectivity—solely through the mediating frameworks of Imaginary-Symbolic reality. The Real is "impossible" qua epistemologically unavailable. Therefore, references to a substantial biomaterial base as a ground beneath the images and signifiers available to the theory and practice of analytic thought can be only mythlike fictions and illusions projected beyond the proper boundaries of analysis, rather than legitimate and legitimizing scientific corroborations.

But, instead of consistently sticking to a Kantian-style critique at the level of epistemology alone in criticizing other analysts' attempts to appropriate the authoritative aura of the natural sciences, Lacan quickly traverses a path parallel to those paths leading from Kant to Hegel. To be more exact, as with Hegel's ontologization of what Kantian transcendental idealism treats as deontologized epistemological topics, Lacan transforms what at first presents itself as a barrier or impediment to comprehending the essence of nature in and of itself into the basis for transubstantiating the very being of this material ground. Put differently, instead of simply denying other analysts theoretical and practical access to the noumenal Real of a substantial natural substratum by insisting on the constraints imposed upon them by their total immersion in a phenomenal reality of images and signifiers, Lacan performs the Hegelian gesture of insisting that this Real is dialectically entangled with and affected by reality. The ostensibly natural Real is always-already partially denaturalized through having been infiltrated and perforated by (in Hegelian parlance) the "objective spirit" of sociohistorical symbolic orders. Lacan's famous metaphor for the id of the hydroelectric dam (referenced in several discussions of his engagement with Freud's science-inspired energetics)[53] precisely illustrates this point as regards the Real qua corporeal nature. He introduces this metaphor immediately after dismissing the material reality of non-Lacanian psychoanalytic orientations as mythical.[54]

Lacan protests that he doesn't deny the existence of something before or prior to the advent of the "I" (*Je*), the emergence of the *parlêtre* ensconced in Imaginary-Symbolic reality. In other words, he can be heard as cautioning that his teachings shouldn't be interpreted as an idealist/antimaterialist doctrine in which everything is collapsed into the inescapable enclosure of the representational spheres of selfhood and subjectification. Lacan proclaims that the anterior thing (preceding the "I") whose being he indeed acknowledges is none other than the id/it (*ça*).[55] Freud's *Es* (id/it), not to be confused and conflated with the unconscious (*das Unbewusste*), is one of the concepts in Freudian metapsychology most closely associated with quasinatural soma, with the tangible physical body. As the seat of the drives, the reservoir of drive sources whose workings are described as the energetic dynamism of an embodied libidinal economy, the *Es* of Freud's second topography (fully inaugurated with the publication of *The Ego and the Id* in 1923) might appear to be a notion through which the later Freud reverts to positing crude animalistic instinctual tendencies as the ultimate base of a human nature reduced to the nature of an unsophisticated naturalism. But, as explained previously, the naturalized Freudian id in and of itself, as a conflict-ridden vortex of elements in tension, pulls away from nature qua integrated, organic harmony; Lacan, through his metaphor of the hydroelectric dam, seeks to demonstrate that the id's energies cannot be conceived of save for as inextricably bound up with and modulated by the signifiers of the big Other (an assertion relying on the implicit assumption of the "natural" id's plasticity in relation to denaturalizing sociosymbolic mediation).

The real materiality of water doesn't become hydroelectric energy per se until this moving matter is channeled through special sets of structures built at the behest of conceptually guided interests entwined with the economic, social, or political practices of humans and their histories (i.e., structures bringing to bear unnatural frameworks upon this matter). Thus, Lacan maintains that there is a world of difference between "energy" and "natural reality."[56] Energy is produced through the calculation of this presupposed reality, namely, through diverting this material substance into the defiles of signifiers and everything connected with them (such as the equations of the natural sciences and technological implements of registration and storage).⁵⁷ Departing from Freud's comparison of the libido (as the energy of the id) to an ever-flowing liquid continually diverted through elaborate labyrinths of pipes⁵⁸ (an image that resembles of a dam), Lacan mobilizes these threads of thought spun out from this metaphor to argue against any sort of vitalist conception of the id. He contends that "there is nothing less fastened to a material support than the notion of libido in analysis."⁵⁹

Instead, the Lacanian id, at least at this moment in 1956, is the "It" that becomes the "I" of the speaking subject, along the lines of Lacan's repeatedly explained and exegetically crucial (re-)translation of Freud's "*Wo Es war, soll Ich werden*" (i.e., this statement isn't, as per Anglo-American interpretive translations, a prescriptive injunction demanding that the agency of the ego must come to dislodge and master the unruliness of a wild, untamed id, but rather a descriptive statement according to which first-person subjectivity is an outgrowth of third-person inter/transsubjective structures preceding its genesis). Additionally, this *Es* that becomes the "S" of the subject-as-$ is, in its protosubjective being, already organized in fashions akin to sociosymbolic signifying configurations.⁶⁰ Right at this point in his discourse, Lacan links the hydroelectric dam of the id, the prefabricated factory of the *Es* producing its subject-effects, with the Holy Spirit, claiming that such a *Saint-Esprit* is the agency responsible for constructing this apparatus.⁶¹ What is this mysterious Lacanian *Geist*? He explains that "the Holy Spirit is the entrance of the signifier into the world."⁶²

Why does Lacan, an adamant atheist, appeal to the notion of the Holy Spirit in describing the inaugural advent of signifying structures, of the big Others of symbolic orders, in the midst of being? Again making reference to the metaphor of the dam, he argues that analytic experience, as rooted in a specific form of practice (itself shaped by the framework of a particular theory), necessarily assumes the effective operation of an already-existent "factory,"⁶³ namely, the id/it, not as the vital flux of an animalistic-organic libido, but as a self-organizing set of consciously "misunderstood" or "impenetrable" (*incompris*) signifiers-in-the-Real automatically functioning according to the dynamics of their own autonomous logics.⁶⁴ Lacan's remarks at this point indicate that, for him, the origins of language, as those events in history (whether phylogenetic or, in the case of an individual's acquisition of language, ontogenetic) when signifiers first appear on the scene, are unknowable. For a knowledge (be it that of an analyst, analysand, or anyone else) thoroughly immersed in and made possible by linguistic structures, the genesis of these structures, their emergence against the backdrop of a presignifying state of being (as an extralinguistic outside), must be nothing more than a mythical moment rendered through confabulations internal to a given symbolic Other.⁶⁵ Hence, a theological rather than a scientific discourse seems appropriate here: insofar as the advent of (in Hegelese) the objective *Geist* of the symbolic order is cognitively inaccessible and incomprehensible for those participating in this same order, its elusive mysteriousness brings it into resonant proximity with what is evoked by the holiness associated with the signifying textures of certain religious rituals and communities. Moreover, given that the individual *parlêtre*, the speaking subject of the signifier, isn't the one responsible for creating the symbolic orders to which he or she is subjected, such Others must be related to a power of creation beyond subjectivity.[66]

But, capitalizing on the fortuitous homophony in English between "holy" and "holey" (of course, this doesn't work in French), maybe there's a "holey-ness" at stake in this same session of the fourth seminar that cuts against the grain of what sounds like Lacan's somewhat Kantian emphasis on the impossibility of knowing anything beyond the limits of Imaginary-Symbolic reality (save for through indirect ideational renditions of a regulative, quasireligious sort). Going back through this 1956 seminar session a second time reveals that what Lacan initially appears to depict as obstacles blocking epistemological access to a natural Real in itself actually are ontological facets of this very Real. Prior to having holes bored in it by the impacts of signifiers (by language introducing nothingness, nonexistence, and so on into being), the Real of nature already is holey, riddled with negativities propelling it into the denaturalizing arms of Symbolic Otherness.

Twice during this session of the fourth seminar, Lacan insists, as he does elsewhere in his teachings, that the pre–Symbolic Real prefigures the Symbolic. First, speaking of his hydroelectric dam, he proposes that aspects of material nature present themselves in ways foretelling and leading to their uptake into the machinery of human activities as occurring in and through symbolic orders.[67] (The second instance of this insistence involves Lacan describing the biomateriality of the human body as exhibiting aspects simultaneously heralding the yet-to-come arrival of specific signifiers as well as being retroactively altered through linking up with these signifiers once they arrive.)[68] When subsequently discussing the id/it in terms of the dam metaphor, he is careful to use the word "like" (*comme*)—"le *Es* est déjà organisé, articulé, comme est organisé, articulé, le signifiant."[69] It isn't that the id/it is itself identical to the signifying chains that come to structure it once its plastic nature is denaturalized by the mortifying effects of cadaverization/corpsification brought about by the deeply penetrating infusion of signifiers into the rock-bottom material foundations of the libidinal economy. (Lacan compares the entry of signifiers as the Holy Spirit to Freud's death drive to the extent that mere, bare life is thereby interrupted through the introduction within it of various literal and non-literal senses of "death.")[70] Obviously, to posit this transfiguring transformation of the *Es* is to engage in an ontological level of analysis (rather than an epistemological reflection on the essentially unknowable nature of this id/it). However, through the *déjà* in addition to the *comme* here, Lacan indicates that there's a further underlying dimension to this ontological analysis: the materiality of the natural Real, before "the entrance of the signifier into the world" (i.e., the Lacanian *Saint-Esprit*), prepares the way for this entrance.

In fact, were it not for the material Real being previously arranged in constellations resembling subsequent signifying structures—which amounts to insinuating that nature itself is a delicate, fragile tissue of mutually interconnected bundles of relations vulnerable and open to incalculable changes over time (i.e., a weak nature)—the Otherness of Symbolic Spirit might not emerge and take hold in the first place (in his later speculations on nature from the 1970s, Lacan hints at this exact axiomatic proposition). The already-there, signifier-like Real is alleged to lack any "pre-established harmony."[71] In other words, there is no strong Nature qua synthesized, synchronized cosmos, a virile sphere both impenetrably closed in upon itself and able to exert an unwavering control keeping everything within its deterministic jurisdiction. If, as Lacan indicates, his "Holy Spirit is the very opposite of the notion of nature,"[72] it's opposed specifically to this protoconceptual image of it as strong rather than weak. By reading him as a Hegelian-style materialist (and not a Kantian-style idealist) in this context, one cannot construe Lacan as maintaining merely that the id-level material Real of human being is denaturalized by the external imposition of the signifiers of the symbolic order as arising from God knows where beyond the material Real. Instead, he must be understood as asserting that the denaturalizing negativity of *Geist*, as the Other of nature, is nonetheless immanent to disharmonious nature itself, originating out of the internally induced autodisruptions of a self-sundering biomateriality thereafter receptive to dialectically reciprocal modifications by this thus-generated more-than-natural Otherness.

The Hegelian philosophical rendition of Christianity can sound as though it proposes that the body of Christ is the point of convergence for the human and the divine merging in the form of an embodied spirituality. Christ is here a "concrete universal" in which the external opposites of the natural and the supernatural are sublated, intersecting in a material incarnation of something transcending what is material. Heaven comes down to earth as eternity walking and talking in, through, and amongst mortal flesh. By contrast, a materialism combining Freudian-Lacanian psychoanalysis with certain contemporary sciences of nature turns this religious figure on its head: unlike the body of Christ, the body of this new materialism is the point of divergence (not convergence) between the material and the more-than-material, the lone immanent ground from which the dichotomies put in relation to each other by Christianity originally arise. There is only a weak nature as the sole creator, and all things spiritual are its monstrous progeny: out-of-control specters whose very existences bear witness to this impotent creator's lack of absolute authority.[73]

NOTES

1. Jonathan Lear, *Happiness, Death, and the Remainder of Life* (Cambridge, Mass.: Harvard University Press, 2000), pp. 80–81, 84–85.
2. Ibid., p. 85.
3. Sigmund Freud, *The Complete Psychological Works of Sigmund Freud: The Standard Edition*, trans. James Strachey and Anna Freud (London: Hogarth Press, 1975), vol. 18, pp. 23, 32. Hereafter abbreviated *SE* followed by volume and page numbers.
4. *SE* 18:36, 37–38, 38–39, 40–41, 60–61, 258–259; *SE* 19:40–41; *SE* 21:118–119, 122; *SE* 22:210–211; *SE* 23:148–149, 197–198, 243, 245–246, 246–247.
5. *SE* 1:169, 170–171.
6. Adrian Johnston, *Žižek's Ontology: A Transcendental Materialist Theory of Subjectivity* (Evanston, Ill.: Northwestern University Press, 2008), p. 241; Adrian Johnston, "Slavoj Žižek's Hegelian Reformation: Giving a Hearing to *The Parallax View*," *Diacritics* 27, no. 1 (2007): 3–20.
7. Adrian Johnston, "Conflicted Matter: Jacques Lacan and the Challenge of Secularizing Materialism," *Pli: The Warwick Journal of Philosophy* 19 (2008): 177–182.
8. Adrian Johnston, "What Matter(s) in Ontology: Alain Badiou, the Hebb-Event, and Materialism Split from Within," *Angelaki: Journal of the Theoretical Humanities* 13, no. 3 (2008): 28–44; Johnston, *Žižek's Ontology*, pp. 203–204, 204–205, 277–278; Johnston, "Conflicted Matter"; Adrian Johnston, "Lightening Ontology: Slavoj Žižek and the Unbearable Lightness of Being Free," *Lacanian Ink: The Symptom* 8 (2007), http://www.lacan.com/symptom8._articles/johnston8.html; Catherine Malabou, *La plasticité au soir de l'écriture: Dialectique, destruction, deconstruction* (Paris: Éditions Léo Scheer, 2005), p. 112; Catherine Malabou, *Que faire de notre cerveau?* (Paris: Bayard, 2004), pp. 21, 31–32; Daniel C. Dennett, *Freedom Evolves* (New York: Viking, 2003), pp. 90–91, 93; Joseph LeDoux, *Synaptic Self: How Our Brains Become Who We Are* (New York: Penguin, 2002), pp. 8–9; François Ansermet, "Des neurosciences aux logosciences," in *Qui sont vos psychanalystes?* ed. Nathalie Georges, Jacques-Alain Miller, and Nathalie Marchaison (Paris: Éditions du Seuil, 2002), pp. 377–378, 383.
9. Francisco J. Varela, Evan Thompson, and Eleanor Rosch, *The Embodied Mind: Cognitive Science and Human Experience* (Cambridge, Mass.: MIT Press, 1991), p. 195.
10. Ibid., pp. 196, 205; Humberto R. Maturana and Francisco J. Varela, *The Tree of Knowledge: The Biological Roots of Human Understanding* (Boston: New Science Library, 1987), pp. 115, 117.
11. Varela, Thompson, and Rosch, *Embodied Mind*, p. 196.

12. G. W. F. Hegel, *Phenomenology of Spirit*, trans. A. V. Miller (Oxford: Clarendon Press, 1977), §17, p. 10.
13. Ibid., §18, p. 10.
14. Adrian Johnston, "Ghosts of Substance Past: Schelling, Lacan, and the Denaturalization of Nature," in *Lacan: The Silent Partners*, ed. Slavoj Žižek (London: Verso, 2006), pp. 34–35, 36–37; Johnston, *Žižek's Ontology*, pp. 271–272, 272–273.
15. David Macey, *Lacan in Contexts* (London: Verso, 1988), p. 99; Shuli Barzilai, *Lacan and the Matter of Origins* (Stanford, Calif.: Stanford University Press, 1999), pp. 78–79.
16. Jacques Lacan, "The Mirror Stage as Formative of the *I* Function as Revealed in Psychoanalytic Experience," in *Écrits: The First Complete Edition in English*, trans. Bruce Fink (New York: Norton, 2006), p. 78.
17. Ibid., p. 77.
18. Jacques Lacan, "Some Reflections on the Ego," *International Journal of Psycho-Analysis* 34 (1953): 13.
19. Ibid., p. 13.
20. Malabou, *Que faire de notre cerveau?* pp. 13–14, 15–16, 17, 29–30, 40, 65–66, 145–146; Malabou, *Plasticité au soir de l'écriture*, pp. 110–111; Catherine Malabou, *Les nouveaux blessés: De Freud à la neurologie, penser les traumatismes contemporains* (Paris: Bayard, 2007), pp. 52–53; François Ansermet and Pierre Magistretti, *Biology of Freedom: Neural Plasticity, Experience, and the Unconscious*, trans. Susan Fairfield (New York: Other Press, 2007), pp. xiii–xiv, 6–7.
21. Slavoj Žižek, *The Parallax View* (Cambridge, Mass.: MIT Press, 2006), pp. 6–7, 29, 79, 166, 197, 208–209, 210–211, 213–214; Johnston, "Slavoj Žižek's Hegelian Reformation"; Johnston, *Žižek's Ontology*, pp. 203–204.
22. Catherine Malabou, *The Future of Hegel: Plasticity, Temporality and Dialectic*, trans. Lisabeth During (New York: Routledge, 2005), pp. 192–193; Malabou, *Que faire de notre cerveau?* pp. 161–162, 162–163.
23. Ansermet and Magistretti, *Biology of Freedom*, pp. xvi, 8, 21, 70; Eric R. Kandel, "Psychotherapy and the Single Synapse: The Impact of Psychiatric Thought on Neurobiologic Research," in *Psychiatry, Psychoanalysis, and the New Biology of Mind* (Washington, D.C.: American Psychiatric Publishing, 2005), p. 21; Eric R. Kandel, "A New Intellectual Framework for Psychiatry," in ibid., pp. 42–43, 47; Eric R. Kandel, "From Metapsychology to Molecular Biology: Explorations Into the Nature of Anxiety," in ibid., p. 150; Jean-Pierre Changeux, *The Physiology of Truth: Neuroscience and Human Knowledge*, trans. M. B. DeBevoise (Cambridge, Mass.: Harvard University Press, 2004), p. 32; Antonio Damasio, *Looking for Spinoza: Joy, Sorrow, and the Feeling Brain* (New York: Harcourt, 2003), pp. 162–163, 164, 173–174.
24. Ansermet and Magistretti, *Biology of Freedom*, p. 10.
25. Malabou, *Nouveaux blessés*, pp. 341–342; Ansermet and Magistretti, *Biology of Freedom*, p. 13.
26. Lacan, "Mirror Stage as Formative," p. 77.
27. Ibid., p. 78.

28. *SE* 1:318; *SE* 20:154–155, 167; *SE* 21:17–19, 30; Jacques Lacan, "Les complexes familiaux dans la formation de l'individu: Essai d'analyse d'une fonction en psychologie," in *Autres écrits*, ed. Jacques-Alain Miller (Paris: Éditions du Seuil, 2001), pp. 33–34; Lacan, "Mirror Stage as Formative," p. 78; Dany Nobus, "Life and Death in the Glass: A New Look at the Mirror Stage," in *Key Concepts of Lacanian Psychoanalysis*, ed. Dany Nobus (New York: Other Press, 1998), pp. 108–109.
29. Jacques Lacan, "Aggressiveness in Psychoanalysis," in *Écrits*, p. 92.
30. Jacques Lacan, *Le Séminaire de Jacques Lacan*, book 8, *Le transfert, 1960–1961*, 2nd corrected ed., ed. Jacques-Alain Miller (Paris: Éditions du Seuil, 2001), p. 410.
31. Lacan, "Some Reflections on the Ego," p. 13.
32. Jacques Lacan, *The Seminar of Jacques Lacan*, book 2, *The Ego in Freud's Theory and in the Technique of Psychoanalysis, 1954–1955*, ed. Jacques-Alain Miller, trans. Sylvana Tomaselli (New York: Norton, 1988), p. 306; Jacques Lacan, *The Seminar of Jacques Lacan*, book 7, *The Ethics of Psychoanalysis, 1959–1960*, ed. Jacques-Alain Miller, trans. Dennis Porter (New York: Norton, 1992), pp. 168–169.
33. Lorenzo Chiesa, *Subjectivity and Otherness: A Philosophical Reading of Lacan* (Cambridge, Mass.: MIT Press, 2007), p. 17.
34. Ibid., pp. 7, 17–18, 137, 196.
35. Jacques Lacan, "The Direction of the Treatment and the Principles of Its Power," in *Écrits*, p. 514; Jacques Lacan, *The Seminar of Jacques Lacan*, book 17, *The Other Side of Psychoanalysis, 1969–1970*, ed. Jacques-Alain Miller, trans Russell Grigg (New York: Norton, 2007), p. 33; Jacques Lacan, "Le Séminaire de Jacques Lacan," book 21, "Les non-dupes errent, 1973–1974" (typescript), session of May 21, 1974; Jacques Lacan, *Le Séminaire de Jacques Lacan*, book 23, *Le sinthome, 1975–1976*, ed. Jacques-Alain Miller (Paris: Éditions du Seuil, 2005), p. 12; Jacques Lacan, "Le Séminaire de Jacques Lacan," book 24, "L'insu que sait de l'une-bévue, s'aile à mourre, 1976–1977" (typescript), sessions of April 19 and May 17, 1977.
36. Adrian Johnston, "Against Embodiment: The Material Ground of the Immaterial Subject," *Journal for Lacanian Studies* 2, no. 2 (2004): 250–251; Johnston, "Ghosts of Substance Past," pp. 36, 46, 49–50; Johnston, "Lightening Ontology"; Johnston, *Žižek's Ontology*, pp. 65, 170–171, 272–273; Chiesa, *Subjectivity and Otherness*, p. 123.
37. Keith E. Stanovich, *The Robot's Rebellion: Finding Meaning in the Age of Darwin* (Chicago: University of Chicago Press, 2004), p. xii.
38. Ibid., pp. 12, 13, 20–21, 21–22, 67, 247.
39. Ibid., pp. 15, 16, 20, 25, 28, 142.
40. Ibid., pp. 60, 122, 186–187.
41. Ibid., pp. 83–84.
42. Ibid., pp. 66–67.
43. Ibid., p. 53.
44. Ibid., p. 82.
45. Malabou, *Future of Hegel*, p. 73.
46. Ibid., p. 74.
47. Ibid.

48. Jacques Lacan, "Place, origine et fin de mon enseignement," in *Mon enseignement*, ed. Jacques-Alain Miller (Paris: Éditions du Seuil, 2005), p. 46.
49. Johnston, "Ghosts of Substance Past," p. 35; Johnston, *Žižek's Ontology*, p. 272.
50. Slavoj Žižek, *Tarrying with the Negative: Kant, Hegel, and the Critique of Ideology* (Durham, N.C.: Duke University Press, 1993), p. 128; Slavoj Žižek, *For They Know Not What They Do: Enjoyment as a Political Factor*, 2nd ed. (London: Verso, 2002), pp. 94–95; Slavoj Žižek, "Lacan—At What Point Is He Hegelian?" trans. Rex Butler and Scott Stephens, in *Interrogating the Real*, ed. Rex Butler and Scott Stephens (London: Continuum, 2005), pp. 28–29.
51. Slavoj Žižek, *The Puppet and the Dwarf: The Perverse Core of Christianity* (Cambridge, Mass.: MIT Press, 2003), pp. 9–10; Chiesa, *Subjectivity and Otherness*, pp. 127–128, 128–129, 218.
52. Jacques Lacan, *Le Séminaire de Jacques Lacan, book 4, La relation d'objet, 1956–1957*, ed. Jacques-Alain Miller (Paris: Éditions du Seuil, 1994), p. 43.
53. Richard Boothby, *Death and Desire: Psychoanalytic Theory in Lacan's Return to Freud* (New York: Routledge, 1991), p. 62; Adrian Johnston, *Time Driven: Metapsychology and the Splitting of the Drive* (Evanston, Ill.: Northwestern University Press, 2005), pp. 197–198; Chiesa, *Subjectivity and Otherness*, pp. 127–128, 128–129, 218.
54. Lacan, *Séminaire de Jacques Lacan*, book 4, p. 43.
55. Ibid., p. 44.
56. Ibid.
57. Ibid.
58. *SE* 7:170.
59. Lacan, *Séminaire de Jacques Lacan*, book 4, p. 45.
60. Ibid., p. 46.
61. Ibid.
62. Ibid., p. 48.
63. Ibid., p. 50.
64. Ibid., p. 49.
65. Ibid., p. 50.
66. Ibid., p. 56.
67. Ibid., p. 44.
68. Ibid., p. 51.
69. Ibid., p. 46.
70. Ibid., p. 48.
71. Ibid., p. 49.
72. Ibid., p. 50.
73. Johnston, "Conflicted Matter."

9

DISRUPTING REASON

Art and Madness in Hegel and Van Gogh

EDITH WYSCHOGROD

What, after all, of the remain(s) today, for us here, now, of a Hegel?
For us, here, now: from now on that is what one will not have been able to think without him.
For us, here, now: these words are citations, already, always, we will have learned that from him.

—JACQUES DERRIDA, *GLAS*

Whether we envisage Hegel's philosophy as a depiction of the dialectical trajectory of Spirit toward rational self-realization or in some alternative received fashion, it is unlikely that we would view his thought as a source of insight into the deviant psychological life of individuals, into what he terms in the language of the period "madness." However in a segment entitled "Anthropology or the Soul" in his *Philosophy of Mind*, Hegel offers compelling accounts of what he terms "insanity" or "mental derangement," whose characteristics, in turn, bear affinities to attributes he ascribes to the Romantic artist, a pivotal figure in his *Lectures on Aesthetics*.[1] However, far from offering a reductive psychological account of artistic consciousness, he meticulously segregates pathology from creativity. Freud, to whom their conflation is often attributed, in fact strongly disavows this presumptive connection. Richard Wollheim writes, "thus for all the attachment to the central European tradition of romanticism, a work of art remained for Freud what it had always been: a piece of work. And second, art ... at its higher reaches did not for Freud connect up with that other and far broader route by which wish and impulse assert themselves in our lives, neurosis."[2] In Freud's own words, "we have no right to place neurosis in the foreground wherever great accomplishment is involved."[3]

Without falling prey to the danger of reading Hegel's philosophical treatment of madness as biographical extrapolation, inquiring into his affectively charged letters to his sister Christianne, who is thus afflicted, and examining his comments on her condition may provide useful existential clues to disinterring the complex relation between art and madness. In this context, I shall consider some striking parallels in Vincent van Gogh's depiction of the artist and the artwork as revealed in his pained description of his mental states during the periods of breakdown and alleged recovery disclosed in letters to his brother Theo. The correspondence with siblings will provide a crucial site for my analysis of madness in both Hegel and van Gogh. I shall also focus on Hegel's account of the Romantic spirit in art that tracks the complex relation between art and religion and their recoding as secular expressions of morality as they are painstakingly explored in his *Lectures on Aesthetics*. It is important to note that this account unfolds in his analysis of the Idea as ethical substance, a context that must be construed as political. Thus in its immediacy, the Idea begins "as 'immediate' or *natural* mind—the *Family*," proceeds to "the 'relative' totality of the 'relative' relations of the individuals as independent persons to one another in a formal universality—*Civil Society*," and finally ends with "the mind developed to an organic actuality—the *Political Constitution*."[4] As in the relation between mind and madness, the tensions between art, religion, and morality are disclosed in an existential correlative, that of the family: Hegel's troubled relation to his natural son Ludwig as depicted in letters to a trusted friend and to his fiancée, later his wife, Marie.

Despite its importance in the context of postmetaphysical philosophy, I shall refrain from fast forwarding Hegel's concerns by considering Heidegger's oft-cited essay "The Origin of the Work of Art" in which Heidegger turns to van Gogh's painting *Peasant Shoes*, in pondering the essential problematic of art as a concern with the meaning of the being of things.[5] I shall also forgo commenting on the acerbic exchange between Heidegger and Meyer Schapiro in regard to Heidegger's discussion of the *Peasant Shoes* as imaginatively configured by Derrida.[6] In addition, I shall not track Hegel's gloss on Kant's discussion of the aesthetic judgment characterized as a free play of understanding and imagination. In the present context my concern is neither ontological, the thing-being of the thing, nor genealogical, but rather an exploration of the aporia between the ongoing eruptions, the recurring upsurge, of madness and the Romantic spirit in art.

INSANITY AND DERANGEMENT

In his depiction of insanity, Hegel takes for granted that insanity is a disease, a mode of illness. He is then constrained to account for the fact that "disease" is a term generally applied to the body whereas insanity on his view is to be understood as an affliction of the "intelligent conscious subject." As such, it transcends the difficulties of an affective self that is "at the same time the *natural* self of *self-feeling*" as well as "liable to the contradiction between its own free subjectivity and a particularity which, instead of being 'idealized' in free subjectivity remains as a fixed element in self-feeling." Mind as such is free and not subject to this difficulty. However the body does not disappear. Hegel notes that "in older metaphysics mind was treated as a soul, as a thing; and it is only as a thing, i.e. as something natural and existent, that it is liable to insanity—the settled fixture of some finite element in it." For Hegel, however, "insanity is therefore a psychical disease, i.e. it is a disease of mind and body alike."[7]

In contrast to the diseased subject, the healthy subject remains in charge of the ordering of the content of sensation. For the sick subject, the difference between waking and dreaming may be lost, allowing the dream to assume charge of the waking life. The feelings set loose in derangement are at war with the cognitive and moral adjustments that are in place in concrete consciousness. In loosening the hold of ethical precepts and theoretical principles, natural affects and passions are released, evincing a dyadic relation of reason and passion whose roots in Greek metaphysics are apparent. By stressing that the intelligent part remains, treatment for Hegel must take into account the fact that insanity is not a loss of reason but a "derangement," a contradiction between a corporeally embodied feeling and the adjustments in place in consciousness. The "contents which are set free in this reversion to mere nature are the self-seeking affections of the heart, such as vanity, pride ... fancies and hopes ... merely personal love and hatred."[8] It is worth noting that despite his stress upon the unconscious, in his account of delusion, Freud does not repudiate an intellectual residue as operative in its formation. Thus, the patient's belief in his delusion is not a result of "an inversion of his powers of judgment.... Rather in every delusion there is a little grain of truth" that warrants the patient's belief. Having long been repressed, this residue penetrates consciousness in distorted form, one to which the patient attaches a strong conviction that remains fixed upon the "distortion-substitute."[9]

Insanity, Hegel contends, is a clinging to a subjective identity of subjective and objective rather than to their objective unity so that "the two modes of finite mind—the immanently developed, rational consciousness with its objective world, and the world of inner feeling which clings to itself and has its objectivity *within* it—are each developed into a separately existing *totality*, into a separate *personality*." The insane often have an accurate awareness of their surroundings but at the same time "they are *dreaming while awake* and are *dominated* by a *fixed idea*" that does not tally with what is discerned in objective consciousness, whereas rational behavior entails a proper conception of both world and self.[10] The bifurcation of mind depicted by Hegel conforms strikingly to Freud's claim that in dreams contradiction is ignored, that any element can be represented by its opposite. Freud finds in these opposing significations a semantic doubling already embedded in early Egyptian linguistic practice in which many words have two meanings, each the opposite of the other.[11]

In his analysis of insanity, Hegel is less interested in its etiology than in its principal phenomenological manifestations. Turning first to what he calls "idiocy," Hegel depicts idiocy as distractedness, a loss of awareness of the immediate present, a lapse that can occur even among the most acute minds. As an amusing case in point, Hegel writes that Isaac Newton is reputed to have, on one occasion, "taken hold of a lady's finger in order to use it as a tobacco-stopper for his pipe."[12] A more significant manifestation of insanity, its second form, "madness proper," is described as the rambling mind that interests itself in everything without being able to concentrate on anything, a form of madness that may also manifest itself as an unfounded disgust with life that, in turn, may lead to the impulse of suicide. In contrast to the indeterminateness of rambling, Hegel considers the mind that is obsessed with a single idea, the *idée fixe*, to which the individual attributes great significance. In the third form of insanity, "mania or frenzy," the individual, aware of a dichotomy of consciousness, a split between subjective consciousness and the objective world, may attempt to bring the subjective into actuality or to destroy the actual. When this destructive tendency takes an afferent course, the inward turn may eventuate in suspicion and resentment so that, casting restraint aside, the individual may become violent.[13] Hegel stresses that the relation of hatred toward another does not preclude a simultaneous intensity of love for the same individual.

In the intellectual ambience of a world in which exhuming the content of an unconscious mind that escapes the immediate grasp of the subject has played a pivotal role in explaining individual psychological development, Hegel's depiction of psychological life offers an alternative. His account is remarkably premonitory of Jean-Paul Sartre's countervalent discourse that rejects what Sartre would construe as a second consciousness. Thus Sartre contends, "existential psychoanalysis rejects the hypothesis of the unconscious; it makes the psychic act coextensive with consciousness but is rather a pre-reflective lived understanding that requires furnishing us with the brute materials which the psychoanalyst must interpret [so that] the patient will know what he understands."[14] The being of consciousness or the for-itself calls itself into question and can never coincide with itself, unlike the being of the in-itself "which is what it is. In the in-itself there is not that which is not wholly within itself, without distance."[15] As Justus Struller, an early Sartre interpreter, comments, "the for-itself is unsatisfied with the situation in which it finds itself. It is broken apart, split asunder, separated from itself. To be sure, it has nihilated the in-itself to become for-itself but misses the placid self-sufficiency of the in-itself" that it would like to regain, a goal that cannot be realized. Between them stands a "Nothingness, invincible even in the absence of something to be overcome."[16]

Hegel does not refrain from asking what implications his account of consciousness has for therapeutic practice. Without appealing to an unconscious but once again in striking synchrony with Freud, Hegel, following the precepts of French psychiatric practitioner Phillipe Pinel, maintains that the most effective cure for insanity is a talking cure. Therapy consists in appealing to the ideas in consciousness that remain rational and in winning the confidence of the patient. In an approach that is pedagogically heuristic rather than radically authoritarian, Hegel writes, "after the confidence of the insane has been won, one must try to obtain a proper authority over them and to awaken in them the feeling that there are, in general, things of importance and worth" and that it is possible to win the respect of the therapist.[17]

"WHAT IS TO BE DONE?": DEAR CHRISTIANNE

In moving from the speculative analysis of insanity in his philosophical oeuvre to its existential depiction in his correspondence, the conceptual interfacing of the two surfaces in Hegel's letters of response to his sister's psychological breakdown. The messiness of life as it unfolds, the affective ambivalences and managerial tasks this disorder generates as manifested in his letters, require lived responses on Hegel's part that contrast with the distanced intellectual analyses of insanity and derangement in the depiction of madness in his *Philosophy of Mind*. Yet Hegel's philosophy, understood as the dialectical trajectory of successive moments in the history of Spirit, can be tracked in his exchange of letters with Goethe, Hölderlin, Schelling, Schleiermacher, and other luminaries of the day as well as with his sister Christianne such that systematic texts and letters have redactive power in relation to one another. Reading Hegel's letters and his philosophical works as an amalgam revealing his philosophical development, Walter Kaufmann in his study of Hegel, actually reproduces the full texts of letters he considers especially significant.[18] In *Glas*, his intertextual commentary on Hegel and Genet that blurs the distinction between literature and philosophy, Derrida, unlike Kaufmann, reproduces Hegel's letters to his sister in the hope of bringing to light that which resists systematization. Thus for Derrida, "following *Glas* . . . every system excludes or expels something which does not let itself be thought within the terms of the system and lets itself be fascinated, magnetized and controlled by this excluded term, which could, for example, be madness."[19]

In what can be read as an emotionally charged and generous response to his sister's situation, in a letter of April 9, 1814, Hegel in his role as elder sibling informs his sister that what is to be done is clear. If a diversionary trip would facilitate her recovery, Hegel suggests she remain in his home with his wife and himself and return to her position only when she recovers. Moreover, if she is no longer able to meet her responsibilities, he invites her "to move in with us permanently, to live with us and receive the care you need."[20] If employed as a governess, he admonishes, she may in that capacity fail to receive what she most desperately needs: "friendly instruction, even regulation and authority over what [she] should and should not do." Those who do not know what to advise, friends and employers, may be embarrassed and abandon the one who asks for help to her or his own devices to do as he or she wishes.[21] In any case, Hegel counsels Christianne to act as independently as she can in the interest of her young charges. In assuming responsibility for her, Hegel stresses the proximity and sanctity of the brother-sister relationship, one that is crucial in his seminal reading of the *Antigone* as it plays out in his account of tragedy in the *Phenomenology*.[22] Although the warmth of his earlier relation to Christianne cools markedly after her stay with the Hegel family in the summer and fall of 1815, which has been attributed to Christianne's falling out with Hegel's wife, Marie, Hegel never backs away from contributing financially to the support of his sister.

The narrative as it unfolds in the letters continues to chronicle Christianne's downward slide into madness. Ultimately the "nerve problem" with which she was afflicted compelled Christianne to leave the service of Count von Berlichingen and to be placed under the care and in the service of Reverend Goeriz in the town of Aalen, where she was able briefly to resume teaching. In 1820 however she suffered a relapse that Hegel guardedly speculated might be a consequence of a change of life. When her condition failed to improve, he requested that she be placed under legal guardianship and in 1820 confined to an asylum from which she was released in 1821. The alternation of progress and disruption I have chronicled in some detail reaches a turning point that is crucial in the context of my argument. Expressing the hope that she may overcome the bitter memories of the past and cognizant of the anger directed against him, in a significant move that replicates his analysis of the development of the Romantic spirit in art, Hegel urges her to direct her soul to a higher power, "to the thought of God." Although she refuses to return to Aalen as he advises, Hegel advocates a self-reliance that would be anchored in "something higher."[23] After leaving the asylum and ultimately settling in Stuttgart, her therapy continues under the auspices of Karl Eberhard Schelling, the brother of the philosopher. As acknowledgment of Hegel's work grows, including his election to the rectorship of Berlin University, Christianne takes pride in the accolades he receives but her decline is precipitous, culminating in her suicide in 1832, an act that has been linked to Hegel's death a year earlier.[24]

The confessional content of the letters lends support to the contention that in insanity the contents of the mind are set free and revert to mere nature, to a release of "merely personal love and hatred." To be sure, Hegel interprets insanity as one of the stages in the development of the "I" toward complete self-possession, as a necessarily occurring form or stage in the development of the soul. "[It is] naturally not to be understood as if we were asserting that *every* mind, *every* soul, must go through this stage of extreme derangement."[25] Everything does not fall apart. Like crime, insanity is a phase that must be overcome. The soul's development is contingent upon its prior existence as an individual, a singularity that is yet identical with the universal natural soul, a soul that is as yet infrarational, an immediacy, corporeality, and naturalness that must be overcome. The insane subject is, however, "in communion with himself in the negative of himself," so that consciousness includes its negative. Thus Hegel concedes that the negative is not vanquished.[26] For the madman, consciousness in an act of nihilatory erasure substitutes an arbitrary content for the actual concrete world. In parsing the letters, do their tone and content not contest the rationality of the system's claims? Do they not expel, as Derrida might put it, what does not allow itself to be thought within the terms of the system and is controlled by the excluded term, for example, by madness so that reason is under its aegis? Thus Derrida writes that on Heidegger's reading "the idea of philosophy is atheistic" and that the idea of philosophy is "madness" for faith. Philosophy supposes the converse of faith. Most philosophers agree with Heidegger's assertion quoted by Derrida that "belief or faith has no place in thought."[27] Is not that which is inimical to rational thought always already as such madness?

ART AND THE FREEDOM OF SPIRIT

In treating the issue of mental illness, I have maintained that Hegel does not depart from the commonsense view that illness is a failure to distinguish subjective from objective perspectives. Their irreconcilability leads him to aver that at a more profound level they are identical and that the Idea is the term expressing this unity.[28] Art as the embodiment of the Idea in sensuous shape, rather than "in the form of thinking and pure spirituality as such." Art "has its value and dignity in the correspondence and unity of both sides, i.e. the Idea and its outward shape."[29] Such correspondence is not to be understood as the result of the imitation of nature since it is not the resemblance of a copy to an original that is determinative. Art attempting to compete with nature is "like a worm trying to crawl after an elephant," Hegel quips.[30] Art's excellence "will depend on the degree of inwardness and unity in which the Idea and shape appear fused into one."[31]

In arguing for the fusion of idea and shape, it would seem that art's relation to the sensuous offers a sharp contrast to the relation of madness to rationality. But the particularization of the Idea in art does not unfold all at once. Its history begins with expressing the Idea in natural shapes but, failing to find its meaning there, "it staggers round in them, it bubbles and ferments in them, does violence to them, distorts and stretches them unnaturally, and tries to elevate their phenomenal appearances to the Idea by the diffuseness, immensity and splendor of the formations employed."[32] In considering Romantic art I shall return to this refractoriness to show that, like madness, in an afferent movement of inwardization Romantic art extrudes or expels the object as that which is external to itself.

As Charles Karelis points out, in this struggle toward its self-realization, Hegel contends that "with man there emerges in nature the highest form of subjective principle, the rational and self-conscious ego."[33] Hegel also conceives of this unity as freedom, a freedom that must be worked out. In the context of mental illness and in consonance with this view, we have seen that Hegel urges his sister Christianne to discover her freedom through knowing and willing. Aspiring to attain freedom as a therapeutic measure cannot, however, be identified with the freedom expressed in the creation of the artwork, which is instead to be construed as another part of the process of the idea's self-realization.[34]

Artistic activity does not provide a respite from the struggle for freedom, but rather "art's vocation is to unveil the *truth* in the form of sensuous artistic configuration."[35] Unlike objects in nature—"the torch-thistle, which blooms for only one night"—the work of art is "essentially a question, an address to the responsive breast, a call to the mind and the spirit."[36] The excellence of the work is contingent upon the success of the fusion of inwardness and shape in the Idea.

In consonance with this view, Hegel classifies artworks by the perspectives of consciousness through which the Idea is grasped as content (the symbolic, the classical, and the romantic) rather than through the medium of expression (music, poetry, architecture, sculpture, and painting). The first phase, the symbolic, presupposes an affinity between the natural object and the idea so that objects are left as they are and interpreted as if the Idea were not imposed on them but was present in them. The universal meaning that results is merely an abstraction as, for example, the identification of the lion with strength.[37] In the classical art form, the Idea is embodied in the shape appropriate to it, the human body as reflecting an ideal of beauty. No longer merely a natural object, it is now one that has been purified and whose flaws are not visible. But the sheer perfection of form that classical art has achieved brings to light the defect in art itself, the depiction of spirit in sensuous concrete form when, in fact, spirit, that is "the infinite subjectivity of the Idea . . . as absolute inwardness," cannot be given appropriate bodily form.[38] The unity of subjective and objective does not express a quiescent identity but is for Hegel parsed theologically: God in his spiritual original nature passes into a unity of mankind. It is Romantic art that undoes the unity of classical art, finding itself in Christianity's assertion of God as spirit; but when brought to the fore as spirit, God is not an individual.[39] The unity of the human and the divine is not tied to sensuous presentation but is freed from immediate existence. Yet Hegel concedes that, like all art, Romantic art requires an external medium for its expression and assigns this role to the heart. But can the heart be an external medium? Is the heart then for Hegel a medium that is an outside that is inside and an inside that is outside supporting his contention that "what is apparent to the senses alone sinks into worthlessness"? He goes on to say, "external existence is consigned to contingency and abandoned to the adventures devised by an imagination [that] can mirror what is present to it, exactly as it is, just as readily as it can jumble the shapes of the external world and distort them grotesquely." It can become reconciled to itself "in all misfortune and grief, and indeed even in crime."[40]

The overcoming of an individual's sense of unworthiness as the "supreme and sole task of man" occurs within the religious domain of Romantic art, the conceptual space in which the Romantic ideal first specifies itself as Christian love. To this end, self-inflicted torments or pains imposed by others are the means for securing reconciliation with God. Hegel acknowledges that the scourges, "the physical torments, the scaffolds, the beheadings, roastings, burning at the stake, boiling in oil," are repugnant and resist conversion into the beauty of the artwork.[41] Although one may respect the original "germ" of religious feeling, modern consciousness, he acknowledges, must be revolted by these extremes. Artistry in this context consists in transforming grief into bliss, into rendering visible the doubleness of a piety that conveys joy in torment as rendered explicit in traditional portrayals of Mary Magdalene. Hegel endorses her self-perception insofar as it magnifies her bliss and beauty but insists that she errs when she perceives herself as a sinner. A second example (which recurs in terms of its more moderate secularized version, honor) is the tale of the man who loves and is loved by his wife and family, who departs on a pilgrimage and returns disguised as a beggar but does not disclose his identity. In sympathy for his plight, he is allowed to stay beneath the stairs of his home for twenty years during which time he becomes a spectator of his family's grief and reveals himself only on his deathbed. For Hegel, this supposed sanctity is fanaticism.

With increasing secularization, the reality of inner life as Christian love comes into increasing conflict with the objective world of family, political life, and ethics. "The aims of love cannot be achieved in concrete reality without collision," so that love itself undergoes a dimming down. Astonishingly, in light of Hegel's life as revealed in his letters to which I shall turn in due course, Hegel contends: "The duty of honour may demand the sacrifice of love.... For example, it would be contrary to the honor of a man in a higher class to love a girl of a lower class. The difference of classes is necessary and given in the nature of civil life," while differences proceeding from birth and honor tend to become fixed as absolute.[42] Hegel affirms that love can be beautiful and noble if it does not remain purely sexual, but the love for an individual woman falls short of universality: "It is only the personal feeling of the individual subject" and lacks the objective aspects of existence, "duties rising from one's calling or class."[43] Clearly uncomfortable with what could be construed as a summary dismissal of love, he must ask whether love directed to a particular person can be made to satisfy the claims of the universal, claims that inhere in the political realm. In an effort to retain both love and universality, Hegel appeals not to duty but to rights, arguing that "every man does have a heart for love and a right to become happy through it," but if he does not achieve this end in relation to one specific chosen girl, "no wrong has occurred" and he is free to seek elsewhere. Hegel asks whether we "are therefore supposed to be interested in supreme contingency, in the man's caprice which has neither universality nor any scope beyond itself."[44]

Do the tensions to which I have alluded reflect a deeper, inexpungeable ambivalence in Hegel's attitude toward art? Robert Wicks asks whether Hegel does not "ennoble art insofar as it conveys metaphysical knowledge," while also "temper[ing] his assessment in view of his belief that art's sensory media can never adequately convey what completely transcends sensation."[45] If so, I would ask further whether the scientific, political, and ethical norms, the laws and maxims that govern contemporary life, require a spirit of reflection, whether general considerations regulate the particular as Hegel contends, and, if so, whether the Romantic intensities of affect I have stressed must give way to the advances in Spirit's development of the subject in revealed religion and philosophy. Does art not in "its highest vocation remain for us a thing of the past"? If art has lost "its truth and life," does it not now require philosophical interpretation, which itself supplants the creation of artworks? This is also a political question.

Art now invites us to know what art is.[46] Yet Hegel also insists that art remains a basic human need and will continue according to its concept, the self-unfolding idea of beauty: "Its architect and builder is the self-comprehending spirit of beauty but to complete it will need the history of the world in its development through thousands of years."[47] If so, the negative as the affective driving force of both art and madness, something that does not let itself be thought, is not vanquished but rather "fascinates, magnetizes and controls." I can now significantly invoke the political by considering what is more than a casual remark: Hegel insists that "the state is no ideal work of art. It stands on earth and so in the sphere of caprice, chance and error." However, "the ugliest of men, or a criminal or an invalid or a cripple, is always a living man . . . the affirmative life subsists despite its defects."[48]

LUDWIG, THE HIDDEN SON

In considering the various modalities of love manifested in the spirit of the Romantic, we have seen that love may appear independently of religious aims even in expressions of love that themselves may morph into less intense forms of social and cultural codes of honor. The link between erotic love and social code is played out in Hegel's relation to Christianna Charlotte Johanna Burkhardt, the abandoned wife of a servant of a count, with whom Hegel, without benefit of marriage, sired a son, Ludwig.[49] Whereas Walter Kaufmann contends that Hegel is responding to conceptual dilemmas connected with the writing of the *Phenomenology,* the conflicts of love and duty explicated in the *Aesthetics* are played out in life. Not wishing to jeopardize his engagement to Marie Tucher, the woman for whom he professes love and hopes to marry, he attempts to keep his engagement to her secret until matters with Christianna are settled. Striving to behave in a manner he deems responsible, Hegel arranges for Ludwig's care in Jena and later brings him to his own home in Heidelberg. In his letter to Frommann, his principal confidant, Hegel attempts to protect Christianna Burkhardt, Ludwig's mother, whom he felt he had wronged.[50] Expressing regret for the pain he caused her, Hegel vows to perform his obligations to "the mother of my child."

The ambivalence of his feelings toward Christianna is attested in his letter to Frommann, to whom he confides that, when learning of her death, Ludwig was affected by the event, but "[his own heart] had long ago finished with her," a negative affect that on occasion seeps into his relation to Ludwig.[51] Denying that Ludwig was suited for the liberal professions, Hegel argues in his 1814 letter to Frommann that there was "some promise in [the boy's] natural abilities" but "that the most appropriate thing will probably be to make a businessman of him."[52] Further, Ludwig complained that Marie's ambivalence toward him and preference for her natural sons left him to live in constant fear; but, lacking the necessary means, he was unable to leave. Yet, contrary to Hegel's aims for him, Ludwig eventually went his own way. Joining the Dutch military, he was dispatched to the East Indies where he met a premature death in August 1831, a fate that remained unknown to Hegel, who died in November of that year.[53] In sum, retreating from the madness of passion, refusing to endorse "free love" as advocated by Friedrich Schlegel and other contemporaries, Hegel submits to duty, to responsibility for one's action precisely as laid out in the social codes defended in the *Aesthetic*s.

Must we not ask whether Hegel's submission to "the way things were done" remained unaffected by Romantic sensibility, whether Romantic sensibility when construed as love itself could arise again as Spirit? Writing in 1811, Hegel declared, "to be complete, love requires a still higher moment than that in which it consists in and for itself. What perfect satisfaction—i.e. being entirely happy—means can only be completed by religion and the sense of duty." But does feeling resist sublation and continue to erupt? Rejecting Hegel's claim, Marie, who is troubled by the subordination of feeling to that which is putatively higher, duty, reads social obligation as tainting the purity of passion. Hegel pleads that his appeal to duty does not undermine the depth of his feeling, that his affect "lies for [him] in the words *dear Marie.*"[54] Does "what the heart likes," as embodied in the words "dearest,

dearest most lovely Marie," continue as that which "magnetizes, is excluded and does not let itself be thought"?

LETTERS TO THEO

According to a widely held stereotypical view of Vincent van Gogh as the mad artist, his insanity is seen to coincide with his artistic genius and indeed is its necessary precondition. Antonin Artaud writes, "what van Gogh cared about most in the world was his idea of a painter, his terrible fanatical idea of a visionary.... No one has ever written, painted, sculpted, modeled, built or invented except literally to get out of hell."[55] However, in conformity with my claim that Hegel viewed the tension between art and Christianity as integral to the Romantic spirit, Artaud observes of van Gogh that he did not die of "delirium" but rather of having been the corporeal site of "the problem of the predominance of flesh over spirit, or of body over flesh or of spirit over both."[56] So we would perhaps not be remiss to compare madness at the individual level with the violence and willfulness of the state of nature from which Hegel thought we must depart. Like Hegel, van Gogh reflects upon the complex relation of Christianity to painting. Despite his early attraction to classical Christianity, van Gogh reverses course, renouncing its contemporary expressions while maintaining that "its founder was sublime" and worshipped, in an antinomian gesture, the love that was once proclaimed to be sin.[57] To be sure, van Gogh does not undertake an extended philosophical analysis of subjectivity. His position unfolds in the unfolding of his life as exhibited in his correspondence with his brother Theo, a life that is lived as a search for its meaning. The life of art for van Gogh remains a quest whose object is sought but cannot be found so that being an artist means "looking for something all the time without ever finding it in full.... I am looking, I am hunting for it, I am deeply involved."[58] To be sure, for the artist natural aptitude is required but talent is not enough. As Hegel holds, "mere talent ... if it is to be perfect in itself, it still requires always over again the capacity for art in general, and the inspiration which genius alone confers."[59] Yet if the object of van Gogh's quest cannot be found, it is manifested in the reciprocal imbrications of depression, love, and the meanings attributable to art. I shall turn to them seriatum by revisioning the texts of van Gogh's letters.

In depicting the persona of madness, van Gogh does not describe his mental illness while an episode of illness is in progress but rather after it seems to be over. Thus he writes that as he was emerging from the hospital, he imagined that there had been nothing wrong with him, but only some time afterward admitted he felt he had been ill.⁶⁰ His madness is seen to culminate in the famous dramatic moment when, in response to a violent argument with Gauguin in December 1888, he cuts off a piece of his ear, appears at a brothel, asks for one of the prostitutes, and hands her the severed lobe. Van Gogh is then admitted to a local hospital. In a letter of December 31, 1888, a Reverend Salles writes to Theo from Arles that Vincent is currently calm but "that as the result of the insane act which required his admission to the hospital and his more than strange behavior [there] the doctors found it necessary . . . to place him in an isolated room which they can keep locked. It is their opinion that he must be transferred to a lunatic asylum."⁶¹ Vincent fears that moving to an asylum as an ultimate fate portends the prospect of living under perpetual surveillance. Upon moving to Paris he is placed under the care of Dr. Gachet, a homeopathic physician whom van Gogh alleges is as ill as he. His decline continues, culminating in his suicide. On July 27, 1890, van Gogh shoots himself in the chest and dies two days later.⁶² In a comment crucial for interpreting what drives yet undoes art, van Gogh maintains that the relation of madness to art is not only disjunctive but enabling. Thus he acknowledges that in regard to the episodes of breakdown that he suffered that, if he recovers, he will never again attain the heights to which the illness led him.⁶³

In his relation to love van Gogh, like Hegel, succumbs to erotic temptation. Seeing love as a relation of proximity, he writes to Theo in March 1881 that he fell so much in love with his cousin Kee Vos that it was as if he and she were the closest persons to one another, but when he informed her of his feelings, she maintained that she could not reciprocate, "never, no, never."⁶⁴ Despite his intense passion for her, he insists that if she "cold-shoulders" him, he will not "allow [himself] to become frozen and [his] mind crippled because of her."⁶⁵ Although he feels less passion for her, he later finds solace in the affection of Sien, "an ordinary woman of the people."⁶⁶ In July 1888, she gives birth to a child and Vincent then assumes the responsibilities of a "paterfamilias."⁶⁷ Like Hegel, in conformity with duty, he maintains that he will not forsake her. Moreover, in his regard for institutional norms he went so far as to claim that, because of the seriousness with which he regarded marriage, were he married to a woman who took up with another, he would try to bring her back.

In what comports with Hegel's view, van Gogh contends that art "is something greater and higher than our own skill or knowledge or learning. . . . [T]hough produced by human hands, [art] is not wrought by hands alone, but wells up from a deeper source, from man's soul, while much of the proficiency and technical expertise associated with art reminds me of . . . self-righteousness in religion."⁶⁸ For Hegel the assumption of a deeper source, if warranted, must entail a fusion of the subject matter and sensibility so that the subjective and factual sides of representation are not "strangers to one another." The work must exhibit the most personal inner life of the artist and the nature of the object as it proceeds from his productive activity. Yet does the intensity of affect as expressed, for example, by color, not continue to disrupt the formal relations of planes and surfaces? Is Hegel not carried away by color when he writes, "in painting, e.g., the atmospheric tone, the foliage, the distribution of light and shade, the whole tone of colour as a whole, permit of an infinite variety"?[69] It is in this regard that the greatest differences among painters can be found. A tone others may not have noticed is observed by an artist "who has made it his own."[70]

IN/CONCLUSION

It would seem that van Gogh's life as it unfolds in his correspondence is cut to fit Hegel's depiction of the artist: "art does indeed consume the accidental idiosyncrasy of the artist, but it absorbs it only so that the artist can follow the pull and impetus of his own genius, filled as it is with his subject alone, and can display his own self, instead of fantasy and empty caprice, in the work he has completed in accordance with its truth."[71] Does this assertion not comport with van Gogh's view cited earlier that art is not wrought by hands alone but "wells up from a deeper source"?

Can Hegel's philosophical writings and his correspondence be viewed not only as mutually extending one another as text and commentary but also as undoing or contaminating one another? Are van Gogh's writing and painting similarly related as symbiotic and disjunctive, so reciprocally imbricated that, as Artaud notes, only van Gogh can "piece" it, whether "not being the creator of a van Gogh canvas you could describe it as miraculously" as he does?[72] What interpretive prospects are opened when the life attested in letters and the account of art in Hegel's philosophical system are read in tandem? Or should one in the manner of Derrida find no criterion for their separability so that the distinction between books and letters remains open?[73] For Derrida, is life not a text? Yet, if each is seen as a series of terms, do we not have multiple series "each giving us to read not so much 'full' terms subsequently mounted together like pearls on a string" but rather their difference?

> Each term of this series names an event of interruption: the serialization marks the interruption between these interruptions and in doing so prevents them from being clean or absolute cuts. There is therefore relation and contamination between the interruptions and what they interrupt. In the very fact of the series [as bond]. Tension of liaison and deliaison ... of gathering and dispersion.[74]

Van Gogh and Hegel, Theo and Christianne, contiguity and separation—the madness and artistry of the work of art.

NOTES

1. *Hegel's Philosophy of Mind: Part Three of the Encyclopedia of the Philosophical Sciences (1830), Translated by William Wallace, Together with the Zusätze in Boumann's Text (1845)*, trans. A. V. Miller (Oxford: Clarendon Press, 1971), pp. 122–140. For an account of the sources and methods used in assembling the *Zusätze* and justifying their inclusion, see J. N. Findlay, foreword to ibid., pp. vi–xix. References to the conception of the artist will be found in G. W. F. Hegel, *Aesthetics: Lectures on Fine Art*, trans. T. M. Knox, vol. 1 (Oxford: Clarendon Press, 1975). Page references to the introduction to Hegel's *Aesthetics* are drawn from another volume, *Hegel's Introduction to Aesthetics*, trans. T. M. Knox (Oxford: Clarendon Press, 1979), to facilitate references to an interpretive essay by Charles Karelis included in the latter volume.
2. Richard Wollheim, "Freud and the Understanding of Art," in *The Cambridge Companion to Freud*, ed. Jerome Neu (Cambridge: Cambridge University Press, 1991), p. 264.
3. Hermann Nunbeg and Ernest Fedora, eds., *The Minutes of the Vienna Psychoanalytic Society* (New York: International Universities Press, 1962), vol. 2, p. 39, quoted in ibid.
4. *Hegel's Philosophy of Mind*, p. 255. See also G. W. F. Hegel, *Philosophy of Right*, trans. T. M. Knox (Oxford: Oxford University Press), p. 110.
5. Martin Heidegger, "The Origin of the Work of Art," in *Poetry, Language, Thought*, trans. Albert Hofstadter (New York: Harper & Row, 1971).
6. Jacques Derrida, "Restitutions," in *The Truth in Painting*, trans. Geoff Bennington and Ian McLeod (Chicago: University of Chicago Press, 1987).
7. *Hegel's Philosophy of Mind*, p. 123.
8. Ibid., p. 124.
9. Sigmund Freud, "Delusion and Dream," trans. Harry Zohn, in *Delusion and Dream and Other Essays*, ed. Philip Rieff (Boston: Beacon Press, 1956), p. 104.
10. *Hegel's Philosophy of Mind*, p. 126.
11. Sigmund Freud, "The Antithetical Sense of Primal Words," in *On Creativity and the Unconscious: Papers on the Psychology of Art, Literature, Love, Religion*, ed. Benjamin Nelson (New York: Harper & Row, 1958). [Reprinted from *Collected Papers*, vol. 4, trans. supervised Joan Riviere (London: Hogarth Press, 1925)]
12. *Hegel's Philosophy of Mind*, p. 132.
13. Ibid., p. 135.
14. Jean-Paul Sartre, "Existentialist Psychoanalysis," in *Existentialism and Human Emotions*, trans. Bernard Frechtman (New York: Philosophical Library, 1957), pp. 72–73.
15. Jean-Paul Sartre, *Being and Nothingness: An Essay on Phenomenological Ontology*, trans. Hazel E. Barnes (New York: Philosophical Library, 1956), p. 74. Although the nineteenth century's allegedly scientific practices of phrenology, the examination of the skull, and physiognomy, the reading of facial expressions in the interest of psycho-

logical interpretation, are rejected by Hegel, his analyses are seen to raise issues that are premonitory of recent biochemical and neurophysiological accounts of psychological states as sufficient causes of human action. See Alasdair MacIntyre, "Hegel on Faces and Skulls," in *Hegel: A Collection of Critical Essays*, ed. Alasdair MacIntyre (Notre Dame, Ind.: University of Notre Dame Press, 1972). The complexity of recent scientific developments renders the assumption of a deep connection to nineteenth-century accounts somewhat tenuous.

16. Justus Streller, *Jean-Paul Sartre: To Freedom Condemned: A Guide to His Philosophy*, (New York: Philosophical Library, 1960), p. 153. This work is a composite of Sartre's texts (translated by Wade Baskin) and Streller's interpretations.
17. *Hegel's Philosophy of Mind*, p. 137.
18. Walter Kaufmann, *Hegel: A Reinterpretation* (Notre Dame, Ind.: University of Notre Dame Press, 1978), pp. 298–370.
19. Derrida, "Restitutions," pp. 283–284.
20. *Hegel: The Letters*, trans. Clark Butler and Christianne Seiler, commentary by Clark Butler (Bloomington: Indiana University Press, 1984), p. 407.
21. Ibid., p. 408.
22. Terry Pinkard, *Hegel: A Biography* (Cambridge: Cambridge University Press, 2000), pp. 315ff. See also Horst Althaus Aujard, *Hegel: An Intellectual Biography*, trans. Michael Tarsh (Oxford: Blackwell, 2000), pp. 164–165.
23. Hegel to Christianne, August 12, 1821, in *Hegel: The Letters*, p. 418.
24. Editorial comment, in ibid., p. 421.
25. *Hegel's Philosophy of Mind*, p. 124.
26. Ibid., p. 126.
27. Jacques Derrida, *Acts of Religion*, ed. Gil Anidjar (New York: Routledge, 2002), p. 94.
28. Charles Karelis, "Hegel's Concept of Art: An Interpretive Essay," in *Hegel's Introduction to Aesthetics*, pp. xix–xx.
29. *Hegel's Introduction to Aesthetics*, p. 72.
30. Ibid., p. 43.
31. Ibid., p. 72.
32. Ibid., p. 76.
33. Karelis, "Hegel's Concept of Art," p. xxiv.
34. Ibid., p. xxvi.
35. *Hegel's Introduction to Aesthetics*, p. 55.
36. Ibid., p. 71.
37. Ibid., p. 76.
38. Ibid., p. 79.
39. Ibid.
40. Ibid., p. 81.
41. Hegel, *Aesthetics*, p. 545.
42. Ibid., p. 565.
43. Ibid., pp. 566–567.
44. Ibid., p. 568.

45. Robert Wicks, "Hegel's Aesthetics: An Overview," in *Cambridge Companion to Hegel*, ed. Frederick C. Beiser (Cambridge: Cambridge University Press, 1993), p. 350.
46. *Hegel's Introduction to Aesthetics*, pp. 10–11.
47. Ibid., p. 90.
48. Hegel, *Philosophy of Right*, p. 279. See also Pinkard, *Hegel*, pp. 602–603.
49. Kaufmann, *Hegel*, p. 72.
50. Editorial comment, in *Hegel: The Letters*, p. 423.
51. Hegel to Karl Friedrich Ernst Frommann, April 19, 1817, in ibid., p. 434.
52. Hegel to Frommann, September 2, 1814, in ibid., p. 428.
53. Editorial comment, in ibid., p. 437.
54. Hegel to his fiancée, Marie von Tucher, summer 1811, in ibid., pp. 243–244.
55. Atonin Artaud, "The Man Suicided by Society," in *Selected Writings*, ed. Susan Sontag, trans. Helen Weaver (New York: Farrar, Straus and Giroux, 1976), p. 497.
56. Ibid., p. 487.
57. Van Gogh to Theo van Gogh, October 1884, in *The Letters of Vincent van Gogh*, ed. Ronald de Leeuw, trans. Arnold Pomerans (London: Penguin, 1996), p. 279. Van Gogh's brother Theo is the addressee of the all letters by Vincent van Gogh that are cited unless otherwise indicated.
58. Letter of May 3–12, 1882, in ibid., p. 150.
59. Hegel, *Aesthetics*, p. 284.
60. Letter of February 3, 1889, in *Letters of Vincent van Gogh*, p. 432.
61. Reverend Salles to Theo van Gogh, December 31, 1888, http://webexhibits.org/vangogh/letter/18/etc-Salles-1-Theo.htm?qp=hea.
62. Commentary, in *Letters of Vincent van Gogh*, p. 509.
63. Letter of January 9, 1889, in ibid., p. 426.
64. Letter of March 1881, in ibid., p. 99.
65. Letter of December 21, 1881, in ibid., p. 122.
66. Letter of June 1 or 2, 1882, in ibid., p. 167.
67. Commentary, in ibid., p. 171.
68. Letter to Anthon von Rappard, March 18, 1884, in ibid., p. 272.
69. Hegel, *Aesthetics*, p. 292.
70. Ibid.
71. Ibid., p. 298.
72. Antonin Artaud, "Man Suicided by Society," p. 499.
73. Jacques Derrida, *The Post Card: From Socrates to Freud and Beyond*, trans. Alan Bass (Chicago: University of Chicago Press, 1987), p. 61.
74. Jacques Derrida and Geoffrey Bennington, *Jacques Derrida*, trans. Geoffrey Bennington (Chicago: University of Chicago Press, 1993), p. 309.

10

FINITE REPRESENTATION, SPONTANEOUS THOUGHT, AND THE POLITICS OF AN OPEN-ENDED CONSUMMATION

THOMAS A. LEWIS

Hegel's system has often been seen as the apex of a drive toward totalizing completion, hegemony, and closure. His apparent claims to having developed an all-inclusive system marking the end of history have appeared as politically perilous philosophical folly. While these concerns stalk Hegel's thought as a whole, the contemporary political environment—with the recently more visible power of the "Religious Right" in the United States, debates over the role of Islam in terrorism, and calls for "crusades" in the Middle East—highlight the potential stakes of Hegel's claim that Christianity is the consummate religion. The very notion of a consummate religion and the claim that Christianity is this religion, for instance, provoke a wide range of negative reactions, from postmodernists who reject closure and postcolonialists who reject the apparent ethnocentricity, to name just two groups.[1]

Recently, however, whether by reading Hegel against himself or arguing that Hegel was successful in safeguarding the element of difference he claimed to preserve, a number of scholars have drawn upon Hegel to support theoretical projects that seek to remain—in one way or another—open. One strategy for doing so has been to defend *Vorstellung*, or representation, against the pretensions of a philosophical thinking, *Denken*, that claims to comprehend all that is important in representations. Tied to the particular, representation can appear to preserve difference in the face of a mode of thinking that assimilates all to the system. Because of the close association between religion and representation, however, such a strategy would also need to defend religion against philosophy's claims to express its content in a higher, more adequate form. The "turn to religion" thus appears as no coincidence in the context of attempts to resist or undermine the models of reason with which Hegel's thought is often associated.[2]

Yet, to turn away from philosophy toward religion raises more dangers than it dispels. Rather than quelling concerns about closure in Hegel's system, his account of religion—particularly his view of Christianity as the consummate religion—constitutes a stumbling block that can only be overcome by appreciating the way in which religious representations are sublated in philosophical thought.[3] Only then can the idea of a consummate religion be interpreted so that even it avoids a perilous form of closure.

In developing this interpretation, I will argue that more promising avenues for an open-ended interpretation of Hegel's system lie in a group of recent reinterpretations of the basic character of Hegel's idealism—thus, reinterpretations of the guiding aims of his philosophical project as a whole. Emphasizing Hegel's debt to Kant and his intention to complete rather than repudiate the critical project, interpreters such as Robert Pippin and Terry Pinkard have rejected the interpretation of Hegel's logic as principally metaphysical in favor of a reading that focuses on the spontaneous and social character of thought.[4]

One of the greatest challenges to this interpretation concerns how to interpret the completion claimed for the system. Hegel's philosophy of religion is particularly relevant in this regard precisely because its claims for the consummation of religion in Christianity are easily taken as some of Hegel's most dramatic and problematic claims for closure. Moreover, this style of argument seems to have underwritten colonialist projects of the nineteenth century as well support more recent neoimperial interventions. While not denying that others have found in Hegel and closely related discourses resources to justify a wide range of repressive practices, I will argue that it is precisely in exploring consummation in relation to this distinctly post-Kantian reading that we will find Hegel's philosophy of religion—and consequently his system as a whole—to be much more open to further development than has often been thought. Doing so also contributes to a broader project of vindicating this general strategy for interpreting Hegel against those who think it necessarily ignores his treatment of religion.

SPONTANEITY AND THE QUESTION OF CLOSURE IN HEGEL'S LOGIC

Recent debate over how to understand the aims of Hegel's logic is largely a debate over how to situate Hegel in the broader context of German idealism—especially how to understand his relationship to Kant. Though Hegel claims to extend Kant's critical project, he has often been interpreted as repudiating its central claims by denying the limits of knowledge set out in Kant's *Critique of Pure Reason*. As scholars have raised powerful arguments against this interpretation, the ensuing discussion has been lively, heated, and extensive. Consequently, even a comprehensive introduction to the debate is impossible in this context. Instead of tracing the debate as a whole, this section sketches a few of the crucial elements of the line of interpretation that eschews the cosmic monism so often attributed to Hegel in the past. The sketch is not intended to be an adequate defense but simply to provide a treatment of the position sufficient to serve as a background to the discussion of closure in the philosophy of religion.

Hegel appears to reject Kant's claims about the limits of knowledge insofar as he rejects the idea of unknowable things-in-themselves and instead argues for the identity of thought and being. Thus, in a crucial passage toward the end of the logic, Hegel writes that

> everything actual *is* only in so far as it possesses the Idea and expresses it. It is not merely that the object, the objective and subjective world in general, *ought to be congruous with the Idea*, but they are themselves the congruence of concept and reality; the reality that does not correspond to the concept is mere *appearance*, the subjective, contingent, capricious element that is not the truth.... What anything actual is supposed in truth *to be*, if its concept is not in it and if its objectivity does not correspond to its concept at all, it is impossible to say; for it would be nothing. (*WL* 2:464/756)[5]

Though this passage initially appears to reinstate the metaphysical claims that Kant's heirs reject, Pippin argues that passages such as this seek to articulate "the conditions necessary for objects to be objects at all."[6] Without the concepts and categories that are produced by thinking itself—not derived from the object—there would be no objects. Hegel here extends Kant's insight that categories coming from the mind rather than from objects themselves are necessary for us to have experience. Yet for Hegel it is nonsensical to even speak of "objects" abstracted from such categories and concepts. Kant's mistake was to posit some object, what Hegel refers to as the "spectral thing-in-itself," that is left outside of or only approached by thinking and its conceptual activity (*WL* 1:41/47).[7] Hegel's claim is not that we can cross over limits to reason highlighted by Kant but that the so-called things-in-themselves are merely chimeras generated by metaphysical presuppositions. As Hegel writes in the passage just quoted, "what anything actual is supposed in truth *to be*, if its concept is not in it and if its objectivity does not correspond to its concept at all, it is impossible to say; for it would be nothing."[8] Hegel's claims regarding the role of thinking in constituting objects, then, do not entail that these objects are metaphysical substances or that they are created by some supersensible being.

Interpreting Hegel's project in these terms requires attending to the elements of Kant's thought that Hegel wants to extend. Kant seeks to rescue knowledge from the twin perils of skepticism and rationalist metaphysics through a two-source view of knowledge, in which knowledge is possible for sensible creatures such as ourselves only as a result of two, coessential elements: sensibility, which is responsible for intuition, and understanding. The account of sensibility functions to explain subject-independent "input," avoiding solipsism. Yet—contra empiricist accounts of knowledge—sensibility alone cannot provide knowledge. In addition, we require that this "data" be assembled or combined. Without this uniting or combining of representations, Kant argues, we could not have experience and there would be no objects, for "an *object* is that in the concept of which the manifold of a given intuition is *united*" (*KrV* B137).[9] This combination is not given or caused by objects of experience but is produced by the understanding itself. The pure concepts of the understanding, or categories, provide the rules according to which this combination occurs.

In setting up the deduction of these categories, Kant argues that for any representation to be mine, it must be capable of being accompanied by "I think" (*KrV* B131). For all of these representations to be *mine*, I must be capable of uniting them in one self-consciousness (*KrV* B134). This self-consciousness regarding representations—which makes this combining possible—is what Kant refers to as apperception (*KrV* B132). As Kant writes, "synthetic unity of the manifold of intuitions, as generated *a priori*, is thus the ground of the identity of apperception itself, which precedes *a priori* all *my* determinate thought.... [Combination] is an affair of the understanding alone, which itself is nothing but the faculty of combining *a priori*, and of bringing the manifold of given representations under the unity of apperception" (*KrV* B134). This combination cannot be explained by an object independent of the understanding but rather must be seen as the spontaneous activity of the understanding itself.

Hegel focuses on this activity of combination and holds that in the latter part of the deduction, particularly in the B version, Kant partially undermines the strict separation of intuition and understanding that initially seemed central to his account of knowledge. At points, Kant suggests that the synthetic unity of apperception places constraints on sensibility and ultimately on objects themselves (see especially *KrV* B150–152); the power of combining places limits on what can be combined and thus on intuitions. Insofar as sensibility itself is constrained by the understanding, Kant seems to undermine the strict separation that he initially posits between these two sources of knowledge.[10]

Hegel picks up and advances the focus on spontaneity and takes it to entail that the relation between the understanding and sensibility cannot be fixed in a general manner. Yet neither does he collapse the distinction. Instead, he argues this distinction should be understood as a "relative antithesis" that allows for sensible input and does not aspire to be a divine intellect (*GuW* 305/70).¹¹ The significance of the input of the senses, however, is always determined by concepts that are ultimately the products of thinking itself.

Hegel provides his most extensive account of the self-determining character of thought in the *Science of Logic*. As Hegel conceives of his logic, it has thinking itself for its object: "Logic is to be understood as the system of pure reason, as the realm of pure thought" (*WL* 1:44/50). This system has an inner dynamism, however, and elucidating it is therefore a matter of thought thinking itself—what Hegel refers to as the "inner self-movement of the content of the logic" (*WL* 1:49/53). This focus on self-movement extends the Kantian concern with spontaneity—of the understanding for Kant, of thought for Hegel. The project cannot consist of examining thought from some position outside itself or of somehow discovering rules whose origin is independent of thinking itself: "It is in this way that the system of concepts as such has to be formed—and has to complete itself in a purely continuous course in which nothing extraneous is introduced" (*WL* 1:49/54). To provide external input to this process would undermine the notion of self-determination central to Hegel's conception of thinking. (Crucially, however, thought's determining of its own categories does not preclude its taking up content from without; Hegel is not here simply adopting the intuitive understanding that Kant proposes in the *Critique of the Power of Judgment*.)¹² One key, then, is to grasp thought as self-moving, generating a process of unfolding through distinct determinations. Only in this manner, by tracing thought's own, spontaneous activity, can we grasp the forms of thought that are necessary for objects to be objects. If his idealism is understood along these lines, Hegel's logic does not involve some superhuman entity or being such as a deity positing the universe. Nor is it a form of spirit monism. Hegel does not reinstate the metaphysical projects that Kant sought to undermine or return to a pre-Kantian, precritical metaphysics, but rather extends a central element of Kant's own idealism.

Perhaps the greatest challenges to interpreting Hegel's logic along these lines concerns the character of the completion achieved at the end of the work. Hegel seems to indicate that the Concept, or Notion, with which the logic concludes is the necessary outcome of all possible forms of thought, making it the final and highest possible form of thinking. Here, the immanent development—thought's spontaneous self-determination—seems to come to an end. Such a view can easily appear to be at odds with an interpretation in which thought's movement is spontaneous rather than preordained or determined by a structure or entity exterior to this thinking itself.

While acknowledging that Hegel does at points claim a more substantive form of closure, Pippin contends that Hegel's argument in the logic supports a weaker, more formal conception of closure: "The resolution in question is an absolute comprehension of the nature of the incompleteness of thought's determination of itself, of the necessity for reflectively determined Notions, and yet the instability and ultimate inadequacy of those Notions."[13] Here, the emphasis on the criteria of judgment always being immanent to the practices, rather than appealing to some standard external to the practices, seems to find its only appropriate completion, one that leaves these practices always open to further transformation. The completion here consists in a comprehension of the recurring movement and instability of any particular concepts. For Pippin, this comprehension is the only rest achieved.

While I believe that the latter interpretation provides for the most consistent reading of Hegel's project as a whole, my point here is not to argue that point. Rather, the ambiguity itself provides a useful lens for considering the form of closure offered in Hegel's philosophy of religion: does the end of the system entail an end of change altogether or merely a new level of self-transparency that leaves open and even anticipates further movement and change?

PHILOSOPHY OF RELIGION

Keeping these elements of Hegel's thought in mind, I turn now to the philosophy of religion to ask what insight it sheds on the question of closure. Hegel's philosophy of religion begins by distinguishing the mode of cognition characteristic of religion, representation (*Vorstellung*), from the mode of cognition characteristic of philosophy, thought (*Denken*). Representation begins from content that appears as merely given rather than self-determined by cognition itself. It is characterized by images, symbols, and allegories and consequently presents objects as finite and standing over against each other. Thought, by contrast, overcomes the givenness of content characterizing representation and abstracts from the particularity of representations.[14] This distinction enables Hegel to argue that religion and philosophy have the same object—the Absolute—and ultimately the same content yet express this shared content differently. Sharing a common object entails that religion and philosophy neither stand in conflict nor are simply relegated to distinct realms. "The Absolute" initially functions as a placeholder for that which Hegel's philosophy identifies as Spirit. Hegel's system as a whole seeks to articulate in the language of philosophy what religious representations express in metaphors, symbols, and narratives.

A central task of Hegel's philosophy of religion is to demonstrate the way in which historical religions have sought to represent the Absolute. Thus, after the introduction and part 1 set out the concept of religion—particularly the relationship between religion and philosophy—he turns in part 2 to the history of religions: "Determinate Religion." Here he examines a wide range of religious traditions with regard to how they conceive of the Absolute.[15] In doing so, he seeks to trace the developments in conceptions of the Absolute toward greater and greater adequacy. This development culminates in what he identifies as the consummate religion, Christianity, which finally represents Spirit as Spirit.

THE CONSUMMATE RELIGION

Hegel begins his introduction of the consummate religion with a concise, formal definition: The consummate religion is "the religion that is for itself, that is objective to itself" (*VPR* 3:177). He makes this point each time he lectures on the topic, and it is even more prominent in the 1824 lectures than in the more widely read 1827 lectures (*VPR* 3:99–105). The fundamental task of the final section of the lectures is to unpack this definition.

At the most comprehensive level, this definition entails that the consummate religion is religion that has religion as its object. As he states in the 1824 lectures,

> Now, therefore, God is as consciousness, or the consciousness of God means that finite consciousness has its essence, this God, as its object; and it knows the object as its essence, it objectifies it for itself. In the consciousness of God there are two sides: the one side is God, the other is that where consciousness as such stands. With the consciousness of God we arrive directly at one side, which is what we have called religion. This content is now itself an object. It is the whole that is an object to itself, or religion has become objective to itself. It is *religion* that has become objective to itself—religion as the consciousness of God, or the self-consciousness of God as the return of consciousness into itself. (*VPR* 3:99)

Since religion is understood as consciousness of the Absolute, the consummate religion is religion that is a consciousness of this consciousness. Thus, in the consummate religion, religion's object is not simply the object itself, "God," but precisely the consciousness of this object.

Crucial to the interpretation of Hegel's thought as a whole is the question, to whom does this latter consciousness belong? If Spirit is understood as Other to human beings, this conception falls into contradictions: it becomes impossible to clarify whether we are dealing with the consciousness of human beings or of some transcendent being referred to as Spirit. Hegel's claim, however, is that human beings collectively constitute Spirit through our social practices, and in the consummate religion we grasp this. That is, as the passage from 3:99 indicates, in the consummate religion we, humans, grasp that Absolute as our own essence. The consummate religion is not a consciousness of some other, but rather Spirit's consciousness of itself—and specifically of itself as conscious of itself in this religion. It is thus self-consciousness. While the entire history of religions is the history of attempts to grasp the Absolute, here the consummate religion is achieved precisely because the Absolute is conceived as grasping itself in religion: "This means that *spirit* is the object of religion, and the object of the latter—essence knowing itself—is spirit. Here for the first time, spirit is as such the object, the content of religion, and spirit *is* only *for* spirit" (3:179). The distinctive feature of Spirit that comes to the fore in the consummate religion is precisely Spirit's self-consciousness. The consummate religion will be the religion that provides a satisfactory representation of Spirit as self-conscious.

For this reason, the religion's content is essential to its being the consummate religion. What makes it consummate is that it represents the Absolute in this manner. Because the consummate religion must *cognize* Spirit through representation, Hegel links this general definition of religion to the notion of a revelatory [*offenbar*] religion: "This absolute religion is the *revelatory* religion that has itself as its content and fulfillment" (3:179). Hegel develops this account of religion as revelatory largely in relation to the idea of positivity. Thus, the sentence continues, "but it is also called the *revealed* [*geoffenbart*] religion—which means, on the one hand, that it is revealed by God, that God has given himself for human beings to know what he is; and on the other hand, that it is a revealed, *positive* religion in the sense that it has come to humanity from without, has been given to it" (3:179).[16]

The consummate religion is necessarily revealed, then, in two senses: First, it provides a representation of God; the Absolute is not hidden. This decisive characteristic of Hegel's consummate religion stands in marked opposition to conceptions of religion as fundamentally mysterious or Other to human understanding. Second, it is positive, which is to say that it comes to human beings from outside. The discussion of positivity is particularly important because of the light it sheds on the ways in which the particulars of Christian doctrine are essential to Christianity's being the consummate religion. In stressing "revelation," Hegel could be seen as linking the consummation of religion to Christian Scripture. That interpretation, however, neglects Hegel's distinctive understanding of positivity. Religion is positive in one sense in that it comes to individual human beings as something external and given. As with ethical mores, institutions such as churches and the family teach religion to children, and it initially appears to these children as a simple given: "even the ethical comes to us in an external mode, chiefly in the form of education, instruction, doctrine: it is simply given to us as something valid as it stands" (3:180). This initial relationship, however, is only the beginning. *This* aspect of positivity concerns the process through which individual human beings are brought to these truths, not the nature of content itself.

That these representations come to us in this manner is irrelevant to their validity. The positive form does not preclude the rationality of their content—though neither does it secure it. Their validity derives from their rationality, from their expressing Spirit, rather than from their positive form. Continuing the parallel with ethics, Hegel states, "when we grasp or recognize the law, when we find it rational that crime should be punished, this is not because law is positive but rather because it has an essential status for us. . . . Positivity does not in any way detract from its character as rational and therefore as something that is our own" (3:180).

Yet there is a remainder, an element of the positivity that cannot be justified simply by reason. While the basic shape can be rational, determinate existence requires specificity that cannot be justified by reason. While imprisonment for a crime may be rational, for instance, reason cannot justify 365 days as intrinsically more rational than 360 or 370 as the punishment for a given infraction. Hegel describes this *merely* positive element—what is "positive according to its nature"—as "without reason" (3:181, my translation). These merely contingent aspects of positivity are present in the sphere of religion as well: "Since historically, externally appearing elements are found in it, there is also present a positive and contingent [feature], which can just as well take one form as another" (3:181). Although consummate religion requires determinacy—it cannot be merely abstract—the nonrational particulars are not in and of themselves essential to its being consummate. They could be otherwise without undermining the consummate character of the religion. That which is merely historical, for instance, cannot be essential to its being the consummate religion, for the merely positive elements do not determine whether or not the religion represents Spirit as self-conscious.

This point is crucial in seeking to answer what makes Christianity the consummate religion. It is not the historical particulars in and of themselves but rather the account of spirit provided by its representations.[17] That which is *merely* positive and therefore not justified by reason is not what makes it the consummate religion.

The next step in the articulation of the consummate religion is the setting forth of the content of its representation of Spirit. The images, narratives, and doctrines of the consummate religion must represent the essence of Spirit. This framing of the consummate religion sets a double task for the substantive sections.[18] They must both give an account of what spirit is and demonstrate that Christian doctrine provides this account. Hegel executes this double task simultaneously through the explication of Christian doctrines. To do so, he must present Christian doctrine, including its narratives and practices, in such a way that it represents the essence of spirit (as this has been developed in philosophical terms earlier in Hegel's system). Doing so will both set forth the elements of the characterization of spirit that are essential to being the consummate religion and demonstrate that Christianity possesses these elements.

In the schematic account of these elements in the final section of the introduction to the consummate religion, we find three moments, corresponding to the three moments of the Concept set out in Hegel's logic: universality, particularity, and singularity (3:198). These moments also track the three segments of Hegel's system: the logic, the philosophy of nature, and the philosophy of Spirit. The consummate religion must represent these three moments and thereby the self-determining and ultimately self-conscious movement that is spirit. While these moments are explicitly identified with the moments from the logic, the philosophy of religion examines how they are expressed in Christian doctrine. Thus, the philosophy of religion discusses these three moments not in the most abstract forms of the logic but as they are represented in the Trinity. The first moment is expressed in terms of "the eternal idea of God for itself, what God is for himself, i.e., the eternal Idea in the soil of thinking as such" (3:197). This is the consideration of the Absolute in itself—in the realm of thinking, not as manifest in determinate existence. The second moment is "the determinate being that God gives himself for the sake of representation" (3:197). This second moment includes the creation of nature, humanity, and the Incarnation. While this second moment begins the process of reconciliation, it is completed in the third moment, in which "reconciliation, the sublation of that separation, is made actual; here God as spirit is in his community" (3:198). God is known as present in—not other than—the community itself. In its consciousness of God, then, the community is conscious of itself, not of some deity that is other.

The remainder of the lectures elaborates these three moments as represented in Christian doctrine. The key to interpreting this discussion lies in appreciating Hegel's conception of representation. Hegel's account is replete with traditional Christian language regarding the Trinity. One of the central tasks of the section is to demonstrate that his philosophy of spirit reveals the truth of Christianity. Yet he understands these doctrines to present this truth in representational form, so that any analysis of these doctrines must take this *form* into account. Hegel is remarkably explicit on this point. After discussing the first two moments of the Trinity in terms of the Father and the Logos, he states,

> These are the forms in which this truth, this idea, has fermented. The main point is to know that these appearances, wild as they are, are rational—to know that they have their ground in reason, and to know what sort of reason is in them. But at the same time one must know how to distinguish the form of rationality that is present and not yet adequate to the content. For this idea has in fact been placed beyond human beings, beyond the world, beyond thought and reason; indeed, it has been placed over against them, so that this determinate quality, though it is the sole truth and the

whole truth, has been regarded as something peculiar to God, something that remains permanently above and beyond. (3:214)

For the philosophy of religion, the task of interpreting these doctrines is the task of identifying what is rational in them, which is to say the way in which they represent spirit. Accordingly, in the analysis of the story of the events in the Garden of Eden, we find such language as, "What it really means is" and "This, too, is expressed in a simple, childlike image" (3:225, 227). Interpreting these materials requires seeing through the images to discover their rational meanings. This is the key to unlocking both Christian doctrine and Hegel's discussion of this doctrine.

Human cognition is easily misled in this interpretive task because the representational form provides images of this object as somewhere beyond and Other than human beings. That is, religious representation projects spirit beyond us.[19] Many of the crucial features of Feuerbach's theory of religion as projection are already present here. In the penultimate chapter of the *Phenomenology of Spirit*, Hegel argues that even in its highest instantiations religion remains intrinsically alienating due to its representational form: The reconciliation that is represented in Christian doctrine "remains burdened with the antithesis of a beyond. Its own reconciliation therefore enters its consciousness as something *distant*, as something in the distant *future*, just as the reconciliation which the other *self* [Christ] achieved appears as something in the distant *past*" (*PhG* 574/para. 787). Even in the *Phenomenology*'s consummate religion, satisfaction remains elsewhere. Alienation is only overcome with the transition to philosophy.[20]

By the time of the 1827 Berlin *Lectures on the Philosophy of Religion*, however, Hegel's view has subtly shifted: Though Hegel still portrays the representational form of religion as projecting, he no longer depicts it as intrinsically alienating.[21] Rather, as we will see in a moment, the modern, Lutheran cultus provides the reconciliation that was always projected beyond in the *Phenomenology*'s account of religion. In the 1827 version of the philosophy of religion, then, conceiving of religion as projection is not, in Hegel's eyes, a criticism of religion. While religion does not thereby achieve a status equal to philosophy's—due to the limitations of its representational form—its relative significance for reconciliation increases significantly. Thus, in Hegel's final view, understanding the truth of Christian doctrine requires an interpretation that sees these representations for what they are: metaphorical and mythical expressions of the Absolute, which mislead if—but only if—they are taken to be in tension with the philosophical expressions of the same content.

The three moments represented by the Trinity are precisely what make Christianity the consummate religion. The claim is not that these three moments are the content of the consummate religion because they are represented by the Christian Trinity but the other way around: Christianity is the consummate religion because its doctrines express these moments. The consummate religion needs to represent each of these moments, though the particular images, narratives, and ritual practices that it uses to do so could in principle vary; such particularities are *merely* positive.

While this distinction between necessary content and mere positivity presents itself in each of the three moments, the third—the cultus—illustrates it most powerfully. Here we see that the essential content of the consummate religion is the self-consciousness of Spirit. The conception of the Holy Spirit as present within the Christian community—to use religious language—represents the reconciliation of humanity with the Absolute by portraying the Absolute as present within the religious community itself: "Thus, the community itself is the existing spirit, the spirit in its existence, God existing as community" (*VPR* 3:254). The practices of the community—the more obviously religious practices such as prayer but also the ethical practices—make spirit actual: "Participation in this reconciliation that is implicitly and explicitly accomplished is the action of the cultus" (1:332). God is no longer conceived as other to the community. What is known here in the third moment is "the identity of the divine and the human. The third element, then, is this consciousness—God as spirit. This spirit as existing and realizing itself in the community" (3:254). Through participating in the cultus, members come to grasp the Absolute as Spirit, that is, as self-conscious in and through the cultus's practices. Through the church, "they as subjects *are* the active expression [*das Betätigende*] of spirit" (3:256). They thereby bring about the realization of spirit as self-conscious.

This reconciliation and overcoming of difference has both practical and theoretical—or conscious—dimensions (1:331). Hegel emphasizes the church's role in transmitting the established doctrines or content of the faith. The church presents these teachings as something given and positive, which is then internalized by the individual participants in the community. Consequently, "the church is essentially a teaching church" (3:257). In this respect, the doctrines are positive in the first sense discussed earlier: they come to the individual from without. Appropriating this content, however, is not simply a matter of memorizing doctrines but of internalizing them, cultivating a consciousness. This process, in Hegel's view, entails a vital role for a wide range of devotional practices, sacraments, and other external forms through which this reconciliation is realized. Hegel's appreciation of the practical dimensions of the cultus is worth underscoring: religious practices play an essential role in shaping the consciousness that achieves this reconciliation: "This is the concern of education, practice, cultivation. With such education and appropriation it is a question of becoming habituated to the good and the true"

(3:259). These practices shape us to accord with the truth of and participate in Spirit. Their ultimate significance lies not in the particularities of their form but in their role in enabling us to appropriate this conception of spirit: "Therefore it is the concern of the church that this habituating and educating of spirit should become ever more identical with the self, with the human will, and that this truth should become one's volition, one's object, one's spirit" (3:260). They bring about the overcoming of the apparent division between particular human beings and infinite spirit.[22]

The final section of the discussion of the community focuses on the forms of consciousness that correspond to different historical forms of Christian community. Hegel sketches the history of Christian notions of community and illuminates the representation of spirit contained in each of these stages. This development within Christianity culminates in the knowledge of spirit achieved in the present, post-Enlightenment age, in which philosophy provides the highest justification for religion—"the witness of spirit" in thought (3:268). In this highest stage of the consummate religion, "it is free reason, which has being on its own account, that develops the content in accord with its necessity and justifies the content of truth. This is the standpoint of a knowledge that recognizes and cognizes a truth" (3:267). What is essential to the consummate religion is only that which is validated by philosophy. The latter knows the limits of the form of representation and is able to distinguish what is rational from what is merely contingent and arbitrary in these representations. Accordingly, the fundamental requirement for the community of the consummate religion is that it recognize that spirit is manifest, is present, in its practices. The teachings and practices must represent this insight, though the particular, accidental features of the rituals are not in themselves essential. Moreover, the consummate religion must itself—in its representations and not only in a corresponding philosophy—somehow draw this distinction between what is essential and what is merely positive, between the spirit and the letter.

Regarding the question of open-endedness in the consummate religion, this point entails that the accidental features of the practices can change. They are not necessary for the consummate religion. Other rituals that represent and preserve this self-consciousness might be equally appropriate. The implications, however, extend beyond the mere compatibility of the Notion of a consummate religion and the possibility of further development. This religion's consciousness necessarily incorporates this awareness of what is essential and what is merely accidental. Consequently, this openness to the further transformation and development of practices that express this consciousness is an essential feature of the consummate religion itself.

The openness to further development that exists at this level returns us to the question of the fundamental openness of this conclusion. Does Hegel's consummate religion support or undermine a conception of closure that is not some final Notion but rather, as Pippin writes, "an absolute comprehension of the nature of the incompleteness of thought's determination of itself, of the necessity for reflectively determined Notions, and yet the instability and ultimate inadequacy of those Notions"?[23]

While the account of the community provides part of an answer, Hegel's treatment of the consummate religion as a whole intends to demonstrate that this religion represents the same content as his philosophy. By doing so, the discussion of the consummate religion simultaneously refers us elsewhere: to the larger structure of the system. The consummate religion simply sets out in the forms of representation, or *Vorstellung*, the same moments that are treated in more philosophical terms by Hegel's system as a whole.[24] To ask whether the conclusion of this larger system allows for further movement leads us to the final sphere of the system, Absolute Spirit, which consists of art, religion, and philosophy. The insufficiency of art lies in the finitude of its conception of Spirit; it cannot provide the answer.

To be returned to the philosophy of religion itself suggests a circularity, but this circularity need not be viewed as vicious. The circularity stresses once more the centrality of self-consciousness as the key to the consummation. Spirit's consciousness of itself stands as the defining feature of the consummation, and any particular content that makes this self-knowledge possible is commensurate with the consummate religion. This circularity itself supports the idea that the completion or consummation consists not in a particular content but in a consciousness of particular content and its instability.

Let me briefly suggest two other places we must look: There are two other versions of the conclusion of the system in Hegel's mature thought: the *Lectures on the History of Philosophy* and the *Encyclopaedia*.[25] Both are striking in suggesting that the completion consists not in some new final concept but in the consciousness or knowledge of the dynamism within all determinate concepts. As Hegel states in final pages of the *Lectures on the History of Philosophy*, "eternal life consists in the very process of continually producing the opposition and continually reconciling it" (*VGP* 3:460/551). This movement continues. The completion is in the knowledge of this movement as continuing. Thus, the paragraph continues: "to know opposition in unity, and unity in opposition—this is absolute knowledge; and science is the knowledge of this unity in its whole development" (3:460/551).

THE POLITICS OF AN OPEN-ENDED HEGELIANISM

At the broadest level, by offering a consummation that is not closure, this interpretation challenges a number of the readings that have linked systematic closure in

Hegel to practical and political exclusions of the other. It suggests that the criticisms of thinkers such as Emmanuel Levinas and Enrique Dussel have at least in part missed their target.[26] The end of development that Hegel proclaims is often seen as precluding genuine difference or alterity; or the alterity is forcibly reduced to sameness in a process that occurs at the level of logic as well as in political struggles. Adorno expresses this view well: "a seamless system and an achieved reconciliation are not one and the same; rather, they are contradictory: the unity of the system derives from unreconcilable violence."[27] But if even the consummate religion is not a definitive endpoint, then perhaps Hegel's larger system need not be understood as negating—or justifying the negation of—all differences. Hegel's "totality" is not as totalizing as these criticisms claim. Although these points can be pursued at many levels, I want to suggest their import for the political significance of his philosophy of religion in particular.

The openness of the consummation has specific implications for the attitude toward other religions that Hegel's project *should* justify. Despite the hierarchy of religions that Hegel establishes in the second part of the philosophy of religion (Determinate Religion), the conception of mere positivity that is integral to his conception of the consummate religion entails that what we tend to think of as other religions might themselves have greater resources for fostering the consciousness and habits that Hegel associates with Protestantism than Hegel himself thought. In making this point, I do not mean to downplay how problematic and disturbing the account of Determinate Religion is. Nonetheless, precisely the open closing of the consummate religion provides Hegelian resources for a greater appreciation of other traditions. If we shift the focus from the larger rubric, "Christianity," to the specific features that constitute its consummateness, we can begin to examine particular religious communities with a more fine-grained lens, appreciating precisely what self-conception and conception of others are produced by that cultus. In this respect, Hegel's philosophy of religion generates a research agenda, studying religions specifically for the self-understandings they inculcate in participants. For such queries, our categories will need to be much more specific than "Christianity" or "Islam," attending closely to differences within these two larger categories, for instance. Doing so may enable us to perceive—much more clearly than Hegel could—a wider range of doctrines and practices that cultivate the self-conceptions he finds uniquely instantiated in Protestantism.[28]

Even this way of interpreting closure, however, still places constraints. Given that so much of this discussion has focused on finding a spirit of openness in Hegel's project, it is also worth emphasizing the way in which these same elements of his thought challenge widespread religious practices. One might argue, in fact, that much of the contemporary political bite of Hegel's philosophy of religion—particularly in relation to United States politics—comes in his implicit condemnation of much of what calls itself Christianity today. Hegel's entire conception of consummation turns upon the notion of a religion that has religion for its object, which means that it represents Spirit as self-conscious in the community itself. As we have seen, one aspect of doing so is that it must include within itself at least some consciousness of which features are intrinsic to its being consummate and which are merely positive elements of the particular representations. His philosophy of religion thereby cuts against religions that take as essential that which is merely positive. Perhaps ironically, precisely those communities that are so focused on the specifics—which are most often the merely positive elements—of the purportedly consummate religion, Christianity, are those that fall farthest from it.

More significantly, however, Hegel's account of the consummate religion illuminates the connection between an inordinate focus on merely positive elements and a failure to cultivate attitudes that support modern self-governance. To take what is merely positive as essential is to fail to grasp the genuine significance of consummate religion: that we collectively constitute Spirit. Instead, such an attitude hangs on precisely the particulars that we have not determined. Failing in this regard, such a religion may thwart one of the most important tasks of the consummate religion: teaching us to conceive of ourselves as the kinds of agents who give ourselves our own norms.[29] And for Hegel, as for many others, it is only by being formed in this way that we become capable of participating fully in what Hegel conceives as modern political institutions—specifically, agents who view authority as grounded in our collective life.[30] Consequently, to take as essential that which is merely positive is not simply to fall short of the highest form of religion; it is to threaten the self-conceptions that support participation in a politically self-determining society. In this respect as well, many of those in the contemporary United States who most loudly proclaim their Christianity and its impact on their political commitments ultimately offer something very far from what Hegel conceives as the consummate religion.

At the same time, Hegel's claim does not entail that individuals who do not participate in the consummate religion are necessarily incapable of participating in modern political institutions. While we should attend to religions' impact on cultivating the attitudes and dispositions that sustain political life—thereby registering a crucial aspect of the relation between religion and politics that is often neglected—religious training is not the unique site of this formation of individuals. Hegel conceives of home, school, and church all working together to instill the proper intuitions; but they may not always do so. Education in the schoolroom, for instance, may do a great deal to nurture relevant attitudes that are not being supported by an individual's church. In such an environment, one's self-conception may be conflicted, but it may still support robust political involvement of the relevant kind. Recently, Jeffrey Stout has drawn attention to the wide range of practices that function to inculcate democratic intuitions in the United States.³¹ These are by no means limited to what goes on in self-described "religious" settings. On the one hand, Hegel's conception of religion should lead us to consider many of these "religious"—by virtue of their use of representation and their constituting our consciousness of Spirit. Yet they are not necessarily part of more conventionally religious traditions, such as Christianity and Islam. And this is no surprise: Hegel should be seen as a major figure in a long line—or perhaps several strands—of reflection on what some have called civil religion, which need not be identified with one of these "conventional" religions.³² Precisely as we think about the significance of Hegel's consummate religion today, we are directed toward broader considerations of the symbols and imagery that inform our self-understanding and, simultaneously, shape our deepest intuitions about our collective life.

Of course, even if interpreting Hegel along these lines opens up greater possibilities for the appreciation of other religions than Hegel's own explicit statements suggest, the resulting view will still not be palatable to all. Doing so may leave open the possibility of further development and suggest strategies for a greater appreciation of other religions than Hegel's own lectures claim, but elements deep within his project—and manifest in the philosophy of religion as well as elsewhere—affirm the superiority of modern Western political institutions and corresponding religious practices. Even if we can reasonably interpret the latter more broadly than Hegel did, we are still faced with a hierarchical view of distinct religions closely associated with distinct political conceptions. Moreover, as we examine religious traditions with these concerns in mind, we are still asking whether or not we find them supportive of what is important to "us." Hegel is neither a relativist nor a radical pluralist. Yet he also forces us to ask whether we would be willing to accept the kind of relativism that rejecting any sense of hierarchy would imply.³³

NOTES

1. See, for instance, Jacques Derrida, *Margins of Philosophy*, trans. Alan Bass (Chicago: University of Chicago Press, 1982), esp. "The Pit and the Pyramid: Introduction to Hegel's Semiology"; Stuart Barnett, ed., *Hegel After Derrida* (London: Routledge, 1998); Enrique D. Dussel, *Método para una filosofía de la liberación: Superación analéctica de la dialéctica hegeliana* (Salamanca: Ediciones Sígueme, 1974); Tomoko Masuzawa, *The Invention of World Religions: Or, How European Universalism Was Preserved in the Language of Pluralism* (Chicago: University of Chicago Press, 2005), esp. pp. 12–13, 42; and Ngũgĩ wa Thiong'o, "The Language of African Literature," in *Colonial Discourse and Post-Colonial Theory: A Reader*, ed. Patrick Williams and Laura Chrisman (New York: Columbia University Press, 1994), pp. 443, 454n.9. Of course, liberals have also claimed to find in Hegel the roots of totalitarianism. For one of the classic formulations,

see Karl Popper, *The Open Society and Its Enemies*, vol. 2, *The High Tide of Prophecy: Hegel, Marx, and the Aftermath* (London: Routledge and Kegan Paul, 1966).

2. For an important example, see Hent DeVries, *Philosophy and the Turn to Religion* (Baltimore: Johns Hopkins University Press, 1999).

3. Although I focus here on religion in Hegel's system, Hegel's argument against placing religion above philosophy is no less relevant to a wide range of other conceptions of religion.

4. Robert B. Pippin, *Hegel's Idealism: The Satisfactions of Self-Consciousness* (Cambridge: Cambridge University Press, 1989); Robert B. Pippin, *Idealism as Modernism: Hegelian Variations* (Cambridge: Cambridge University Press, 1997); Robert B. Pippin, "Naturalness and Mindedness: Hegel's Compatibilism," *European Journal of Philosophy* 7, no. 2 (1999): 194–212; Terry Pinkard, *Hegel's Phenomenology: The Sociality of Reason* (Cambridge: Cambridge University Press, 1994); Terry Pinkard, *Hegel: A Biography* (Cambridge: Cambridge University Press, 2000); Terry Pinkard, *German Philosophy, 1760–1860: The Legacy of Idealism* (Cambridge: Cambridge University Press, 2002). For important recent interpretations that offer alternatives to this current, see Paul W. Franks, *All Or Nothing: Systematicity, Transcendental Arguments, and Skepticism in German Idealism* (Cambridge, Mass.: Harvard University Press, 2005); Frederick C. Beiser, *German Idealism: The Struggle Against Subjectivism, 1781–1801* (Cambridge, Mass.: Harvard University Press, 2002); Stephen Houlgate, *The Opening of Hegel's Logic: From Being to Infinity* (West Lafayette, Ind.: Purdue University Press, 2006); Robert M. Wallace, *Hegel's Philosophy of Reality, Freedom, and God* (Cambridge: Cambridge University Press, 2005); and Merold Westphal, "Hegel and Onto-Theology," *Bulletin of the Hegel Society of Great Britain* 41–42 (2000): 142–165.

5. See also *WL* 1:44/50 and *PR* § 1. References to Hegel's writings and lectures are abbreviated as follows. In citing Hegel, I have made use of previously published translations when available, yet have altered them as I have deemed appropriate. Except as otherwise noted, texts are cited by the page number in the German text followed by a slash and the page number in the English translation, if available. Within quotations, italics are Hegel's unless otherwise noted. *Werke*: *Werke*, ed. Eva Moldenhauer and Karl Markus Michel, 20 vols. (Frankfurt: Suhrkamp, 1969–1971). *Enz*: *Enzyklopädie der philosophischen Wissenschaften* (1830), in *Werke*, vols. 8–10 (cited by paragraph [§] number; remarks are indicated by an "A" [*Anmerkung*] and additions by a "Z" [*Zusatz*]); English translations: *The Encyclopaedia Logic: Part I of the Encyclopaedia of Philosophical Sciences with the Zusätze*, trans. T. F. Geraets, W. A. Suchting, and H. S. Harris (Indianapolis: Hackett, 1991); *Hegel's Philosophy of Mind: Part Three of the Encyclopedia of the Philosophical Sciences (1830), Translated by William Wallace, Together with the Zusätze in Boumann's Text (1845)*, trans. A. V. Miller (Oxford: Clarendon Press, 1971); *Hegel's Philosophy of Subjective Spirit*, trans. Michael J. Petry, 3 vols, bilingual ed. (Dordrecht: Reidel, 1978). *GuW*: *Glauben und Wissen oder Reflexionsphilosophie der Subjektivität in der Vollständigkeit ihrer Formen als Kantische, Jacobische und Fichtesche Philosophie*, in *Werke*, vol. 2, pp. 287–433; English translation: *Faith and Knowledge*, trans. Walter Cerf and H. S. Harris (Albany: State University of New York Press, 1977). *PhG*: *Phän-*

omenologie des Geistes, in *Werke*, vol. 3; English translation: *Phenomenology of Spirit*, trans. A. V. Miller (Oxford: Clarendon Press, 1977). *PR*: *Grundlinien der Philosophie des Rechts*, in *Werke*, vol. 7 (cited by paragraph [§] number; remarks are indicated by an "A" [*Anmerkung*], additions by a "Z" [*Zusatz*], and Hegel's marginal notes by an "N"); English translation: *Elements of the Philosophy of Right*, trans. H. B. Nisbet, ed. Allen W. Wood. (Cambridge: Cambridge University Press, 1991). "TE": "Fragmente über Volksreligion und Christentum, 1," in *Werke*, vol. 1, pp. 9–44; English translation: "Tübingen Essay," in *Three Essays, 1793–1795*, trans. Peter Fuss and John Dobbins (Notre Dame, Ind.: University of Notre Dame Press, 1984), pp. 30–58. *VGP*: *Vorlesungen über die Geschichte der Philosophie*, in *Werke*, vols. 18–20; English translation: *Lectures on the History of Philosophy*, trans. E. S. Haldane and Frances H. Simson, 3 vols. (Lincoln: University of Nebraska Press, 1995). *VPR*: *Vorlesungen über die Philosophie der Religion*, ed. Walter Jaeschke, 3 vols. (Hamburg: Felix Meiner Verlag, 1983–1985) (cited by the German page number, which is included in the margin of the English translation); English translation: *Lectures on the Philosophy of Religion*, ed. Peter C. Hodgson, trans. R. F. Brown, P. C. Hodgson, and J. M. Stewart, 3 vols. (Berkeley: University of California Press, 1984–1987). *WL*: *Wissenschaft der Logik*, in *Werke*, vols. 5–6; English translation: *Hegel's Science of Logic*, trans. A. V. Miller (Atlantic Highlands, N.J.: Humanities Press, 1969).

6. Pippin, *Hegel's Idealism*, p. 176.
7. See also *WL* 1:25–26/36.
8. See also *WL* 2:560/833.
9. Immanuel Kant, *Kritik der reinen Vernunft* (Hamburg: Felix Meiner Verlag, 1998); Immanuel Kant, *Critique of Pure Reason*, trans. Norman Kemp Smith (New York: St. Martin's Press, 1965). Cited by edition and paragraph number.
10. As Karl Ameriks notes, these issues continue to be a source of much disagreement in contemporary Kant scholarship. See Karl Ameriks, *Interpreting Kant's Critiques* (Oxford: Clarendon Press, 2003), pp. 98–99.
11. My argument at this point is deeply indebted to Robert Pippin, "Hegel's Original Insight," *International Philosophical Quarterly* 33, no. 3 (1993): 291.
12. Immanuel Kant, *Critique of the Power of Judgment*, trans. Paul Guyer and Eric Matthews (Cambridge: Cambridge University Press, 2000), § 77. As Pippin notes, Hegel's account allows for "access to 'extra-conceptual content'" ("Hegel's Original Insight," p. 291).
13. Pippin, *Hegel's Idealism*, p. 257.
14. I have discussed representation and thought at much greater length in *Freedom and Tradition in Hegel: Reconsidering Anthropology, Ethics, and Religion* (Notre Dame, Ind.: University of Notre Dame Press, 2005), pp. 86–94.
15. His treatment reveals not only the paucity of information on other traditions available to him but also the alarming distortions of the material he did have to fit these groups into his system. See, for instance, Robert Bernasconi, "Hegel at the Court of Ashanti," in *Hegel After Derrida*, ed. Barnett, pp. 41–63. To focus on the account of completion he does offer, I leave aside here the many important problems raised by Hegel's account of "Determinate Religion."

16. While the English translation by Hodgson et al. divides this into two sentences, the German is one sentence.
17. A final aspect of positivity concerns the role that historical events, particularly miracles, should play in the verification of faith. Anticipating much of the subsequent discussion of the relation between faith and history, Hegel's point here is that no historical event can provide proof of Spirit. With an understanding of Spirit in which consciousness is so central, no historical event could in and of itself prove its existence; no historical event can demonstrate self-consciousness. Only the witness of Spirit is "authentic witness," and "the witness of sprit in its highest form is that of philosophy, according to which the concept develops the truth purely as such from itself without presuppositions" (*VPR* 3:183). The highest—and ultimately the only entirely adequate—proof for religion is the justification that philosophy provides.
18. That these two tasks coincide for Hegel is no coincidence. It derives from Spirit's self-manifesting Nature, such that the consummate religion must be manifest in the world for us to recognize it as such. It is only because this religion has existed that we are in a position to know that Spirit has these particular moments.
19. See also *Enz.* §§ 565–566.
20. I have developed this interpretation at length in "Religion and Demythologization in Hegel's *Phenomenology of Spirit*," in *Hegel's Phenomenology of Spirit: A Critical Guide*, ed. Dean Moyar and Michael Quante (Cambridge: Cambridge University Press, 2008).
21. Although the 1821 lecture manuscript provides some indication of this shift (*VPR* 3:76), it is not fully worked out until the 1827 lectures. The concluding pages of the 1824 lectures, for instance, still posit a contradiction that is only completely overcome in philosophy (*VPR* 3:174–176).
22. I have discussed these points at greater length in *Freedom and Tradition in Hegel*, chap. 8.
23. Pippin, *Hegel's Idealism*, p. 257.
24. One of the places to which we are referred is the treatment of these three moments in the realm of thought itself: the logic. Yet the consummate religion represents the larger movement of Hegel's system as a whole, not only the treatment of these movements within the logic.
25. There are also multiple versions of each of these, in addition to multiple versions of the lectures on the philosophy of religion.
26. Emmanuel Levinas, *Totality and Infinity: An Essay on Exteriority*, trans. Alphonso Lingis (Pittsburgh: Duquesne University Press, 1969); Dussel, *Método para una filosofía de la liberación*.
27. Theodor W. Adorno, *Hegel: Three Studies*, trans. Shierry Weber Nicholsen (Cambridge, Mass.: MIT Press, 1993), p. 27.
28. Moreover, while Hegel's claim that "religion constitutes the *foundation* which embodies the ethical realm in general, and, more specifically, that nature of the state as the divine will" may initially raise concerns about theocracy, his account of the relation between religious representation and philosophical thought grounds his explicit rejection of theocracy (*PR* § 270 A). Although religions play an important role for Hegel in cultivating

the habits and dispositions necessary for political life, the state and its policies must ultimately by justified by appeals to Reason, not to religious authorities or scripture. To subordinate the state to religious authority is to fail to appreciate the proper significance of religious representations as metaphorical and narrative expressions of what we are—which can be given a more authoritative discursive formulation by philosophy. I have dealt with this issue at length in "Cultivating Our Intuitions: Hegel on Religion, Politics, and Public Discourse," *Journal of the Society of Christian Ethics* 27, no. 1 (2007): 205–224.

29. For further development of this point, see Lewis, "Cultivating Our Intuitions."
30. My phrasing here is intended to be broad and inclusive. Even within considerations of Christianity alone, theorists from Alexis de Tocqueville to Robert Bellah to Cornel West suggest the variety of forms of religion that may support democracy. Of course, there are important differences between Hegel's views and theirs (as well as among theirs), but those differences remain beyond the scope of the present paper. See Alexis de Tocqueville, *Democracy in America*, trans. Arthur Goldhammer (New York: Library of America, 2004); Robert N. Bellah, *The Broken Covenant: American Civil Religion in Time of Trial*, 2nd ed. (Chicago: University of Chicago Press, 1992); Robert N. Bellah, "Civil Religion in America," in *Beyond Belief: Essays on Religion in a Post-Traditionalist World* (Berkeley: University of California Press, 1970); and Cornel West, *Democracy Matters: Winning the Fight Against Imperialism* (New York: Penguin Press, 2004).
31. Jeffrey Stout, *Democracy and Tradition* (Princeton, N.J.: Princeton University Press, 2004).
32. Bellah, for instance, describes American civil religion as "exist[ing] alongside of and rather clearly differentiated from the churches" ("Civil Religion in America," p. 168). Hegel's concern with *Volksreligion*, which in this context is best rendered "civil religion," comes out in his earliest surviving essay ("TE").
33. These issues are central to my current book project on religion, modernity, and politics in Hegel.

11

HEGEL AND SHITTING

The Idea's Constipation

SLAVOJ ŽIŽEK

One of the topics of the pseudo-Freudian dismissal of Hegel is to regard his system as the highest and most overblown expression of oral economy: is the Hegelian Idea not a voracious eater that "swallows" every object upon which it stumbles? No wonder Hegel perceived himself as Christian: for him, the ritual eating of bread transubstantiated into Christ's meat signals that the Christian subject can himself integrate and digest, without remainder, God himself. Is, consequently, the Hegelian conceiving/grasping not a sublimated version of digestion? So when Hegel writes:

> If the individual human being does something, achieves something, attains a goal, this fact must be grounded in the way the thing itself, in its concept, acts and behaves. If I eat an apple, I destroy its organic self-identity and assimilate it to myself. That I can do this entails that the apple in itself, already, in advance, before I take hold of it, has in its nature the determination of being subject to destruction, having in itself a homogeneity with my digestive organs such that I can make it homogeneous with myself.[1]

Is what he offers not a lower version of the cognition process itself in which, as Hegel likes to point out, we can only grasp the object if this object itself already "wants to be with/by us"? One should carry this metaphor to the end: the standard critical reading constructs the Hegelian Absolute Substance-Subject as thoroughly *constipated*—keeping in itself the swallowed content. Or, as Adorno put it in one of his biting remarks (which, as is all too often the case with him, misses the mark),

Hegel's system "is the belly turned mind,"[2] pretending that it swallowed the entire indigestible Otherness. But what about the countermovement, the Hegelian shitting excremenation? Is the subject of what Hegel calls "Absolute Knowing" not also a thoroughly *emptied* subject, a subject reduced to the role of pure observer (or, rather, registrator) of the self-movement of the content itself?

> The richest is therefore the most concrete and most *subjective*, and that which withdraws itself into the simplest depth is the mightiest and most all-embracing. The highest, most concentrated point is the pure personality which, solely through the absolute dialectic which is its nature, no less *embraces and holds everything within itself*.[3]

In this strict sense, subject itself is the abrogated/cleansed substance, a substance reduced to the void of the empty form of self-relating negativity, emptied of all the wealth of "personality"—in Lacanese, the move from substance to subject is the one from S to $, that is, subject is the barred substance. (Adorno and Horkheimer, in *The Dialectic of Enlightenment*, make the critical point of how the Self, bent on mere survival, has to scarify all content that would make survival worthy; this very move is what Hegel asserts.) Schelling referred to this same move as *contraction* (again, with the excremental connotation of squeezing the shit out of oneself, dropping it out): subject is the contracted substance.

Does, then, the final subjective position of the Hegelian system not compel us to turn around the digestive metaphor? The supreme (and, for many, the most problematic) case of this countermovement occurs at the very end of logic, when (after the notional deployment is completed, reaching the full circle of the Absolute Idea) the Idea, in its resolve/decision, "freely releases itself"[4] into Nature: lets Nature go, leaves it off, discards it, pushes it away from itself, and thus liberates it. This is why, for Hegel, the philosophy of nature is not a violent reappropriation of this externality; it rather involves the passive attitude of an observer to watch nature sublate its own externality.

The same move is accomplished by God himself who, in the guise of Christ, this finite mortal, also "freely releases itself" into temporal existence. The same goes for the early modern art, which is how Hegel accounts for the rise of the "dead nature" paintings (not only landscapes, flowers, etc., but even pieces of food and dead animals). Because of the development of art, subjectivity no longer needs the visual medium as the principal medium of its expression. For example, because the accent shifted to poetry as a more direct presentation of a subject's inner life, the natural environs is "released" of the burden to express subjectivity and thus gains freedom and can be asserted on its own. And, furthermore, as some perspicuous readers of Hegel have already pointed out, the very sublation of art in philosophical sciences (in conceptual thought), the fact that art is no longer obliged to serve as the principal medium of the expression of the Spirit frees it, thus allowing it to gain autonomy and stand on its own: is this not the very definition of the birth of modern art proper—that it is no longer subordinated to the task of representing spiritual reality?

The way abrogation relates to sublation is not that of a simple succession or external opposition; not "first you eat, then you shit." Shitting is the immanent *conclusion* of the entire process: without it, we would be dealing with the "spurious infinity" of an endless process of sublation. The process of sublation itself can only reach its end by the countermove:

> Contrary to what one would initially imagine, these two processes of sublation and abrogation are completely interdependent. Considering the last moment of absolute spirit (*Philosophy*), one readily notes the synonymy between the verbs *aufheben* and *befreien* ("to liberate"), as well as *ablegen* ("to discard," "to remove," "to take away"). Speculative abrogation, in no way alien to the process of *Aufhebung*, is indeed its fulfillment. Abrogation is a *sublation of sublation*, the result of the *Aufhebung*'s work on itself and, as such, its transformation. The movement of suppression and preservation produces this transformation at a certain moment in history, the moment of Absolute Knowledge. Speculative abrogation is the *absolute sublation*, if by "absolute" we mean a relief or sublation that frees from a certain type of attachment.[5]

A true cognition is thus not only the notional "appropriation" of its object: the process of appropriation goes on only as long as cognition remains incomplete. The sign of its completion is that it liberates its object, lets it be, drops it. This is why and how the movement of sublation has to culminate in the self-relating gesture of sublating itself. And is this shift from sublation to abrogation not structurally homologous to Alain Badiou's shift from destruction to subtraction? After "destroying" the Substance in its immediacy—appropriating it through its mediation, applying on it the "work of the negative"—the subject has to subtract itself from it, set it free. So what about the obvious counterargument: is the part that is abrogated/released (not precisely the arbitrary, passing aspect of the object) that which the notional mediation/reduction can afford to drop as the part that is in itself worthless? This is precisely the illusion that is to be avoided on two points. First, the released part is, on the contrary, if one may be permitted to insist on the excremental metaphorics, precisely discarded as much as the *manure* of the spiritual development, the ground out of which further development will grow. The release of Nature into its own thus lays the foundation of Spirit proper, which can itself develop only out of Nature, as its inherent self-sublation. Second, and more fundamentally, what is released into its own being in speculative cognition is ultimately the object of cognition itself, which, when truly grasped (*begriffen*), no longer has to rely on the subject's active intervention, but develops itself following its own conceptual automatism with the subject reduced to a passive observer who, without its contribution (*Zutun*), lets the thing deploy its potentials and merely registers the process. This is why the Hegelian cognition is simultaneously active and passive, in a sense that radically displaces the Kantian notion of cognition as the unity of activity and passivity. In Kant, the subject actively synthesizes (confers unity on) the content (the sensuous multiplicity), by which the subject is passively affected. For Hegel, on the contrary, at the level of Absolute Knowing, the cognizing subject is thoroughly passivized: he no longer intervenes into the object, but merely registers the immanent movement of the subject's self-differentiation/self-determination (or, to use a more contemporary term, the object's autopoietic self-organization). The subject is thus, at its most radical, not the agens of the process: the agens is the system (of knowledge) itself, which "automatically" deploys without any need for external pushes or impetuses. However, this utter passivity simultaneously involves the greatest activity: it takes the most strenuous effort for the subject to "erase himself" in its particular content (as the agent intervening into the object) and to expose oneself as a neutral medium, the site of the system's self-deployment. Hegel thereby overcomes the standard dualism between system and freedom, between the Spinozist notion of a substantial *deus sive natura* of whom I am part, caught in its determinism, and the Fichtean notion of subject as the agent opposed to the inert stuff, trying to dominate and appropriate it: *the supreme moment of subject's freedom is to set free its object*, to leave it to freely deploy itself: "The Idea's absolute freedom consists in . . . that it resolves to freely let go out of itself the moment of its particularity."[6] "Absolute freedom" is here literally absolute in the etymological meaning of *absolvere*: releasing, letting go. Schelling was the first to criticize this move as illegitimate: after Hegel completed the circle of logical self-development of the Notion, being aware that all this development took place in the abstract medium of thought, outside real life, he had to somehow make the passage to real life. There were, however, no categories in his logic to accomplish this passage, which is why he had to resort to terms like "decision" (the Idea "decides" to release Nature from itself), which are not categories of logic but of will and practical, actual life. This critique clearly misses the way that this act of releasing the other is thoroughly *immanent* to the dialectical process and its conclusive moment: the sign of the conclusion of a dialectical circle. Is this not the Hegelian version of *Gelassenheit*?

This is how one should read Hegel's "third syllogism of Philosophy," Spirit-Logic-Nature: the starting point of the speculative movement rendered by this syllogism is spiritual substance into which subjects are immersed. Then, through strenuous conceptual work, the wealth of this substance is reduced to its underlying elementary logical/notional structure. Once this task is accomplished, the fully developed logical Idea can release Nature out of itself. Here is the key passage:

> The Idea, namely, in positing itself as absolute unity of the pure Notion and its reality and thus contracting itself into the immediacy of being, is the totality in this form—nature.
>
> But this determination has not issued from a process of becoming, nor is it a transition, as when above, the subjective Notion in its totality becomes objectivity, and the subjective end becomes life. On the contrary, the pure Idea in which the determinateness or reality of the Notion is itself raised into Notion, is an absolute liberation for which there is no longer any immediate determination that is not equally posited and itself Notion; in this freedom, therefore, no transition takes place; the simple being to which the Idea determines itself remains perfectly transparent to it and is the Notion that, in its determination, abides with itself. The passage is therefore to be understood here rather in this manner, that the Idea freely releases itself in its absolute self-assurance and inner poise. By reason of this freedom, the form of its determinateness is also utterly free—the externality of space and time existing absolutely on its own account without the moment of subjectivity.⁷

Here Hegel repeatedly insists on how this "absolute liberation" is thoroughly different from the standard dialectical "transition." But how? The suspicion lurks that Hegel's "absolute liberation" relies on the absolute mediation of all otherness: I set the Other free after I completely internalized it. However, is this so?

One should reread here Lacan's critique of Hegel: what if, far from denying what Lacan calls the "subjective disjunction," Hegel asserts an unheard-of division that *runs through the (particular) subject as well as through the (universal) substantial order of "collectivity," uniting the two*? That is to say, what if the "reconciliation" between the particular and the universal occurs precisely through the division that cuts across the two? The basic "postmodern" reproach to Hegel—that his dialectics admits antagonisms and splits only to resolve them magically in a higher synthesis-mediation—strangely contrasts the good old Marxist reproach to Hegel (already formulated before Marx by Schelling), according to which Hegel resolves antagonisms only in "thought," through conceptual mediation, while in reality they remain unresolved. One is tempted to accept this second reproach at its face value and use it against the first one: what if this is the proper answer to the accusation that Hegelian dialectics magically resolves antagonisms? What if, for Hegel, the point, precisely, *is* not to "resolve" antagonisms "in reality," but just to enact a parallax shift by which antagonisms are recognized "as such" and thereby perceived in their "positive" role?

The passage from Kant to Hegel is thus much more convoluted than it may appear. Let us approach it again through the opposition of Kant and Hegel with regard to the ontological proof of God's existence. Kant's rejection of this proof takes as the starting point his thesis that being is not a predicate: if one knows all predicates of an entity, its being (existence) doesn't follow; for example, one cannot conclude being from a notion. (The anti-Leibniz is clear here, according to whom two objects are indiscernible if all of their predicates are the same.) The implication for the ontological proof of God is clear: in the same way that I can have a perfect notion of one hundred thalers and still not have them in my pocket, I can have a perfect notion of God without God existing. Hegel's first remark on this line of reasoning is that "being" is the poorest, most imperfect notional determination (everything "is" in some way, even my craziest phantasmagorias); it is only through further notional determinations that we get to existence, to reality, to actuality, which are all much more than mere being. His second remark is that the gap between notion and existence is precisely the mark of finitude; it holds for finite objects like one hundred thalers but not for God: God is not something I can have (or not have) in my pocket.

In a first approach, it may seem here that the opposition of Kant and Hegel is ultimately the one between materialism and idealism: Kant insists on a minimum of materialism (the independence of reality with regard to notional determinations), while Hegel totally dissolves reality in its notional determinations. However, Hegel's true point lies elsewhere: it involves the much more radical "materialist" claim that a complete notional determination of an entity, to which one would only have to add "being" in order to arrive at its existence, is in itself an abstract notion, an empty abstract possibility. The lack of (a certain mode of) being is always also an inherent lack of some notional determination—say, for a thing to exist as part of opaque material reality, a whole set of notional conditions-determinations have to be met (and other determinations to lack). With regard to one hundred thalers (or any other empirical object), this means that their notional determination is abstract, which is why they posses an opaque empirical being and not full actuality. So when Kant draws a parallel between God and one hundred thalers, one should ask a simple and naive question: but does he *really* possess a (fully developed) *concept* of God?

This brings us to the true finesse of Hegel's argumentation, which is directed both against Kant and against Anselm's classic version of the ontological proof of God. Hegel's argument against Anselm's proof is not that it is too conceptual, but that it is not conceptual enough: Anselm does not develop the concept of God, he just refers to it as the sum of all perfections, which, as such, is precisely beyond the comprehension of our finite human mind. Anselm merely presupposes "God" as an impenetrable reality beyond our comprehension (i.e., outside the notional domain). For example, his God is precisely not a concept (something posited by our conceptual work), but a purely presupposed pre- or nonconceptual reality. Along the same lines, albeit in the opposite sense, one should mention the irony that Kant talks about thalers, that is, *money*, whose existence *as money* is not objective, but depends on notional determinations. True, as Kant says, it is not the same to have a concept of one hundred thalers and to have them in your pocket; but let us imagine a process of rapid inflation that totally devalues the one hundred thalers is my pocket. Yes, the same object is there in reality, but it is no longer money, just a meaningless and worthless coin. In other words, money is precisely an object whose status depends on how we think about it: if people no longer treat this piece of metal as money, if they no longer believe in it as money, it no longer *is* money.

With regard to material reality, the ontological proof of God's existence should thus be turned around: the existence of material reality bears witness to the fact that the Notion is not fully actualized. Things "materially exist" not when they meet certain notional requirements, but when they *fail* to meet them. Material reality is, as such, a sign of imperfection. With regard to truth, this means that, for Hegel, the truth of a proposition is inherently notional, determined by the immanent notional content, not a matter of comparison between Notion and reality—in Lacanian terms, there is a non-All *pas-tout* of truth. It may sound strange to evoke Hegel apropos non-All: is Hegel not the philosopher of All par excellence? However, the Hegelian truth is precisely without the external limitation/exception that would serve as its measure-standard, which is why its criterion is absolutely immanent: one compares a statement with itself, with its own process of enunciation.

When Alain Badiou emphasizes the undecidability of a Truth-Event,[8] his position is radically different from the standard deconstructionist notion of undecidability. For Badiou, undecidability means that there are no neutral "objective" criteria for an Event: an Event appears as such only to those who recognize themselves in its call; or, as Badiou puts it, an Event is self-relating: it includes itself—its own nomination—into its components. While this does mean that one has to *decide* about an Event, such an ultimately groundless decision is not "undecidable" in the standard sense; it is rather uncannily similar to the Hegelian dialectical process in which, as Hegel already made clear in the introduction to his *Phenomenology*, a "figure of consciousness" is not measured by any external standard of truth but in an absolutely immanent way, through the gap between itself and its own exemplification/staging. An Event is thus "non-All" in the precise Lacanian sense of the term: it is never fully verified precisely because it is, for example, infinite/illimite-

unlimited because there is no external limit to it. And the conclusion to be drawn here is that, for the very same reason, the Hegelian "totality" is also "non-All."

So, back to our main line, this means that the externality of Nature with regard to the Idea is not that of the Idea's constitutive exception: it is not that Nature is set free as the exception that guarantees the wholeness of the Idea's self-mediation. It is not that, after this mediation is completed (i.e., after the Idea's dialectical progress can no longer be propelled by the Idea's own incompleteness, its failure to correspond to its own notion), the completed Idea needs an external Other (Nature) to sustain the complete and closed circle of its self-mediation. Nature is, rather, the mark of the non-All of Idea's totality. Here is how the early Hegel, still struggling to differentiate himself from the legacy of other German Idealists, formulated this self-relating non-All totality, starting from Kant's great philosophical breakthrough: in the Kantian transcendental synthesis, "the determinateness of form is nothing but the identity of opposites. As a result, the a priori intellect becomes, at least in principle, a posteriori as well; for a posteriori is nothing but the positing of the opposite."[9]

In principle, the meaning of this dense passage seems clear: the "determinateness of form" is another name for concrete universality, for the fact that the universal form of a concept generates out of itself its particular content, that it is not merely a form imposed on an independent empirical content. And since the notional universality and the particularity of its content—in short, the a priori of the universal form and the a posteriori of its content—are opposites (precisely the opposites that Kant keeps apart and that are ultimately external to each other, since the immanent transcendental form is imposed onto a content that affects the subject from the outside), the determinateness of form equals the unity of opposites and the fact that content is generated by its form. The trick is how are we to concretely read this identity of the opposites? The standard critical reading satisfies itself by seeing in it the very model of how the Idea mediates/posits all of its particular content, for example, as the extreme "idealist" affirmation of the primacy of a priori over a posteriori. What such a reading clearly misses is the opposite movement: the irreducible "umbilical cord" on account of which every a priori universality remains attached to (colored, "overdetermined" by) the a posteriori, a particular content. To put it somewhat bluntly: yes, the universal notional form imposes necessity upon the multitude of its contingent content, but *it does so in a way that remains marked by an irreducible stain of contingency*. Or, as Derrida would have put it, the frame itself is always also a part of the enframed content. The logic here is that of the Hegelian *gegensaetzliche Bestimmung*, the "oppositional determination" in which the universal genus encounters itself among its particular-contingent species. (Marx's classic example: Among the species of production, there is always one that gives the specific color on the universality of production within a given mode of production. In feudal societies, artisanal production itself is structured like another domain of agriculture, while in capitalism, agriculture itself is "industrialized," that is, it becomes one of the domains of industrial production.) Hegel introduces this notion of "oppositional determination" in his logic of essence, when he discusses the relationship between identity and difference. His point there is not only that identity is always the identity of identity and difference, but that difference itself is also always the difference between itself and identity. In the same way, it is not only necessity that encompasses itself and contingency, but—also and more fundamentally—it is contingency itself that encompasses itself and necessity. Or, with regard to the tension between essence and appearance, the fact that essence has to appear means not only that essence generates/mediates its appearances, but also that the difference between essence and appearance is internal to appearance: essence has to appear within the domain of appearances, as a hint that "appearances are not all" but "merely appearances."

Insofar as (in a language) this opposition appears as the opposition between the universal content of meaning and its expression in a contingent particular form (of the signifier), it is no wonder that language provides the ultimate example of this dialectical unity of the opposites:

> There is no such thing as a superior language or benchmark idiom. Every language is an instance of the speculative. Philosophy's role is to show how, in each language, the essential is said and exhibited through the idiom's accidents.[10]

The starting point of a thought has to be all the contingency of one's own language as the "substance" of one's thinking: there is no direct path to universal truth through abstracting from the contingencies of one's "natural" tongue and constructing a new artificial or technical language whose terms would display a precise meaning. This, however, does not mean that a thinker should naively rely on the resources of his language: the starting point of his reflection should rather be the *idiosyncrasies* of this language, in a way, the redoubled contingencies, contingencies within a contingent (historically relative) order itself. Paradoxically, the path from the contingency (of one's natural language) to the necessity (of speculative thought) leads through the redoubled contingency: one cannot escape thinking in one's language, this language is one's unsurpassable substance; however, thinking means thinking *against* the language in which one thinks. Language inevitably ossifies our thoughts; it is the medium of the fixed distinction of understanding par excellence. But, while one has to think against the language in which one thinks, one has to do this *within* language; there is no other option. This is why Hegel precludes the possibility (developed later, especially by Anglo-Saxon analytic philosophy) of purifying our natural language of its "irrational" contingencies or of constructing a new artificial language that would faithfully reflect conceptual determinations. In what, then, in language itself are we to find a support for thinking against it? Hegel's answer is: in what, in language, is not language proper as a formal system—in that which, in a language, is most inconsistent, contingent, idiosyncratic. The paradox is that one can combat the "irrationality" of language on behalf of the immanent notional necessity only if this necessity relies on what is the most "irrational" in language, on redoubled irrationality/contingency, which is similar to the Freudian logic of the dream in which the Real announces itself in the guise of a dream within a dream. What Hegel has in mind here is often uncannily close to Lacan's notion of *lalangue*: wordplays, double meanings, and so on. His great example in German is words with opposite or multiple meanings, such as *zu Grunde gehen*, "disintegrate/fall apart" *and*, literally, "to go to, to reach, one's ground," not even to mention the notorious *Aufhebung* with its three meanings: to cancel/annihilate, to preserve, to elevate at a higher level. *Aufhebung* is often put forward as the very example of what is "idealist-metaphysical" about Hegel: does it not signal the very operation by which all external contingency is overcome and integrated into the necessary self-deployment of the universal notion? Against this operation, it is hence fashionable to insist how there is always a remainder of contingency, of particularity, which cannot be *aufgehoben*, which insists and resists its conceptual (dis)integration. The irony here is that the very term Hegel uses to designate this operation is marked by the irreducible contingency of an idiosyncrasy of the German.

There is no conceptual clarity without *lalangue* as a starting point, or, to put it in more conceptual terms, not only does necessity express itself in the appearance of contingency, but this necessity itself does not preexist the contingent multitude of appearances as their ground. It itself emerges out of contingency, as a contingency (say, the contingent multiple meaning of *Aufhebung*) elevated to the necessity of a universal concept.[11] Does Freud not intend something strictly homologous with his notions of symptoms, jokes, and slips of the tongue? An inner necessity can only articulate itself through the contingency of a symptom, *and*, vice versa, this necessity (say, the constant urge of a repressed desire) comes to be through this articulation. Here, also, necessity does not only preexist contingency: when Lacan says that repression and the return of the repressed (in symptomal formations) are the front and the obverse of one and the same process, the implication of this is precisely that the necessity (of the repressed content) hinges on the contingency (of its articulation in symptoms). Critics of Hegel emphasize only the first aspect (necessity as the inner principle dominating its contingent expressions), neglecting the second one, for example, how this necessity itself hinges on contingency, how it *is* nothing but contingency elevated into the form of necessity.

So, to pursue our rather tasteless metaphor, Hegel was not a sublimated coprophague, as the usual notion of the dialectical process would lead us to believe. The matrix of the dialectical process is not that of excrementation-externalization followed up by swallowing up (reappropriation) of the externalized content, but, on the contrary, of appropriation followed up by the excremental move of dropping it, releasing it, letting it go. What this means is that one should not equate externalization with alienation: the externalization, which concludes a cycle of dialectical process, is not alienation; it is the highest point of disalienation: one really reconciles oneself with some objective content not when one still has to strive to master and control it, but when one can afford the supreme sovereign gesture of releasing this content from oneself, of setting it free. This is why, incidentally, as some perspicuous interpreters pointed out, far from subduing Nature totally to man, Hegel opens up an unexpected space for ecological awareness: for Hegel, the drive to technologically exploit nature is still a mark of man's finitude; in such an attitude, nature is perceived as an external object, an opposing force to be dominated, while a philosopher, from his standpoint of Absolute Knowing, does not experience nature as a threatening foreign field to be controlled and dominated, but as something to be left to follow its inherent path.

What this means is that the Hegelian Subject-Substance has nothing to do with some kind of mega-Subject who controls the dialectical process, pulling its strings: there is no one pulling the strings and controlling the process—the Hegelian system is a plane without a pilot. Here Louis Althusser was wrong when he opposed the Hegelian Subject-Substance, the "teleological" process-with-a-subject, to the materialist-dialectical "process without a subject." The Hegelian dialectical process is the most radical version of a "process without a subject" in the sense of an agent controlling and directing it, be it God or humanity or class as a collective subject—in his late writings, Althusser starts to become aware of this. What Althusser is thoroughly unaware of is how the fact that the Hegelian dialectical process is a "process without a subject" (in the sense of a controlling agent) means exactly the same as Hegel's fundamental thesis that "it is crucial to grasp the Absolute not only as Substance, but also as Subject": the emergence of a pure subject qua void is strictly correlative to the notion of "system" as the self-deployment of the object itself with no need for any subjective agent to push it forward or to direct it.

What critics of Hegel's voracity need is, perhaps, a dosage of a good laxative.

NOTES

1. G. W. F. Hegel, *Lectures on the Philosophy of Religion* (Berkeley: University of California Press, 1985), vol. 3, p. 127.

2. Theodor W. Adorno, *Negative Dialectics* (New York: Continuum, 1973), p. 34.
3. G. W. F. Hegel, *Science of Logic* (London: Humanities Press, 1976), p. 841.
4. Ibid., p. 843.
5. Catherine Malabou, *The Future of Hegel: Plasticity, Temporality and Dialectic*, trans. Lisabeth During (London: Routledge, 2005), p. 156.
6. G. W. F. Hegel, *Philosophy of Nature* (Oxford: Clarendon Press, 1970), para. 244.
7. G. W. F. Hegel, *Philosophy of Mind*, para. 577.
8. Alain Badiou, *L'etre et l'evenement* (Paris: Editions de Minuit, 1989).
9. G. W. F. Hegel, "Glauben und Wissen," in *Jenaer Kritische Schriften* (Hamburg: Felix Meiner Verlag, 1968), vol. 3, p. 26.
10. Malabou, *Future of Hegel*, p. 171.
11. And Hegel was far from conceding any priority to German language—an interesting biographical detail: when, in the 1810s, he was considering the invitation of a Dutch friend to accept a university post in Amsterdam, he not only started to learn Dutch but immediately bombarded his friend with requests to inform him on Dutch-language idiosyncrasies such as wordplays, so that he would be able to develop his thoughts in Dutch.

CONTRIBUTORS

BRUNO BOSTEELS is professor of romance studies at Cornell University. He is the author of *Alain Badiou, une trajectoire polémique*; *Badiou and Politics*; and *The Actuality of Communism*.

JOHN D. CAPUTO is the Thomas J. Watson Professor of Religion and Humanities and professor of philosophy at Syracuse University. His newest books are *What Would Jesus Deconstruct? The Good News of Postmodernism for the Church*; *After the Death of God* (with Gianni Vattimo); and *The Weakness of God: A Theology of the Event*.

CLAYTON CROCKETT is associate professor and director of religious studies at the University of Central Arkansas. He is the author of three books, including *Radical Political Theology: Religion and Politics After Liberalism*.

CRESTON DAVIS is an assistant professor in the Department of Philosophy and Religion at Rollins College. He is the co-author (with John Milbank and Slavoj Žižek) of *Paul's New Moment: Continental Philosophy and the Future of Christian Theology* and editor of *The Monstrosity of Christ: Paradox or Dialectic?* and the forthcoming *Truth After the Death of Meaning*.

WILLIAM DESMOND is professor of philosophy at the Institute of Philosophy, Katholieke Universiteit Leuven, Belgium. He is the author of *Being and the Between*; *Ethics and the Between*; *Hegel's God: A Counterfeit Double?*; and *God and the Between*.

ADRIAN JOHNSTON is a professor in the Department of Philosophy at the University of New Mexico and an assistant teaching analyst at the Emory University Psychoanalytic Institute. He is the author of *Time Driven: Metapsychology and the Splitting of the Drive*; *Žižek's Ontology: A Transcendental Materialist Theory of Subjectivity*; and *Badiou, Žižek, and Political Transformations: The Cadence of Change*.

THOMAS A. LEWIS is associate professor of religious studies at Brown University. His books include *Freedom and Tradition in Hegel: Reconsidering Anthropology, Ethics, and Religion* and *Religion, Modernity, and Politics in Hegel*.

CATHERINE MALABOU teaches philosophy at the University of Paris, Nanterre. Her books in English include *The Future of Hegel: Plasticity, Temporality, and Dialectic*; *What Should We Do with Our Brain?*; *Plasticity at the Dusk of Writing: Dialectic, Destruction, Deconstruction*; and the forthcoming *Changing Difference: The Question of the Feminine in Philosophy*.

ANTONIO NEGRI has taught at the University of Padua and the University of Paris. He is the author of *The Savage Anomaly*; *Insurgencies: Constituent Power and the Modern State*; and *Thirty-three Lessons on Lenin*.

KATRIN PAHL is assistant professor of German at Johns Hopkins University. She is the author of *Tropes of Transport: Hegel and Emotion* and editor of "Emotionality," special issue of *Modern Language Notes*.

MARK C. TAYLOR is chair of the Department of Religion and co-director of the Institute for Religion, Culture, and Public Life at Columbia University. His most recent books include *After God*; *Crisis on Campus: A Bold Plan to Reform Our Colleges and Universities*; and the forthcoming *Refiguring the Spiritual: Beuys, Barney, Turrell, and Goldsworthy*.

EDITH WYSCHOGROD (1930–2009) was J. Newton Rayzor Professor of Philosophy and Religious Thought at Rice University. Her books include *Crossover Queries: Dwelling with Negatives*; *Embodying Philosophy's Others*; *An Ethics of Remembering: History, Heterology, and the Nameless Others*; *Saints and Postmodernism: Revisioning Moral Philosophy*; and *Spirit in Ashes: Hegel, Heidegger, and Man-Made Mass Death*.

SLAVOJ ŽIŽEK is a senior researcher in the Department of Philosophy at the University of Ljubljana, Slovenia, and co-director of the Center for Humanities at Birkbeck College, University of London. He is the author of *Living in the End Times*; *The Parallax View*; and *The Sublime Object of Ideology*.

INDEX OF NAMES

Adorno, Theodor, 75–76, 82, 84–85, 213, 221–222
Althusser, Louis, 230
Anselm, Saint, 226
Ansermet, François, 165
Aristotle, 5, 117, 124
Artaud, Antonin, 192
Augustine, Saint, 27

Badiou, Alain, 5, 9, 79, 83, 223, 227
Barth, Karl, 56
Bauer, Bruno, 127
Benjamin, Walter, 51, 60
Bergson, Henri, 5, 60
Berlichingen, Count von, 186
Blanchot, Maurice, 109
Bosteels, Bruno, 9–10
Buck-Morss, Susan, 74
Burkhardt, Christianna Charlotte Johanna, 191
Butler, Judith, 28, 153

Caputo, John D., 9, 12
Chiesa, Lorenzo, 167, 171
Cohn-Bendit, Daniel, 79
Cohn-Bendit, Gabriel, 79
Coleridge, Samuel Taylor, 110
Crockett, Clayton, 26

Dawkins, Richard, 168
Deleuze, Gilles, 5, 53–55, 61–62
Demeter, 153
Derrida, Jacques, 3–5, 7, 9–10, 25–27, 51, 54, 61, 76, 78, 91–92, 94, 111, 181–182, 185, 187, 194, 228
Descartes, René, 70, 72, 75
Desmond, William, 11–12
Dionysos, 151, 153–154
Dussel, Enrique, 68, 72–74, 213

Echevarría, Bolívar, 79
Eckhart, Meister, 59
Empedocles, 161

Fanon, Franz, 26
Feinmann, José Pablo, 72, 74
Feuerbach, Ludwig, 12, 129
Fichte, Johann Gottlieb, 56, 94, 102, 106, 108, 110
Fink, Eugen, 141
Freud, Sigmund, 13, 87, 159–164, 166, 171–174, 183, 185, 230
Frommann, Carl Friedrich Ernst, 191

Gachet, Paul, 193
Galileo Galilei, 87
Gasché, Rodolphe, 78, 103
Gaugin, Paul, 193
Genet, Jean, 185
Genghis Khan, 87
Gentile, Giovanni, 38
Goeriz (reverend), 186
Goethe, Johann Wolfgang von, 21, 185

Habermas, Jürgen, 73
Hegel, Christianne (sister), 14, 181, 185–186, 188, 195
Hegel, Ludwig (son), 14, 190–191
Hegel, Marie von Tucher (wife), 181, 186, 191–192
Heidegger, Martin, 12, 48, 58, 75, 94, 104, 107–108, 131, 182, 187
Henrich, Dieter, 99, 102
Hergé (Georges Prosper Remi), 67
Hitler, Adolf, 82
Hölderlin, Friedrich, 185
Horkheimer, Max, 222
Hume, David, 163
Hyppolite, Jean, 21

Jaar, Alfredo, 67
Jesus, 2, 62, 87
Johnston, Adrian, 13–14, 16

Kant, Immanuel, 2, 10–11, 15, 64, 70, 72, 75, 84, 94–109, 111, 117–122, 128, 130–132, 137, 171, 182, 200–203, 224, 226–228
Karelis, Charles, 188
Kaufmann, Walter, 185, 191
Kierkegaard, Søren, 10, 47, 56, 62, 124
Kimmerle, Heinz, 4
Knox, T. M., 2
Kojève, Alexandre, 14, 75, 83–84, 170

Lacan, Jacques, 13–14, 159, 161, 163–167, 169–175, 225, 227, 230
Landru, Henri Désiré, 87
Lear, Jonathan, 161–162
Lefebvre, Henri, 85
Lenin, Vladimir Ilyich, 79, 87
Levinas, Emmanuel, 3–5, 48, 55, 60, 64, 136, 213
Lewis, Thomas A., 15
Lispector, Clarice, 13, 142, 146, 148, 150
Locke, John, 163
Luther, Martin, 126
Lyotard, Jean-François, 3–5, 53

Magistretti, Pierre, 165
Magritte, René, 67
Malabou, Catherine, 7–9, 12, 14, 16, 70, 75, 78, 165, 169
Marx, Karl, 3, 12, 23, 28, 42, 60, 85, 129, 133, 225, 228
Mary Magdalene, 189
Maturana, Humberto, 162
Meillassoux, Quentin, 12
Michael, Christopher Domínguez, 80
Miller, Jacques-Alain, 170

Nancy, Jean-Luc, 76–78, 103, 109
Napoleon, 87

Negri, Antonio, 8–9, 11–12
Newton, Isaac, 184
Nietzsche, Friedrich, 12, 48, 55, 100, 110, 126, 131–133, 137

Ortega y Gasset, José, 10, 67–72

Pahl, Katrin, 8, 13
Parmenides, 2, 84
Paul, Saint, 58, 62
Pentheus, 151
Peter, Saint, 62
Pinel, Phillipe, 185
Pinkard, Terry, 15, 200
Pippin, Robert, 15, 200–201, 203–204, 212
Plato, 64, 97, 141
Prometheus, 130

Revueltas, José, 10, 79–82, 84–87
Ricardo, David, 37
Rizzolati, Giacomo, 164
Rosch, Eleanor, 162
Rousseau, Jean-Jacques, 7, 19–26, 28
Ruge, Arnold, 85
Rumsfeld, Donald, 68

Sade, Marquis de, 87
Salles (reverend), 193
Sartre, Jean-Paul, 26, 132, 184
Schapiro, Meyer, 182
Schelling, F. W. J., 14, 53, 94, 108, 163, 185, 222, 224–225
Schelling, Karl Eberhard, 186
Schlegel, Karl Wilhelm Friedrich, 94, 109–110, 191

Schleiermacher, F. D. E., 185
Schmitt, Carl, 38
Smith, Adam, 37
Solomon, Robert, 141
Spinoza, Baruch, 52, 56
Spivak, Gayatri Chakravorty, 74
Stalin, Joseph, 81, 87
Stanovich, Keith E., 168–169
Stout, Jeffrey, 214
Struller, Justus, 184

Taylor, Charles, 1–2
Taylor, Mark C., 10–11, 14, 50
Thomas Aquinas, Saint, 124
Thomson, Evan, 162
Tillich, Paul, 52–53, 56

van Gogh, Theo, 14, 182, 192–195
van Gogh, Vincent, 14, 182, 192–195
Varela, Francisco, 162, 165
Vos, Kee, 193

Walcott, Derek, 154
Wicks, Robert, 190
Wollheim, Richard, 181
Wyschogrod, Edith, 11, 14

Zarathustra, 132
Zeus, 130
Žižek, Slavoj, 5–6, 9, 12, 14–16, 26, 47, 49–52, 56–57, 64, 76, 78, 86, 165, 170–171
Zupančič, Alenka, 76

GPSR Authorized Representative: Easy Access System Europe, Mustamäe tee 50, 10621 Tallinn, Estonia, gpsr.requests@easproject.com

www.ingramcontent.com/pod-product-compliance
Lightning Source LLC
Chambersburg PA
CBHW031549300426
44111CB00006BA/227